THE LEGACY OF THE MEXICAN AND SPANISH-AMERICAN WARS

Legal, Literary, and Historical
PERSPECTIVES

Bilingual Press/Editorial Bilingüe

General Editor
  Gary D. Keller

Managing Editor
  Karen S. Van Hooft

Associate Editors
  Barbara H. Firoozye
  Karen Akins Swartz

Assistant Editor
  Linda St. George Thurston

Editorial Consultants
  Ingrid Muller
  Evelyn Partridge

Address:
  Bilingual Press
  Hispanic Research Center
  Arizona State University
  P.O. Box 872702
  Tempe, Arizona 85287-2702
  (480) 965-3867

THE LEGACY OF THE MEXICAN AND SPANISH-AMERICAN WARS

Legal, Literary, and Historical PERSPECTIVES

EDITED BY
Gary D. Keller and Cordelia Candelaria

Bilingual Review/Press
TEMPE, ARIZONA

©2000 by Bilingual Press/Editorial Bilingüe

All rights reserved. No part of this publication may be reproduced in any manner without permission in writing, except in the case of brief quotations embodied in critical articles and reviews.

ISBN 0-927534-90-8

Library of Congress Cataloging-in-Publication Data

The legacy of the Mexican and Spanish-American wars : legal, literary, and historical perspectives / edited by Gary D. Keller and Cordelia Candelaria.
    p.   cm.
   Papers from the 1848/1898@1998 Transhistoric Thresholds conference held at Arizona State University in Dec. 1998.
   Includes bibliographical references.
   ISBN 0-027534-90-8
   1. Mexican War, 1846–1848—Influence—Congresses. 2. Mexican War, 1846–1848—Law and legislation—Congresses. 3. Spanish-American War, 1898—Influence—Congresses. 4. Spanish-American War, 1898—Literature and the war—Congresses. I. Keller, Gary D. II. Candelaria, Cordelia.

E415.L44 1999
973.6'2—dc21   99-058432

PRINTED IN THE UNITED STATES OF AMERICA

Cover and interior design by John Wincek, Aerocraft Charter Services

Acknowledgments

The editors acknowledge the financial support of The Rockefeller Foundation and Philip Morris Companies, Inc., which provided partial funding toward publication of this volume.

The Bilingual Review/Press gratefully acknowledges the *Southwestern Journal of Law & Trade in the Americas* for allowing us to reprint the following: "One Hundred Fifty Years of Solitude: Reflections on the End of the History Academy's Dominance of Scholarship on the Treaty of Guadalupe Hidalgo," "Immigration, Citizenship, and U.S./Mexico Relations: The Tale of Two Treaties," and "Dispute Resolution and the Treaty of Guadalupe Hidalgo: Parallels and Possible Lessons for Dispute Resolution under NAFTA."

Contents

Foreword .... *vii*

One Hundred Fifty Years of Solitude: Reflections on the End of the History Academy's Dominance of Scholarship on the Treaty of Guadalupe Hidalgo
CHRISTOPHER DAVID RUIZ CAMERON 1

Immigration, Citizenship, and U.S./Mexico Relations: The Tale of Two Treaties
KEVIN R. JOHNSON... 23

Dispute Resolution and the Treaty of Guadalupe Hidalgo: Parallels and Possible Lessons for Dispute Resolution under NAFTA
GEORGE A. MARTÍNEZ 39

Border Crossings in the Mexican American War
ROSEMARY KING 63

Puerto Rico lírico: la influencia del "Poeta de América" en el nacionalismo puertorriqueño
SANTIAGO DAYDÍ-TOLSON 87

Dialéctica histórica en el teatro del puertorriqueño Manuel Méndez Ballester
L. TERESA VALDIVIESO... 93

La hispanidad amenazada: Rubén Darío y la Guerra del 98
ALBERTO ACEREDA 99

Mapping Empire in Omaha and Buffalo: World's Fairs and the Spanish-American War
SARAH J. MOORE 111

Foreword

On December 8-12, 1998, Arizona State University mounted an extensive and broadly interdisciplinary conference entitled "1848/1898@1998: Transhistoric Thresholds." Two scholarly products have emerged from this conference. One is the conference CD-ROM, which contains the abstracts of all conference presentations, a considerable number and variety of scholarly papers, some of the art images that were exhibited, and other information. The second is this book, *The Legacy of the Mexican and Spanish-American Wars: Legal, Literary, and Historical Perspectives*, which is the companion to the CD-ROM. It contains the papers that were most suitable for publication in hard copy given our financial resources. The volume offers a multidisciplinary view of the events that surrounded the Mexican War, which culminated in the Treaty of Guadalupe Hidalgo (1848), and the Spanish-American War, which ended with the Treaty of Paris (1898).

Many individuals and organizations made this project possible and they are more fully acknowledged on the CD-ROM. Here we would like to give a general thanks to all those who collectively made this conference and scholarly project so successful. We want to specifically acknowledge with our deepest gratitude the following financial supporters: Arizona Public Service (APS), Motorola Corporation, The Philip Morris Companies, Inc., and The Rockefeller Foundation.

Finally, we wish to acknowledge our institutional partners including: the Inter-University Partnership for Latino Research, Dr. Gilberto Cárdenas, Executive Director; the National Council of La Raza, Raúl Yzaguirre, President; The Smithsonian Institution's Center for Latino Initiatives, Dr. Refugio Rochín, Director; Arizona State University West, and especially Dr. Mildred García, Associate Vice-Provost; the Department of Chicana and Chicano Studies, Arizona State University, Dr. Vicki Ruiz, Chair; and the Bilingual Press/Editorial Bilingüe of the Hispanic Research Center, Arizona State University, Karen S. Van Hooft, Managing Editor.

Gary D. Keller
Cordelia Candelaria
ARIZONA STATE UNIVERSITY

One Hundred Fifty Years of Solitude

REFLECTIONS ON THE END OF THE HISTORY ACADEMY'S DOMINANCE OF SCHOLARSHIP ON THE TREATY OF GUADALUPE HIDALGO

Christopher David Ruiz Cameron*
SOUTHWESTERN UNIVERSITY

> "Science has eliminated distance," Melquíades proclaimed. "In a short time, man will be able to see what is happening in any place in the world without leaving his house."
>
> —Gabriel García Márquez[1]

I. Introduction: The Treaty of Guadalupe Hidalgo as History

For most of its one hundred fifty years, the Treaty of Guadalupe Hidalgo has been the scholarly province of history rather than of law professors. Whereas members of the history academy have produced a rich English-language literature describing both the terms of the Treaty and their interpretation in many of the reported cases,[2] members of the law academy, until now, have produced but a handful of significant law review articles attempting to do likewise.[3]

To be sure, receiving wisdom about the Treaty from historians instead of law scholars has been a blessing. We in the law academy owe a tremendous intellectual debt to historians, especially the Chicano Studies scholars, whose pioneering work on the Treaty has set the standard by which we evaluate the document's influence on law and policy regarding persons of Mexican ancestry in this country.[4] The historians have enriched our understanding of this most important of laws affecting U.S.-Mexico relations by offering at least three distinct ways of ascribing meaning to the document.

The first way that historians ascribe meaning to the Treaty is by what I shall call the traditional perspective: the notion that the Treaty is a sort of recorded deed of the biggest "land grab" in American history,[5] the crowning achievement of an unjust war incited and waged by a stronger, richer, whiter nation against its weaker, poorer, browner neighbor.[6] From the traditional perspective, the Treaty merely codifies as terms of surrender the frustrated diplomatic objectives that the United States went to war to achieve. So it is no surprise that American courts interpreting the Treaty issued decisions that, for example,

---

*Many thanks are due to the folks who inspired this project, especially Rudy Acuña, Arturo Gándara, Regan Grilli, Richard Griswold del Castillo, Cruz Reynoso, Leigh Taylor, and Russ Trice, and to the folks who reviewed and commented on earlier drafts, especially Joe Baca, Kevin Johnson, Guadalupe Luna, George Martínez, and Carlos Vázquez. Generous financial support was provided by the Trustees of Southwestern University School of Law. Valuable research assistance was offered by Matthias Wagener (Class of 1999).

tended to resolve doubts about the validity of Spanish and Mexican land titles against Mexican grantees and in favor of Anglo claimants.[7]

The second way that historians ascribe meaning to the Treaty is by what I shall call the revisionist perspective: the notion that the Treaty provided real protections for the civil and property rights of Mexicans, but that these protections were eroded by the cultural shock waves that rolled over land claimants when Mexico's continental-style civil law system clashed with the United States' Anglo-American common law tradition.[8] From the revisionist perspective, the tribunals that adjudicated Treaty rights generally were fair to Mexicans, and even produced significant results favoring them. If Mexicans lost their properties anyway, then factors other than the Treaty, or the institutions charged with interpreting it, were to blame.

The third way that historians ascribe meaning to the Treaty is what I shall call the reclamation perspective: the notion that the Treaty is a "living" document that not only guaranteed the human rights of displaced Mexicans in 1848, but also guarantees them in 1998.[9] From the reclamationist perspective, Treaty rights have been systematically ignored, or at least have lain dormant, for too long, but could be reclaimed by use of litigation and organizational tools to aid the descendants of the original Mexican settlers of the Southwest and their more recently arrived kin.[10] Thus the Treaty has been a kind of tableau upon which numerous Chicano Studies scholars have projected their hopes for vindicating a whole range of historic claims, including land grant recognition, civil rights, affirmative action, and even bilingual education.

Despite the blessings conferred by these historical perspectives, the dominance of Treaty discourse by historians has also been, in some cases, a curse. Like Melquíades's proclamation that "[s]cience has eliminated distance," the proclamations of traditionalists, revisionists, and reclamationists contain much insight—but also suffer from much oversimplification. Distance has not quite been eliminated. Nor has legal doctrine, whose role in informing, if not manipulating, the decisions of the courts and land commissioners who were charged with implementing Treaty rights is all too often misunderstood. Of course, explaining the more complex truths behind the law and its institutions is the province of law professors, whose participation in Treaty discourse is long overdue.

This article seeks to supplement our understanding of how the Treaty of Guadalupe Hidalgo became the legal document it is today by shedding light on the critical role that legal doctrine—especially the manipulation of that doctrine by legal actors—has played in its interpretation. To understand this role more precisely, I draw on two distinct, but related, themes from the burgeoning literature of Latino Critical ("Lat Crit") Legal Theory: the inherent indeterminacy of rules of law, and the tendency of the law to make Latinos invisible. In so doing, I attempt to build on the path-breaking, yet incomplete, work done by historians, and to develop the complexities that have informed the choices of lawgivers and legal institutions who framed the Treaty and its jurisprudence.

II. Lat Crit Theory: The Treaty of Guadalupe Hidalgo as Law

A. Indeterminacy

A wide range of legal thinkers, including legal realists,[11] pragmatists,[12] and critical legal scholars,[13] have argued that the law is indeterminate in the sense that legal materials—constitutions, treaties, statutes, and the court decisions interpreting them—often permit a judge to justify multiple outcomes to lawsuits.[14] The indeterminacy of the law has permitted jurists to manipulate legal doctrine to produce outcomes adverse to the interests of Latinos, especially Mexican Americans. George Martínez has pointed out that, in cases dealing with bilingual education, public accommodations, restrictive covenants, racial slurs, school desegregation, and, for my purposes, Spanish and Mexican land titles analyzed under the Treaty of Guadalupe Hidalgo, the text of the applicable legal rule was so general that the court, far from being "bound" by precedent to decide against the Mexican American litigant, "could have gone the other way."[15]

Traditionalists, revisionists, and reclamationists each discuss reported decisions on land titles under the Treaty. Whereas revisionists[16] typically attribute Anglo victories and Mexican defeats to the contrast between "exact, clear, and precise" rules of Anglo-American land and the "vagueness" of corresponding Mexican laws, and whereas traditionalists[17] contend that subsequent legislation enacted by Congress to implement the Treaty "was in reality a violation" of the document, reclamationists argue that courts helped make the Treaty "meaningless over the past century and a half."[18] As I demonstrate with the aid of Professor Martínez's work, the truth is more complex. Neither traditionalists, revisionists, nor reclamationists fully appreciate the role that indeterminacy played in shaping the outcomes of cases in which Treaty rights were litigated. I offer two examples: (1) the significance of deleting Article X of the original Treaty and substituting for it the Protocol of Querétaro, and (2) the implementation of Treaty rights in the California Land Act of 1851.

1. Article X and the Protocol of Querétaro

The Mexican and American representatives who negotiated the Treaty "knew well that most of the Mexican citizens occupying land grants in the ceded territories did not have perfect title to their lands and that the majority were still in the process of fulfilling the requirements of Mexican law."[19] In large measure, this was due to changes in the enforcement of land grant policy, if not changes in the policy itself, that accompanied the instability of Mexican federal governments in the years after Mexico broke from Spain in 1821; the notorious slowness of the Mexican bureaucracy; and of course the individual hardships that attended the citizens of the sparsely populated northern territories of Arizona, California, New Mexico, and Coahuila Texas who tried to follow the rules drawn up by unseen authorities in faraway Mexican capitals.[20] Nowhere were these problems more serious than in Texas, where from 1836 to 1845 the short-lived independent Republic of Texas declared so many lands to be in the public domain and purported to grant them to soldiers, settlers, and speculators, thereby creating clouds over Spanish and Mexican land titles.

Anticipating litigation over who owned what in the soon-to-be-ceded territories, Treaty negotiators working in Mexico drafted Article X, which read:

> All grants of land made by the Mexican government or by the competent authorities, in territories previously appertaining to Mexico . . . shall be respected as valid, to the same extent if said territories had remained within the limits of Mexico. But the grantees of Texas . . . [who] may have been prevented from fulfilling all the conditions of their grants, shall be under the obligation to fulfill the said conditions within the periods limited in the same respectively; such periods to be now counted from the date of the exchange of ratifications.[21]

The language "respected as valid, to the same extent if said territories had remained within the limits of Mexico" would have made it clearer that Mexican civil law, not Anglo-American common law, governed the adjudication of land titles. And the language giving more time to "the grantees of Texas" to perfect their claims would have extended the protections of the Treaty to Tejano claimants, many of whom had fled Texas for Mexico after Anglos declared independence in 1836. But the administration of President James K. Polk would have none of Article X. At President Polk's insistence, the Senate deleted Article X before ratifying the Treaty. To add intrigue to the proceedings, upon a motion by Senator Sam Houston of Texas, the chamber voted to conduct its deliberations in secret; as a result, there are no official records of the debate.[22]

Secretary of State James Buchanan summarized the administration's views on Article X when he said that if it were part of the Treaty "it would be a mere nullity" and "the Judges of our courts would be compelled to disregard it."[23] Insisted Buchanan:

> It is to our glory that no human power exists in this country which can deprive the individual of his property without his consent and transfer it to another. If the grantees of lands in Texas, under the Mexican government, possess valid titles, they can maintain their claims before our courts of justice.[24]

Officials of the Mexican government sought clarification of what was intended by the Senate's deletion of Article X and modification of other parts of the Treaty.[25] The result was a document called the Protocol of Querétaro, which provided, among other things, that in deleting Article X the U.S. government "did not in any way intend to annul grants of land made by Mexico in the ceded territories."[26] The Protocol was signed by U.S. and Mexican representatives at Querétaro, where the Mexican government had set up provisional headquarters to escape the U.S. troops that occupied Mexico City during the Treaty negotiation and ratification processes.

But the Polk administration did not like the Protocol any better than it had liked Article X. Secretary Buchanan declared that the document had "no value"; it was merely a record of conversations between diplomats and lacked the force or effect of law.[27] President Polk kept the Protocol secret and did not send it along with the other Treaty documents to the Senate for the ratification vote. When political opponents discovered the Protocol some six months after the president had declared the ratification process to be completed, there ensued a vigorous debate over whether the document had restored the protections of deleted Article X. Democrats in the administration maintained that it had not; Whigs in Congress, not to mention the Republic of Mexico, maintained that it had. In the end, the Polk administration's position became the official U.S. view and created a dispute with Mexico that persists to this day.[28]

The twin ironies of Buchanan's earlier statement should not be missed. The first irony, as noted in the analysis of Supreme Court decisions interpreting land grant cases presented above, is that even though "no human power exists in this country which can deprive the individual of his property without his consent and transfer it to another," some form of power managed to make this happen all the same. As I explain below, between 1854 and 1930, Mexican litigants or their heirs prevailed in just one-quarter of all cases presenting land title claims decided by the Court during the period. The opinions in these cases demonstrate that, far from being "exact, clear, and precise," U.S. land law in the absence of Article X was so indeterminate as to permit tribunals "to have gone the other way."

For example, in 1865, the Court held that title to church lands at Mission San Jose, California, had passed to the claimant by various mesne conveyances from Catholic Bishop Joseph Alemany of Monterey.[29] The result was curious because Bishop Alemany's claim had been based on "ecclesiastical law" and "actual and undisturbed possession" from 1797 through the date of the U.S. conquest, rather than on any "deed or writing" from Spanish authorities of the type that was so important to the courts in other cases.[30] Yet during the same year, in a separate case, the Court held that title to a tract in Northern California had passed into the public domain even though Maria de Valencia and other heirs of Teodora Peralta had produced the original *expediente* containing all papers necessary to document a grant by then-Governor Pío Pico.[31] The trouble seemed to be the claimant's failure adequately to explain why the *expediente* was found in her possession rather than in the official archives, which "contained no record or trace whatever" of Pico's grant to Peralta.[32] According to the Court, following passage of the California Land Act of 1851, which prescribed the procedures by which Spanish and Mexican grantees were to seek patents confirming their titles, there "commenced a struggle . . . to fritter away the act of Congress, and substitute parol evidence for record evidence. [But w]e have refused to allow oral testimony to prevail when archive evidence was necessary [under Mexican law]."[33]

The second irony is that, despite Buchanan's suggestion that "the grantees of lands in Texas . . . [could] maintain their claims before our courts of justice," Tejanos were not permitted to litigate those claims under the Treaty for over 50 years. In 1856, just two years after the first Treaty cases raising land claims reached the Court, the Justices held that the extant provisions of the Treaty—specifically Article VIII, which deals with the property rights of Mexicans "not established" within the ceded territories—"did not refer to any portion of the acknowledged limits of Texas."[34] Thus were Manuel and Pilar Saviego advised that the Treaty of Guadalupe Hidalgo had nothing to do with their right to inherit two and a half leagues of land in Goliad and Refugio Counties from Pilar's mother Gertrudis Barrera. According to the Court, Barrerra, who had acquired the land in 1834, "abandoned" it by relocating to Matamoros, Tamaulipas, to escape the Texas rebellion in 1835, and dying there in 1842.[35]

It is evident that the text of the Treaty did not dictate the outcomes in these cases. In deciding any of them, the Supreme Court could have "gone the other way." That it did not reflects the indeterminacy that the United States insisted upon before the Senate would ratify the Treaty of Guadalupe Hidalgo.

2. The California Land Act of 1851

Article VIII of the Treaty sought to protect the property rights of Mexicans who had left or otherwise were "not established" in the ceded territories. It provided:

> In the said territories, property of every kind, now belonging to Mexicans not established there, shall be inviolably respected. The present owners, the heirs of these, and all Mexicans who may hereafter acquire said property by contract, shall enjoy with respect to it, guarantees equally ample as if the same belonged to citizens of the United States.[36]

Similarly, Article IX of the Treaty sought to protect the property rights of Mexicans who remained in the ceded territories and who became U.S. citizens rather than "preserve the character of citizens of the Mexican Republic." It provided:

> The Mexicans who . . . shall not preserve the character of citizens of the Mexican Republic . . . shall be incorporated into the Union of the United States and be admitted, at the proper time . . . to the enjoyment of all the rights of citizens of the United States according to the principles of the Constitution; and in the mean time shall be maintained and protected in the free enjoyment of their liberty and property. . . .[37]

In the ceded territories, California became the first battleground over which Mexican and Anglo land claimants fought to sort out their respective rights. This prominence was due in no small measure to the discovery there of gold, which quickly attracted thousands of Anglo-American and other settlers, and in just two years' time transformed California into our thirty-fifth state. Even before these events, the leading opponent of Treaty ratification in the Mexican Congress had called Alta California "our priceless flower" and "our inestimable jewel."[38] At any rate, Mexican grants encompassed over 10 million acres and included "some of the best land suitable for development."[39]

As the Supreme Court tells the tale, Congress, "[t]o fulfill its obligations" to Mexican property holders under Articles VIII and IX, and to provide for "an orderly settlement of Mexican land claims,"[40] passed the California Land Act of 1851.[41] The Act set up a "comprehensive settlement claims procedure":[42] a board of land commissioners was established to decide the rights of "each and every person claiming lands in California by virtue of any right to title derived from the Spanish or Mexican government";[43] a claimant was required to present her claim within two years (a period later extended to five years) or be forever barred from asserting it;[44] the board was to decide the validity of any claim according to the "laws, usages, and customs" of Mexico;[45] a decision of the board could be appealed to federal district court for a de novo determination of rights;[46] final appellate jurisdiction was vested in the Supreme Court;[47] and the final decree of the board, or any patent issued under the Act, constituted a conclusive adjudication of the rights of the claimant as against the United States, but not as against the interests of a third party holding superior title.[48]

Traditionalists,[49] and to a certain extent, reclamationists,[50] regard the California Land Act as "in reality a violation of the Treaty of Guadalupe Hidalgo," "an instrument of evil," and the basis for "needless persecution of the grant holders" by representatives of the federal government and by the district courts. Their views seem to be based mainly on a layman's reading of the U.S. Constitution's Supremacy Clause, which declares that "all Treaties [of the United States] shall be the supreme Law of the Land."[51] The reasoning goes something like this: if the Treaty had already conferred property rights on Mexican land grant holders, then Congress should not have created obstacles to the enforcement of these rights by enacting a statute that, among other things, established a board of land commissioners with the power to screw things up.[52] Under the Act's procedures, including its preservation of appeals to the federal courts, claimants were "considered guilty until they had proved them innocent."[53] Hubert Howe Bancroft, whose multi-volume history of California remains a standard in the field, thought "it would have been infinitely better to confirm promptly all the claims, both valid and fraudulent,"[54] than to put California land grant holders to the test of litigation before the board and the courts.

Of course, revisionists reject these conclusions. Paul Gates, who has written extensively about U.S. land policy in general and the treatment of California land claims in particular, suggests that the California Land Act actually worked a much-need reform of the inefficient procedures that had been used to patent land titles in previously acquired territories, including Florida, Illinois, Louisiana, and Missouri.[55] Professor Gates also defends both the Act and the judges who interpreted it as more than fair to the property interests of Mexicans.[56] Taking on Bancroft and other traditionalists, he writes: "Such denunciation of the Land Act of 1851 and of the subsequent history of adjudication under it reveals an astonishing failure to appreciate the careful protection Anglo-Saxon American law has given private property."[57]

Neither the traditionalists, the reclamationists, nor the revisionists have it quite right. As for the view espoused by traditionalists and reclamationists that the Treaty makes the California Land Act of 1851 illegitimate, at least two bodies of law governing the enforcement of treaties in the U.S. courts suggest that there is plenty of room for disagreement: the "later in time" doctrine and the law of "self-executing" treaties.

The "later in time" doctrine holds that, although U.S. treaties are the supreme law of the land, they nevertheless must give way to other supreme laws of the land with which they conflict, such as congressional legislation, that are enacted after the treaty is ratified.[58] So even if we assume that the California Land Act of 1851, with its short statute of limitations and other traps for the unwary, is in actual conflict with Articles VIII or IX, we should not necessarily conclude that the Act is in reality a violation of the Treaty of Guadalupe Hidalgo.

The law of "self-executing" treaties, which "has been correctly described as 'the most confounding [doctrine] in treaty law,'"[59] is even more troublesome for traditionalists and reclamationists. This "law"[60] distinguishes between self-executing treaties, which may be enforced immediately in federal court, and non-self-executing treaties, which are executory in nature and must first be implemented by legislation.[61] Although treaty law experts unanimously agree that a non-self-executing treaty "is unavailing to the litigant relying on it in court,"[62] they sharply disagree, as do the courts, over how to tell the difference between a self-executing and a non-self-executing treaty.[63] Even Chief Justice John Marshall, who first elaborated the self-execution doctrine in 1829, changed his mind in 1833 about whether the identical language in the same treaty governing Spanish land claims in Florida was self-executing or non-self-executing.[64] There is no reason to suppose that the task would be any easier in the case of the Treaty of Guadalupe Hidalgo.

As for the view espoused by revisionists that the Act worked a welcome reform, or that it was fair both on its face and as applied, a few scratches reveal some serious shortcomings just below the surface. The Act certainly represented an improvement over the pork-barrel politicking that characterized the confirmation or rejection of land titles prior to 1851. But surely Professor Gates places too much faith in civil litigation when he calls the statute "a major step forward in the adjudication of land claims" because it "placed full authority for their final determination in the courts."[65] The very structure of the Act ensured that it would take a claimant years of expensive litigation to obtain his patent. In this regard, the short statute of limitations and the lack of Spanish-speaking agents available to assist the board with its work interpreting Mexican statutes and documents, as others have noted,[66] were the least of claimants' problems. Instead, the Act's true evil lay in its formality, which ensured delay, which in turn ensured costly litigation. To negotiate the three levels of adjudicatory apparatus (board, district court, and Supreme Court), a claimant could ill afford to proceed without counsel, who often took a mortgage in the disputed title as part of the fee. And even if a claimant successfully completed this obstacle course, the patent was conclusive only as to the United States; it did not quiet title in the holder, who could be exposed to yet more lengthy, and potentially unsuccessful, litigation with third party claimants in the state courts.[67] Finally, the value of California lands sharply increased with the influx of settlers, which drove up not only land prices but also the property taxes of grantees and their heirs. Small wonder, as Professor Gates notes, that:

> [i]t was to take years before the last claims were confirmed. By that time some owners or their heirs either had lost their rights through tax delinquency, mortgage foreclosures, or intra family litigation, or the titles had been fragmented into so many parts as to make division and sale of the land difficult.[68]

Moreover, the key example offered by Professor Gates to support the notion that the judiciary "leaned so far in the direction of leniency" so as to demonstrate "the greatest readiness . . . to accept any substantial evidence"[69] to confirm Mexican grants—the case of American pioneer and Bear Flag revolt leader John C. Fremont[70]—supports rather than undermines the notion that Mexican grantees suffered discrimination in tribunals adjudicating Treaty rights. On the one hand were claimants like Fremont, an Anglo who possessed questionable papers documenting dubious title. Still the Supreme Court gave him the benefit of the doubt and confirmed his patent.[71] On the other hand were claimants like Dominga Domínguez, a Mexican who possessed unquestionable papers documenting perfect title. Yet the Court brushed aside her claim because she had failed to make a timely application for a patent with the board of land commissioners, and refused to eject the French and Anglo squatters who had overrun her lands east of Mission San Gabriel, California.[72]

In short, the indeterminate nature of the Treaty, and U.S. laws purporting to implement it, could be manipulated to promote the claims of grant holders when it suited the courts and to extinguish them when it did not.

B. Invisibility

Traditionalists view the adjudication of Spanish and Mexican land grant claims by U.S. courts as an unmitigated disaster. In California, "most Californio landholders lost their lands because of the tremendous expense of litigation and legal fees."[73] In New Mexico and Texas, similar fates awaited Mexican grantees.[74] Although there were periods during which the courts seemed more disposed toward the claims of Mexican grantees and their heirs, by 1930 Mexican Americans, through legal defeat, fraud, or financial exhaustion, had been all but wiped out as a landholding class in the Southwestern United States. Their transformation from masters into servants had been completed, and set the stage for a new chapter in U.S.-Mexico relations: the exploitation of low-wage, migratory Mexican and Mexican American labor.[75]

But revisionists view adjudication as having been a great success for persons who asserted title under Spanish and Mexican land grants. For example, from 1852 to 1854, the first three years that the board of land commissioners was in business, 292 claims were confirmed and 103 claims were rejected—a winning percentage of nearly 74 percent.[76] Revisionists assign blame for the occasional failures on "the careless manner in which owners had handled their titles."[77] And failure, when it occurred, was an equal opportunity outcome; by the time that the board had finished its work in 1857, 43 claims asserted by non-Mexicans, covering over 584,000 acres, had been rejected.[78] With some measure of satisfaction, Professor Gates points out that 346 of the 812 claims presented to the board were submitted by non-Mexicans: Americans, English, Scots, Irish, Germans, and members of other nationalities.[79] Among the "poor Californians" who lost all or part of their litigated claims, he notes, were early California empire builders such as Thomas O. Larkin, John C. Fremont, and even John Sutter, at whose mill the gold that started all the trouble was first discovered.[80]

All of which proves precisely the point I wish to make here: that there is more than one way for the law and its institutions to make Mexicans "disappear," to become invisible. In post-conquest California, Mexicans became conspicuous by their absence among not only the landholding class but also the land claimant class. Why this was so is surely due to a complex combination of many factors, including fraud by non-Mexicans, carelessness by California grantees and their heirs, and the financial distresses mentioned earlier. But the fact of their invisibility, which I have explored elsewhere,[81] is noteworthy all by itself and deserves further study. It is one of the great curiosities of life in California, as it is throughout the Southwest, that the names of the former grantees Alvarado, Bandini, Carrillo, Castro, Cota, Estrada, de la Guerra, Lugo, Martínez, Ortega, Pico, and Vallejo, to name but a few[82] are today affixed to cities, streets, and waterways, but no longer to the recorded deeds of the lands in which these points of interest are located. At least one reclamationist has decried this "invisibility" of Mexican Americans for whom the protections of the Articles VIII and IX of the Treaty of Guadalupe Hidalgo were supposedly drafted.[83]

One need look no further than the Supreme Court's docket to find Mexicans becoming invisible. Accordingly, I attempt to answer two related questions about Treaty cases: (1) who won, and lost, land grant claims; and more importantly, (2) who litigated them?

1. Who won, and lost, land grant claims?

From 1854 to 1930, the Supreme Court published decisions in at least 91 cases raising the question whether the Spanish or Mexican land grant of one or more claimants should be upheld or not upheld under the Treaty of Guadalupe Hidalgo and its implementing legislation.[84] Although the litigants in these cases included individuals, families, partnerships, railroads, utilities, land and mining companies, and government agencies, I have classified them into just two racial groups: "Anglos," which includes all non-Mexican persons, entities, or owners of entities; and "Mexicans," which includes Mexicans, Mexican Americans, and Mission Indians and other Indian groups.[85] The Court decided the cases of these groups as set forth in Table 1:

TABLE 1

Outcomes of Land Grant Cases in the Supreme Court, 1854-1930

Upheld		Not Upheld		No Decision
41		34		16
(45.1%)		(36.4%)		(17.6%)
Anglos	Mexicans	Anglos	Mexicans	
21½	19½	15½	18½	
(52.4%)	(47.6%)	(44.3%)	(52.7%)	

Table 1 shows that the 91 cases produced 75 total decisions either upholding or not upholding the grant; the remaining 16 cases produced no decision as to the validity of the grant. Table 1 also shows that, in the 75 decisions, the Court upheld 41 grants but did not uphold 34 others. These outcomes did not seem to differ markedly by race. As to the 41 grants that were upheld, Anglos won 52.4 percent while Mexicans won 47.6 percent—a fairly close spit. As to the 34 grants that were not upheld, Anglos lost 44.3 percent while Mexican lost 52.7—a slightly poorer set of outcomes for Mexicans, but given the sample spread of only 3 cases, not outrageously so.

On the surface, then, Table 1 would seem to support the revisionist view: when we examine who won, or lost, land grant cases decided under the Treaty, Anglos did not fare substantially better than Mexicans, and Mexicans did not fare substantially worse than Anglos.

2. Who litigated land grant claims?

Focusing on the 75 cases in which the Court reached a decision as to the validity of the grant, Table 2 summarizes who litigated these claims:

TABLE 2

Who Litigated Land Grant Cases in the Supreme Court, 1854-1930

Table 2 shows that just over half of all land grant claims reaching the Supreme Court were asserted by Mexicans. On the surface, this fact does not seem to be remarkable; rather, it seems to suggest that the Court was even-handed in its treatment of Anglo and Mexican claimants. But upon closer inspection, this development must be seen as truly curious. Surely the overwhelming majority of original grantees were Mexican. In fact, by Professor Gates' count, at least 73.7 percent of all claimants who filed claims with the board of land commissioners in California alone were Mexican citizens or former Mexican citizens.[86] Therefore, we should expect to find that the overwhelming number of the claimants litigating in the Supreme Court were Mexican. Instead, what we find is that just half of them were Mexican; the other half were Anglo. What happened to the Mexicans? Apparently, they became invisible.

When the territories that now constitute the states of Arizona, California, Colorado, New Mexico, Nevada, Utah, and parts of Wyoming were ceded to the United States, some 120,000 Mexicans occupied scores of millions of square miles of granted lands. How odd it is that, in the decades following annexation, so few Mexican claimants participated, much less succeeded, the litigation process required to protect those claims.

III. Conclusion

Until 1998, the history academy enjoyed 150 years of solitude in the study of the Treaty of Guadalupe Hidalgo. To be sure the traditional, revisionist, and reclamation perspectives have enriched our understanding of the Treaty and its interpretation. We in the law academy are especially indebted to Chicanos Studies scholars, whose pioneering work on the Treaty has reinforced its relevance even today. Nevertheless, "science has not yet eliminated distance"; each of these views tends to oversimplify the complex role that law and legal institutions have played in the adjudication of Treaty rights. The time is long overdue for the law academy to fill this void. I hope this Article, by drawing on the themes of indeterminacy and invisibility from Lat Crit Theory, contributes to the project of doing so.

Cases Interpreting the Treaty of Guadalupe Hidalgo

Case:	Property rights of original Mexican land grantee upheld?	Parties?
Hooker v. Los Angeles, 188 U.S. 314 (1903)	No decision	Anglo v. gov't
Los Angeles Milling Co. v. Los Angeles, 217 U.S. 217 (1910)	No decision	Non-Mexican land co. v. gov't
Boquillas Land & Cattle Co. v. Curtis, 213 U.S. 339 (1909)	Upheld	Mexican land co. v. Anglo
United States v. Coronado Beach Co., 255 U.S. 472 (1921)	Upheld	Gov't v. Mexican land co.
Fremont v. United States, 58 U.S. (17 How.) 542 (1855)	Upheld	Anglo v. gov't
United States v. Pico, 72 U.S. (5 Wall.) 536 (1867)	Upheld	Gov't v. Mexican
Grisar v. McDowell, 73 U.S. (6 Wall.) 363 (1868)	No decision	Mexican v. gov't
Peralta v. United States, 70 U.S. (3 Wall.) 434 (1866)	Not upheld	Mexican v. gov't
Thompson v. Los Angeles Farming Co., 180 U.S. 72 (1901)	Upheld	Anglo v. non-Mexican land co.
Beard v. Federy, 3 Wall. 400 (1864)	Not upheld	Anglo v. Anglo
United States v. Moreno, 68 U.S. (1 Wall.) 400 (1864)	Upheld	Gov't v. Mexican
United States v. Fossatt, 62 U.S. (21 How.) 445 (1869)	No decision	Gov't v. Anglo
Summa Corp. v. California ex rel. State Land Commission, 466 U.S. 198 (1984)	Upheld	Anglo land co. v. gov't
United States v. O'Donnell, 303 U.S. 501 (1938)	Upheld	Anglo v. gov't
United States v. Title Insurance Trust Co., 265 U.S. 427 (1923)	Anglo grant upheld, but Indians' use claim not upheld	Private co. v. gov't on behalf of real party in interest, Mission Indians
Lockhart v. Johnson, 181 U.S. 516 (1901)	Not upheld	Anglos & Mexicans v. Anglos & Mexicans
United States v. Green, 185 U.S. 256 (1902)	Upheld	Anglos v. gov't
Barker v. Harvey, 181 U.S. 481 (1901)	Upheld, but Indians' servitude not upheld	Anglos v. Mission Indians

(continued)

11

Cases Interpreting the Treaty of Guadalupe Hidalgo, cont.

Case:	Property rights of original Mexican land grantee upheld?	Parties?
Ainsa v. New Mexico & Arizona R.R. Co., 175 U.S. 76 (1889)	Upheld	Mexican administrator v. railroad
Cessna v. United States, 169 U.S. 165 (1898)	Not upheld	Gov't v. Anglo grantee's heirs
Basse v. Brownsville, 154 U.S. 610 (1875)	Not upheld	
United States v. Sandoval, 167 U.S. 278 (1897)	Not upheld	Gov't v. Mexicans
Pueblo of Zia v. United States, 168 U.S. 198 (1897)	Not upheld	Pueblo Indians v. gov't
California Power Works v. Davis, 151 U.S. 389 (1894)	No decision	Anglo land co. v. Anglos
Astiazaran v. Santa Rita Land & Mining Co., 148 U.S. 80 (1893)	Not upheld	Mexicans v. mining co.
Palmer v. United States, 65 U.S. (24 How.) 125 (1860)	Not upheld	Anglos v. gov't
Phillips v. Mound City Land & Water Ass'n, 124 U.S. 605 (1888)	No decision	Anglos v. land co.
United States v. Augisola, 68 U.S. (1 Wall.) 352 (1863)	Upheld	Mexican v. gov't
United States v. Moreno, 68 U.S. (1 Wall.) 400 (1863)	Upheld	Mexican v. gov't
Townsend v. Greeley, 72 U.S. 326 (1866)	Upheld	Anglo v. Anglo
Interstate Land Co. v. Maxwell Land Grant Co., 139 U.S. 569 (1891)	Not upheld	Colorado land co. v. Netherlands land co.
Botiller v. Domínguez, 130 U.S. 238 (1889)	Not upheld	Mexican v. French & Anglo squatters
United States v. Reading, 59 U.S. (18 How.) 1 (1855)	Upheld	Anglo v. gov't
United States v. Nye, 62 U.S. (21 How.) 408 (1858)	Not upheld	Gov't v. Anglo
United States v. Bassett, 62 U.S. (21 How.) 412 (1858)	Not upheld	Gov't v. Anglo
United States v. Rose, 64 U.S. (23 How.) 262 (1859)	Not upheld	Gov't v. Anglo
Cramer v. United States, 261 U.S. 219 (1923)	Indians' rights upheld re: actual occupancy only	Anglo on behalf of Indian claimants v. gov't

(continued)

Cases Interpreting the Treaty of Guadalupe Hidalgo, cont.

Case:	Property rights of original Mexican land grantee upheld?	Parties?
United States v. Santa Fe Pacific R.R. Co., 314 U.S. 339 (1941)	Indians' rights upheld re: actual occupancy only	Gov't on behalf of Indian claimants v. R.R. Co.
United States v. DeArguello, 59 U.S. (18 How.) 539 (1855)	Upheld	Heirs of Mexican v. gov't
Fuentes v. United States, 63 U.S. 443 (1859)	Not upheld	Mexican v. gov't
Luco v. United States, 64 U.S. 515 (1859)	Not upheld	Mexicans v. gov't
Rodríguez v. United States, 68 U.S. 582 (1863)	Upheld	Mexican v. gov't
Newhall v. Sanger, 92 U.S. 761 (1875)	Upheld	Anglo v. Anglo
United States v. McLaughlin, 127 U.S. 428 (1888)	No decision	Gov't v. Anglo
Hornsby v. United States, 77 U.S. 224 (1869)	Upheld	Anglos v. gov't
United States v. Rocha, 76 U.S. 639 (1869)	Upheld	Gov't v. Mexicans
United States v. Throckmorton, 98 U.S. 61 (1878)	Upheld	Anglos v. gov't
United States v. Vallejo, 66 U.S. 541 (1861)	Not upheld	Gov't v. Mexican
Henshaw v. Bissell, 85 U.S. 255 (1873)	Upheld	Anglo v. Anglo
United States v. Castro, 65 U.S. 346 (1869)	Not upheld	Gov't v. Mexicans
Romero v. United States, 68 U.S. 721 (1863)	Not upheld	Mexicans v. gov't
United States v. Bolton, 64 U.S. 341 (1859)	Not upheld	Gov't v. Anglo
More v. Steinbach, 127 U.S. 70 (1888)	Upheld	Anglo v. Anglo
United States v. Sutherland, Guardian of Las Pedronenas, 60 U.S. 363 (1856)	Upheld	Gov't v. Anglo guardian of Mexicans
United States v. Knight's Administrator, 66 U.S. 227 (1861)	Administrator's claim not upheld	Administrator of Anglo v. gov't
United States v. Castillero, 67 U.S. 17 (1862)	Not upheld	Mexican's heirs v. gov't

(continued)

Cases Interpreting the Treaty of Guadalupe Hidalgo, cont.

Case:	Property rights of original Mexican land grantee upheld?	Parties?
Hornsby v. United States, 77 U.S. 224 (1869)	Upheld	Anglo v. Gov't
Ely's Administrator v. United States, 171 U.S. 220 (1898)	Upheld	Administrator of Anglo v. gov't
United States v. Coe, 155 U.S. 76 (1894)	No decision	Gov't v. Anglo
United States v. Ritchie, 58 U.S. 525 (1854)	Upheld	Anglo v. gov't
Stoneroad v. Stoneroad, 15 S.Ct. 822 (1895)	No decision	Anglo v. Anglo
United States v. Sepúlveda, 68 U.S. 104 (1863)	No decision	Gov't v. Mexican
United States v. Circuit Judges, 70 U.S. 673 (1865)	No decision	Gov't entity v. judges
United States v. Heirs of Berreyesa, 64 U.S. 499 (1859)	Upheld	Heirs of Mexican v. gov't
United States v. Baca, 184 U.S. 653 (1902)	No decision	Mexican v. gov't
Devine v. City of Los Angeles, 202 U.S. 313 (1906)	No decision	Anglo v. gov't
United States v. Peña, 175 U.S. 500 (1899)	Upheld	Mexican v. gov't
Board of Trustees of Sevilleta do la Joya Grant v. Board of Trustees of Belen Land Grant, 242 U.S. 595 (1916)	No decision	Mexican v. Mexican
United States v. Ortiz, 176 U.S. 422 (1899)	Not upheld	Gov't v. Mexican
Chávez v. United States, 175 U.S. 552 (1899)	Not upheld	Mexican v. gov't
United States v. Camou, 184 U.S. 572 (1902)	Upheld	Gov't v. Mexican
Hayes v. United States, 170 U.S. 637 (1898)	Not upheld	Anglo v. gov't
Bergere v. United States, 168 U.S. 66 (1897)	Not upheld	Mexican v. gov't
United States v. Larkin, 59 U.S. 557 (1855)	Upheld	Gov't v. Anglos

(continued)

Cases Interpreting the Treaty of Guadalupe Hidalgo, cont.

Case:	Property rights of original Mexican land grantee upheld?	Parties?
Crespin v. United States, 168 U.S. 208 (1897)	Not upheld	Anglos v. gov't
United States v. Cervantes, 59 U.S. 553 (1855)	Upheld	Gov't v. Mexican
United States v. Pacheco, 69 U.S. (2 Wall.) 587 (1864)	Upheld	Gov't v. Mexican
De la Paz Valdez de Conway v. United States, 175 U.S. 60 (1897)	Not upheld	Mexican v. gov't on behalf of Pueblo Indians
United States v. Galbraith, 63 U.S. 89 (1859)	Not upheld	Anglos v. gov't
United States v. West's Heirs, 63 U.S. 3s15 (1859)	Upheld	Anglos heirs v. gov't
United States v. Pendell & Excobar, 185 U.S. 189 (1902)	Upheld	Anglo & Mexican gov't
United States v. Cambuston, 61 U.S. 59 (1857)	Not upheld	Gov't v. Anglo
Heirs of Yturbide, 63 U.S. 290 (1859)	No decision	Heirs of Mexican v. gov't
United States v. Johnson, 68 U.S. 326 (1863)	Upheld	Gov't v. Anglo
Whitney v. United States, 181 U.S. 104 (1901)	Not upheld	Anglo v. gov't
DeGuyer v. Banning, 167 U.S. 723 (1897)	Not upheld	Mexican v. gov't
United States v. D'Aguirre, 68 U.S. 311 (1863)	Upheld	Gov't v. Mexican
Castro v. Hendricks, 64 U.S. 438 (1859)	Not upheld	Mexican v. Commissioner of General Land Office
San Pedro & Canon Del Ague Co. v. United States, 146 U.S. 120 (1892)	Not upheld	Mexican land co. v. gov't
Miller v. Dale, 92 U.S. 473 (1875)	Upheld	Anglo v. Anglo
Gwin v. United States, 184 U.S. 669 (1902)	Not upheld	Anglo v. gov't

Appendixes

United States Supreme Court Cases Regarding Land Claims Under the Treaty of Guadalupe Hidalgo, 1854-1940

Appendix A

Cases Upholding Anglos' Land Claims

1. Beard v. Federy, 3 Wall. 400 (1864)
2. Cessna v. United States, 169 U.S. 165 (1898)
3. Crespin v. United States, 168 U.S. 208 (1897)
4. Gwin v. United States, 184 U.S. 669 (1902)
5. Hayes v. United States, 170 U.S. 637 (1898)
6. Interstate Land Co. v. Maxwell Land Grant Co., 139 U.S. 569 (1891)
7. Lockhart v. Johnson, 181 U.S. 516 (1901)*
8. Palmer v. United States, 65 U.S. (24 How.) 125 (1860)
9. United States v. Bassett, 62 U.S. (21 How.) 412 (1858)
10. United States v. Bolton, 64 U.S. 341 (1859)
11. United States v. Cambuston, 61 U.S. 59 (1857)
12. United States v. Galbraith, 63 U.S. 89 (1859)*
13. United States v. Knight's Administrator, 66 U.S. 227 (1861)
14. United States v. Nye, 62 U.S. (21 How.) 408 (1858)
15. United States v. Rose, 64 U.S. (23 How.) 262 (1859)
16. Whitney v. United States, 181 U.S. 104 (1901)

Split decision

Appendix B

Cases Upholding Mexicans' and Indians' Land Claims

1. Astiazaran v. Santa Rita Land & Mining Co., 148 U.S. 80 (1893)
2. Bergere v. United States, 168 U.S. 66 (1897)
3. Botiller v. Domínguez, 130 U.S. 238 (1889)
4. Castro v. Hendricks, 64 U.S. 438 (1859)
5. Chávez v. United States, 175 U.S. 552 (1899)
6. De Guyer v. Banning, 167 U.S. 723 (1897)
7. De la Paz Valdez de Conway v. United States, 175 U.S. 60 (1897)
8. Fuentes v. United States, 63 U.S. 443 (1859)
9. Lockhart v. Johnson, 181 U.S. 516 (1901)*
10. Luco v. United States, 64 U.S. 515 (1859)
11. Peralta v. United States, 70 U.S. (3 Wall.) 434 (1866)
12. Pueblo of Zia v. United States, 168 U.S. 198 (1897)
13. Romero v. United States, 68 U.S. 721 (1863)
14. San Pedro & Canon Del Ague Co. v. United States, 146 U.S. 120 (1892)
15. United States v. Castillero, 67 U.S. 17 (1862)

16. United States v. Castro, 65 U.S. 346 (1869)
17. United States v. Ortiz, 176 U.S. 422 (1899)
18. United States v. Sandoval, 167 U.S. 278 (1897)
19. United States v. Vallejo, 66 U.S. 541 (1861)

    Split decision

Appendix C

Cases Not Upholding Anglos' Land Claims

1. Barker v. Harvey, 181 U.S. 481 (1901)
2. Ely's Administrator v. United States, 171 U.S. 220 (1898)
3. Fremont v. United States, 58 U.S. (17 How.) 542 (1855)
4. Henshaw v. Bissell, 85 U.S. 255 (1873)
5. Hornsby v. United States, 77 U.S. 224 (1869)
6. Miller v. Dale, 92 U.S. 473 (1875)
7. More v. Steinbach, 127 U.S. 70 (1888)
8. Newhall v. Sanger, 92 U.S. 761 (1875)
9. Summa Corp. v. California ex rel. State Land Commission, 466 U.S. 198 (1984)
10. Thompson v. Los Angeles Farming Co., 180 U.S. 72 (1901)
11. Townsend v. Greeley, 72 U.S. 326 (1866)
12. United States v. Galbraith, 63 U.S. 89 (1859)*
13. United States v. Green, 185 U.S. 256 (1902)
14. United States v. Johnson, 68 U.S. 326 (1863)
15. United States v. Larkin, 59 U.S. 557 (1855)
16. United States v. O'Donnell, 303 U.S. 501 (1938)
17. United States v. Pendell & Escobar, 185 U.S. 189 (1902)*
18. United States v. Reading, 59 U.S. (18 How.) 1 (1855)
19. United States v. Ritchie, 58 U.S. 525 (1854)
20. United States v. Throckmorton, 98 U.S. 61 (1878)
21. United States v. Title Insurance Trust Co., 265 U.S. 427 (1923)

    Split decision

Appendix D

Cases Not Upholding Mexicans' and Indians' Land Claims

1. Ainsa v. New Mexico & Arizona R.R. Co., 175 U.S. 76 (1889)
2. Boquillas Land & Cattle Co. v. Curtis, 213 U.S. 339 (1909)
3. Cramer v. United States, 261 U.S. 219 (1923)
4. Rodríguez v. United States, 68 U.S. 582 (1863)
5. United States v. Augisola, 68 U.S. (1 Wall.) 352 (1863)
6. United States v. Camou, 184 U.S. 572 (1902)
7. United States v. Cervantes, 59 U.S. 553 (1855)
8. United States v. Coronado Beach Co., 255 U.S. 472 (1921)

9. United States v. D'A'guirre, 68 U.S. 311 (1863)
10. United States v. De Arguello, 59 U.S. (18 How.) 539 (1855)
11. United States v. Heirs of Berreyesa, 64 U.S. 499 (1859)
12. United States v. Moreno, 68 U.S. (1 Wall.) 400 (1864)
13. United States v. Pacheco, 69 U.S. (2 Wall.) 587 (1864)
14. United States v. Peña, 175 U.S. 500 (1899)
15. United States v. Pendell & Escobar, 185 U.S. 189 (1902)*
16. United States v. Pico, 72 U.S. (5 Wall.) 536 (1867)
17. United States v. Rocha, 76 U.S. 639 (1869)
18. United States v. Santa Fe Pacific R.R. Co., 314 U.S. 339 (1941)
19. United States v. Sutherland, Guardian of Las Pedrorenas, 60 U.S. 363 (1856)

*Split decision

Appendix E
Cases Reaching No Decision Regarding Land Claims

1. Board of Trustees of Sevilleta do la Joya Grant v. Board of Trustees of Belen Land Grant, 242 U.S. 595 (1916)
2. California Power Works v. Davis, 151 U.S. 389 (1894)
3. Devine v. City of Los Angeles, 202 U.S. 313 (1906)
4. Grisar v. McDowell, 73 U.S. (6 Wall.) 363 (1868)
5. Heirs of Yturbide, 63 U.S. 290 (1859)
6. Hooker v. Los Angeles, 188 U.S. 314 (1903)
7. Los Angeles Milling Co. v. Los Angeles, 217 U.S. 217 (1910)
8. Phillips v. Mound City Land & Water Ass'n, 124 U.S. 605 (1888)
9. Stoneroad v. Stoneroad, 15 S.Ct. 822 (1895)
10. United States v. Baca, 184 U.S. 653 (1902)
11. United States v. Circuit Judges, 70 U.S. 673 (1865)
12. United States v. Coe, 155 U.S. 76 (1894)
13. United States v. Fossatt, 62 U.S. (21 How.) 445 (1869)
14. United States v. McLaughlin, 127 U.S. 428 (1888)
15. United States v. Sepulveda, 68 U.S. 104 (1863)

Notes

[1] GABRIEL GARCÍA MÁRQUEZ, ONE HUNDRED YEARS OF SOLITUDE (Harper Collins 1st ed. 1991).
[2] See, e.g., 6 HUBERT HOWE BANCROFT, HISTORY OF CALIFORNIA (1888); MALCOLM EBRIGHT, LAND GRANTS AND LAWSUITS IN NORTHERN NEW MEXICO (1994); PAUL GATES, LAND AND LAW IN CALIFORNIA: ESSAYS ON LAND POLICY (1991); RICHARD GRISWOLD DEL CASTILLO, THE TREATY OF GUADALUPE HIDALGO: A LEGACY OF CONFLICT (1990); DOUGLAS MONROY, THROWN AMONG STRANGERS: THE MAKING OF A MEXICAN CULTURE IN FRONTIER CALIFORNIA (1990); JIM BERRY PEARSON, THE MAXWELL LAND GRANT (1961); LEONARD PITT, THE DECLINE OF THE CALIFORNIOS (1970); WILLIAM W. ROBINSON, LAND IN CALIFORNIA (1948); AARON M. SAKOLSKI,

THE GREAT AMERICAN LAND BUBBLE (1932); WILLIAM W. MORROW, SPANISH AND MEXICAN PRIVATE LAND GRANTS (1923); Paul W. Gates, *The California Land Act of 1851*, 50 CALIF. HIST. Q. 395 (1971); Rodolfo O. de la Garza & Karl Schmitt, *Texas Land Grants and Chicano-Mexican Relations: A Case Study*, 21 LAT. AM. RES. REV. 123 (1986); Robert D. Shadow & María Rodríguez-Shadow, *From Repatriation to Partition: A History of the Mora Land Grant, 1835-1916*, 70 N.M. HIST. REV. 257 (1995).

[3] *See* Federico M. Cheever, *A New Approach to Spanish and Mexican Land Grants and the Public Interest Doctrine: Defining the Property Interest Protected by the Treaty of Guadalupe Hidalgo*, 33 UCLA L. REV. 1364 (1986); Richard D. García & Todd Howland, *Determining the Legitimacy of Spanish Land Grants in Colorado: Conflicting Values, Legal Pluralism, and Demystification of the Sangre de Cristo/Rael Cases*, 16 CHICANO-LATINO L. REV. 39 (1995); Plácido Gómez, *The History and Adjudication of the Common Lands of Spanish and Mexican Land Grants*, 25 NAT. RESOURCES L.J. 1039 (1985); Christine A. Klein, *Treaties of Conquest: Property Rights, Indian Treaties, and the Treaty of Guadalupe Hidalgo*, 26 N.M. L. REV. 201 (1996); Guadalupe T. Luna, *Chicana/o Land Tenure in the Agrarian Domain: On the Edge of a Naked Knife*, 3 MICH. J. RACE & L. 39 (1998); Guadalupe T. Luna, *"Agricultural Underdogs" and International Agreements: The Legal Context of Agricultural Workers Within the Rural Economy*, 26 N.M. L. REV. 9 (1996); Peter Reich, *The "Hispanic" Roots of Prior Appropriation in Arizona*, 27 ARIZ. ST. L.J. 649 (1995).

[4] *See* Kevin R. Johnson & George A. Martínez, *Three Cheers for Chicana/o Studies and the Emergence of Lat Crit Theory: Some Thoughts on the Roots of a Movement* (based on papers presented at 1998 Sixth Annual Western Law Teachers at Color Conference, sponsored by University of Oregon) (1998).

[5] Lalo López, *Legacy of a Land Grab*, HISPANIC MAG., Sept. 1997, at 23.

[6] *See, e.g.*, GRISWOLD DEL CASTILLO, *supra* note 2, at xii ("With an arrogance born of superior military, economic, and industrial power, the United States virtually dictated the terms of the settlement. The treaty established a pattern of inequality between the two countries, and this lopsided relationship has influenced Mexican American relations ever since.").

[7] *See, e.g.*, 6 BANCROFT, *supra* note 2, at 576-81; [cfs]John Walton Caughey, California 309 (1964); ROBERT GLASS CLELAND, HISTORY OF CALIFORNIA: THE AMERICAN PERIOD 411-12 (1922); JOSIAH ROYCE, CALIFORNIA FROM THE CONQUEST IN 1846 TO THE SECOND VIGILANCE COMMITTEE IN SAN FRANCISCO 360-83 (1948)[cfn].

[8] *See, e.g.*, GATES, *supra* note 2, at 51 (Anglo-American law respecting land titles is "exact, clear, and precise and does not allow for the vagueness of the Mexican land system in California."); *see also* MORROW, *supra* note 2, at 15; [cfs]Robinson, *supra* note 2, at 109 (1948).

[9] *See, e.g.*, ARMANDO B. RENDÓN, CHICANO MANIFESTO: HISTORY AND ASPIRATIONS OF THE SECOND LARGEST MINORITY 81 (25th Anniversary ed., Ollin & Associates 1996) (1971). ("The Treaty of Guadalupe Hidalgo is the most important document concerning Mexican Americans that exists. From it stem specific guarantees affecting our civil rights, language, culture, and religion."); *see also* PATRICIA BELL BLAWIS, TIJERINA AND THE LAND GRANTS 37 (1970); RICHARD GARDNER, GRITO! REIES TIJERINA AND THE NEW MEXICAN LAND GRANT WARS OF 1967 (1970); Fernando Chacón Gómez, *The Intended and Actual Effects of Article VIII of the Treaty of Guadalupe Hidalgo: Mexican Treaty Rights Under International and Domestic Law*[cfn] (unpublished Ph.D. dissertation), in Griswold del Castillo, *supra* note 2, at 145-46.

[10] *See* López, *supra* note 5, at 24.

[11] *See, e.g.*, JEROME FRANK, LAW AND THE MODERN MIND 7 (1936); KARL LLEWELLYN, JURISPRUDENCE: REALISM IN THEORY AND PRACTICE 122-23 (1962); Felix S. Cohen, Transcendental Nonsense and the Functional Approach, 35 Colum. L. Rev. 809, 833 (1935); Roscoe Pound, The Call for a Realist Jurisprudence, 44 Harv. L. Rev. 697, 707 (1931).

[12] *See, e.g.*, RICHARD A. POSNER, THE PROBLEMS OF JURISPRUDENCE 23 (1990).

[13] *See, e.g.*, DAVID A. KAIRYS, THE POLITICS OF LAW: A PROGRESSIVE CRITIQUE 140, 160-61 (1982); Mark V. Tushnet, *Following the Rules Laid Down: A Critique of Interpretivism and Neutral Principles*, 96 HARV. L. REV. 781, 819 (1983).

[14] *See, e.g.*, H.L.A. HART, THE CONCEPT OF LAW 132 (1961).

[15] George A. Martínez, *Legal Indeterminacy, Judicial Discretion, and the Mexican American Litigation Experience: 1930-1980*, 27 U.C. DAVIS. L. REV. 555, 557-60 (1983); *see, e.g.*, Christopher David Ruiz

Cameron, *How the García Cousins Lost Their Accents: Understanding the Language of Title VII Decisions Approving English-Only Rules as the Product of Racial Dualism, Latino Invisibility, and Legal Indeterminacy,* 85 CAL. L. REV. 1347, 1385-86 (1997) (discussing role that Title VII indeterminacy plays in decisions adjudicating challenges to "English-only" as national origin discrimination); *see also* George A. Martínez, *Some Thoughts on Law and Interpretation,* 50 SMU L. REV. 1651, 1653-62 (1997) (discussing distinctive role that interpretation plays in law).

[16]Gates, *supra* note 2, at 51.

[17]6 BANCROFT, *supra* note 2, at 576-81.

[18]*See, e.g.,* CHACÓN GÓMEZ, *supra* note 9, at 197, in GRISWOLD DEL CASTILLO, *supra* note 2, at 145.

[19]GRISWOLD DEL CASTILLO, *supra* note 2, at 48.

[20]*Id.*

[21]5 TREATIES AND OTHER INTERNATIONAL ACTS OF THE UNITED STATES OF AMERICA 242 (Hunter Miller ed., U.S. Gov't Printing Off. 1937).

[22]Exec. Doc. No. 52, 30th Cong., 1st Sess. 9 (1848).

[23]5 TREATIES AND OTHER INTERNATIONAL ACTS OF THE UNITED STATES OF AMERICA, *supra* note 21, at 255.

[24]*Id.*

[25]Indeterminacy was also injected into the civil and property rights law affecting Mexicans who chose to remain in the U.S. and become citizens. Originally, in Article IX, Treaty negotiators agreed on the following language:

> The Mexicans who, in the territories aforesaid, shall not preserve the character of citizens of the Mexican Republic, conformably with what is stipulated in the preceding Article, shall be incorporated in the Union of the United States as soon as possible.... In the meantime, they shall be maintained and protected in the enjoyment of their liberty, their property, and the civil rights now vested in them according to the Mexican laws. With respect to political rights, their condition shall be on an equality with that of the inhabitants of the other territories of the United States.

Treaty of Peace Friendship, Limits and Settlement Between the United States of America and the Mexican Republic, Feb. 2, 1848, U.S.-Mex., art. IX, 9 Stat. 922, 929; hereinafter Treaty of Guadalupe Hidalgo, *reprinted in* 9 TREATIES AND OTHER INTERNATIONAL AGREEMENTS OF THE UNITED STATES OF AMERICA, 1776-1949, 791, 797 (Charles I. Berans ed., 1972).

[26]Protocol of Querétaro, art. 2, *reprinted in* GRISWOLD DEL CASTILLO, *supra* note 2, at 182; *see also* Geoffrey Mawn, *The Treaty of Guadalupe Hidalgo or the Protocol of Querétaro?,* 14 J. of the West, 57, 58 (1975) (discussing Protocol and its background in detail).

[27]GRISWOLD DEL CASTILLO, *supra* note 2, at 54; Mawn, *supra* note 26, at 59.

[28]GRISWOLD DEL CASTILLO, *supra* note 2, at 54; Mawn, *supra* note 26, at 59.

[29]Beard v. Federy, 70 U.S. (3 Wall.) 478, 489 (1865).

[30]*Id.* For my understanding of both the title confirmation process and the formalities of Spanish and Mexican land law that are an essential component of that process, I am indebted to Professor Luna, whose thorough scholarship on the Treaty has made her its leading expert in the law academy. *See,* e.g., Luna, *supra* note 3.

[31]Peralta v. United States, 70 U.S. (3 Wall.) 434, 440 (1865).

[32]*Id.* at 435.

[33]*Id.* at 440.

[34]McKinney v. Saviego, 59 U.S. (18 How.) 235, 240 (1855).

[35]*Id.* at 237.

[36]Treaty of Guadalupe Hidalgo, art. VIII, reprinted in 9 TREATIES AND OTHER INTERNATIONAL AGREEMENTS OF THE UNITED STATES OF AMERICA, 1776-1949, *supra* note 25, at 796.

[37]Treaty of Guadalupe Hidalgo, *supra* note 25, art. IX, *codified at* 9 Stat. 922 (1948), *reprinted* in 9 TREATIES AND OTHER INTERNATIONAL AGREEMENTS OF THE UNITED STATES OF AMERICA, 1776-1949, *supra* note 25, at 797.

[38]Manuel Crescencio Rejón, *Observations on the Treaty of Guadalupe Hidalgo, in* PENSAMIENTO POLÍTICO 127, 133 (UNAM ed., 1968), *quoted in* GRISWOLD DEL CASTILLO, *supra* note 2, at 50 & n.16.

[39]Summa Corp. v. California ex rel. State Lands Commission, 466 U.S. 198, 202 (1984).
[40]*Id.* at 203.
[41]Act of Mar. 3, 1851, ch. 41, 9 Stat. 632 (1851).
[42]Summa Corp., 466 U.S. at 203.
[43]Act of Mar. 3, 1851, ch. 41, § 8.
[44]*Id.* §13; see, e.g., Botiller v. Domínguez, 130 U.S. 238, 246 (1889).
[45]Act of Mar. 3, 1851, ch. 41, §11.
[46]*Id.* §9; see, e.g., Grisar v. McDowell, 73 U.S. (6 Wall.) 363 (1867).
[47]Act of Mar. 3, 1851, ch. 41, §10.
[48]*Id.* §15.
[49]*See* 6 BANCROFT, *supra* note 2, at 576-81; CAUGHEY, *supra* note 7, at 309; CLELAND, *supra* note 7, at 411-12; ROYCE, *supra* note 7, at 360-83.
[50]*See, e.g.,* RENDÓN, *supra* note 9, at 81 (calling upon Chicanos to learn of the "exact processes by which the Treaty of Guadalupe Hidalgo was made meaningless over the past century and a half"); Chacón Gómez, *supra* note 9, at 197 (contending that, due to New Mexican judges' ignorance of local tradition, "the century-old concept of flexibility of the common law may indeed have been 'bastardized'"), *quoted in* GRISWOLD DEL CASTILLO, *supra* note 2, at 145.
[51]U.S. Const. art. VI, cl. 2.
[52]*See generally* GRISWOLD DEL CASTILLO, *supra* note 2, at 76-77.
[53]6 Bancroft, *supra* note 2, at 576-577.
[54]*Id.* at 579.
[55]*See* Gates, *supra* note 2, at 395, 398. Until 1851, the usual procedure for testing the validity of land claims in newly acquired U.S. territories, including the former French territories of the Louisiana Purchase and the former Spanish territories of Florida, was to establish a board of land commissioners to pass upon claimants' written and oral documentation in the first instance but to reserve for Congress the job of confirming or rejecting titles in the final analysis. Too often, Congress played its role inefficiently or not at all. At the urging of persistent lobbyists, individual bills to confirm or reject titles were passed and sometimes repealed; committees of representatives spent "countless hours" sifting through documents they often did not read or understand; Congress sometimes resorted to "blanket confirmations" of smaller claims that received no serious consideration. Concluded Professor Gates: "By 1851 experience had shown the advisability of placing the burden of adjudication on the courts rather than on Congress." *Id.* at 397-98.
[56]If anything, Professor Gates argues, the courts gave Mexican grantees the benefit of the doubt. He reads the opinions of Justice Stephen J. Field, the great exponent of liberty and property rights under the Fourteenth Amendment, and himself a California lawyer, as disregarding Mexican law when doing so would favor the claimant. He also singles out Judges Ogden Hoffman and I.S.K. Ogier, two of Justice Field's colleagues on the federal district bench in Californian, for their "leniency" toward the claims of grant holders. *See Id.* at 402, 405.
[57]Gates, *supra* note 2, at 405.
[58]*See* Klein, *supra* note 3, at 217; see also, e.g., Ainsa v. Arizona & N.M. RR. Co., 175 U.S. 76, 83-84 (1899); United States v. Sandoval, 167 U.S. 278, 293-94 (1897); California Power Works v. Davis, 151 U.S. 389, 394-95 (1894); but see LOUIS HENKIN, FOREIGN AFFAIRS AND THE CONSTITUTION 156-57, 163-64 (1971) (acknowledging rule but challenging its legitimacy).
[59]Carlos Manuel Vázquez, *Treaty-Based Rights and Remedies of Individuals,* 92 Colum. L. Rev. 1082, 1121 (1992) (quoting United States v. Postal, 589 F.2d 862, 876 [5th Cir. 1979], *cert. denied,* 444 U.S. 832 [1979]).
[60]Professor Vázquez has explained that the sometimes incoherent law of self-executing treaties actually consists of four distinct "doctrines" that are "masquerading as one." Carlos Manuel Vázquez, *The Four Doctrines of Self-Executing Treaties,* 89 Am. J. Int'l L. 695, 695 (1995).
[61]*See* Vázquez, *supra* note 59, at 1117.
[62]*Id.* at 1121.
[63]*See Id.* at 1117-23.
[64]*Compare* Foster v. Neilson, 27 U.S. (2 Pet.) 253, 310, 314 (1829) (rejecting treaty-based claim to title on ground treaty merely provided that Spanish grants "*shall be* ratified and confirmed") (emphasis added), *with* United States v. Percheman, 32 U.S. (7 Pet.) 51, 88 (1833) (embracing treaty-based claim to title on

ground Spanish text of treaty provided such grants were to "*remain* ratified and confirmed") (emphasis added). Neither Article VIII nor Article IX of Treaty of Guadalupe Hidalgo even uses words self-executing terms "ratified" or "confirmed," but non-self-executing term "shall be" appears several times).

[65] Gates, *supra* note 2, at 398.

[66] *See,* e.g., George A. Martínez, *Dispute Resolution and the Treaty of Guadalupe Hidalgo: Parallels and Possible Lessons for Dispute Resolution Under NAFTA,* 5 Sw. J. of L. & Trade 147 (1998).

[67] [cfi]*See,* e.g., Phillips v. Mound City Land & Water Ass'n, 124 U.S. 605, 610-12 (1888) (dismissing for want of a federal question under California Land Act of 1851 an action for partition brought by one private claimant against another in state court).

[68] Gates, *supra* note 2, at 398.

[69] *Id.* at 404.

[70] Fremont v. United States, 58 U.S. (17 How.) 542 (1855).

[71] *Id.* at 565.

[72] Botiller v. Domínguez, 130 U.S., at 255.

[73] GRISWOLD DEL CASTILLO, *supra* note 2, at 73-74.

[74] *Id.* at 78, 83-84.

[75] *See, e.g.,* JUAN GÓMEZ-QUIÑONES, MEXICAN AMERICAN LABOR, 1790-1990 45 (1994); MARY ROMERO, MAID IN THE U.S.A. 9-10 (1992); Luna, *Agricultural Underdogs, supra* note 3, at 14-15. For a general discussion, see RODOLFO ACUÑA, OCCUPIED AMERICA (3d ed. 1988).

[76] Gates, *supra* note 2, at 401-02.

[77] *Id.* at 398.

[78] *Id.* at 408.

[79] *Id.*

[80] *Id.* at 408, 410.

[81] *See* Cameron, *supra* note 15, at 1372-73.

[82] *See* Gates, *supra* note 2, at 408.

[83] Chacón Gómez, *supra* note 9, at 197, in GRISWOLD DEL CASTILLO, *supra* note 2, at 145. The "invisibility" of Latinos in many walks of American life is a theme that runs strongly in the critical literature of the academies of both history, *see, e.g.,* LA RAZA: FORGOTTEN AMERICANS (Julian Samora ed., 1966); George I. Sánchez, Forgotten People (1967), and law, see, e.g., Kevin R. Johnson, *Los Olvidados: Images of the Immigrant Political Power of Noncitizens, and Immigration Law and Enforcement,* 1993 BYU L. Rev. 1139; Juan F. Perea, *Los Olvidados: on the Making of an Invisible People,* 70 NYU L. Rev. 965 (1995).

[85] With some trepidation, I have assigned litigants to these categories based on their surnames, and to a lesser degree, their descriptions, as set forth in the Supreme Court's reported decisions. I am well aware that this method has its limits; for example, it could exclude many persons of Mexican heritage like me. *See,* e.g., Cameron, *supra* note 15, at n. 73. But given the limited data provided by these cases and their historical distance from us, I am satisfied that this method offers a useful sketch of who the litigants were.

[86] *See* Gates, *supra* note 2, at 408 (noting that 133 of 812 claims presented to board of land commissioners were brought by naturalized Mexican, and presumably Anglo, citizens).

Immigration, Citizenship, and U.S./Mexico Relations

THE TALE OF TWO TREATIES

*Kevin R. Johnson**
UNIVERSITY OF CALIFORNIA AT DAVIS

The 1990s have been fascinating times for study of United States-Mexico relations. In the decade's early years, public discussion in the United States centered on the ratification of the North American Free Trade Agreement (NAFTA), a controversial trade accord between the United States, Mexico, and Canada.[1] The NAFTA debate in the United States focused on whether this country should enter into a trade agreement with Mexico; Canada's inclusion as a trading partner provoked considerably less controversy.[2] Free trade forces ultimately prevailed and Congress approved the agreement.[3]

Not long after NAFTA's approval, debate over immigration, particularly undocumented immigration from Mexico, hit a fever pitch in the United States. Tinged by a distinctly anti-Mexican tilt,[4] California's Proposition 187, which swept to a landslide victory in the November 1994 elections,[5] marked the beginning of the restrictionist onslaught. Congress soon after funded monumental efforts to bolster enforcement along the United States-Mexico border through military-style operations.[6] Like the infamous deportation campaign of 1954 known as Operation "Wetback,"[7] in which the United States rounded up and deported Mexican immigrants and United States citizens of Mexican ancestry, recent border enforcement efforts meant tightening migration controls along the nation's southern border with Mexico and increased deportation of Mexican citizens. Tighter enforcement came despite the longstanding charges that U.S. Border Patrol officers all-too-frequently abuse Mexican citizens.[8] At the same time, the federal government stiffened the immigration laws[9] and drastically limited the public benefits available to legal as well as undocumented immigrants.[10] This legislative action disparately impacts Mexican citizens.[11]

---

*Associate Dean for Academic Affairs and Professor of Law, University of California at Davis School of Law. A.B., University of California at Berkeley; J.D., Harvard University. Conversations with George A. Martínez, David López, and Arturo Gándara helped me conceptualize the arguments presented in this article. I presented a draft of this essay at the "Understanding the Treaty of Guadalupe Hidalgo on Its 150th Anniversary" conference held in February 1998 at Southwestern University School of Law in Los Angeles, California. My thanks to Chris Cameron, who organized the conference and invited me to participate. I appreciate the comments and encouragement of the conference participants, especially Rudy Acuña, Refugio Rochín, Eileen Gauna, Louis A. Martínez, and James F. Smith. I also presented this paper in March 1998 at Southern Methodist University School of Law at a conference entitled "A Tale of Two Treaties: United States/Mexico Relations Through the Lens of the Treaty of Guadalupe Hidalgo and NAFTA." I thank Joseph J. Norton and George A. Martínez for inviting me to participate in that conference. Chris Cameron, George A. Martínez, Sushil Narayanan, Guadalupe Luna, and David López offered helpful comments on a draft of this article. Roberta S. Hulit provided much-appreciated editorial assistance.

One might wonder what this modern history has to do with the Treaty of Guadalupe Hidalgo, which in 1848 ended the United States-Mexican War.[12] As part of the price for peace and a large piece of Mexican land, the Treaty, among other things, purported to protect the rights of Mexican citizens in the territory surrendered to the United States.[13] However, as many have carefully documented, the spirit, if not the letter, of the Treaty went largely unfulfilled.[14] Most fundamentally, many Mexican citizens, transformed by the Treaty into United States citizens of Mexican descent, and their descendants, never enjoyed full membership rights in this society, despite the Treaty's promise that they would.[15]

Though dealing with issues of citizenship, the Treaty of Guadalupe Hidalgo did not address future migration between the United States and Mexico, as the nations were reconfigured under the Treaty and later the Gadsden Purchase.[16] Thus, the Treaty drafters failed to confront a question that ultimately came to dominate relations between the two nations. This omission is understandable in light of the fact that the U.S. government did not enact the first comprehensive immigration laws until several decades after Mexico and the United States consummated the Treaty.[17] Unlike modern times, immigration did not preoccupy the national consciousness.

Like its predecessor, NAFTA failed to deal generally with the question of migration. Unlike the omission of migration from the Treaty of Guadalupe Hidalgo, however, the modern failure is striking because migration had emerged as one of the most, if not the most, contentious issues in United States-Mexico relations during the latter half of the twentieth century.[18] A high level of migration between the two nations is a simple fact of modern life. Indeed, not long after NAFTA's ratification, Mexico, for the first time in its history, allowed its citizens to become U.S. citizens while maintaining Mexican nationality,[19] thereby legally recognizing—in a way that NAFTA did not—the transnational identity of a segment of its population.[20]

Against this backdrop, one might expect the NAFTA partners to at least discuss immigration.[21] From the outset, however, NAFTA "was limited to free trade as opposed to a common market, which would allow for the free flow of all factors of production."[22] In any event, if NAFTA had dealt with immigration, it presumably would have responded to domestic political pressures in the United States and restricted, not liberalized, migration from Mexico to this country.

Suppose, however, that the political climate changed dramatically in a way that "open borders" advocates might endorse. Assume that the United States agreed to permit labor migration between the two nations while (to be fair) prohibiting the exploitation of Mexican labor.[23] Would the terms of such an agreement be enforceable? Unfortunately, significant evidence suggests that they would not be, at least under present political, economic, and social conditions. Experience with the lax enforcement of the Treaty of Guadalupe Hidalgo, and United States anti-discrimination laws generally, suggest that undue confidence in the effectiveness of such a compact would not be justified.[24]

Economic and social forces shape the rate of legal and illegal immigration to the United States and the legal and social status of migrants in the country. Business gains in the United States result from a low wage labor force provided by migration from Mexico.[25] The public in the United States, however, resists formalizing the immigration status of Mexican immigrants, who are viewed as racially and culturally different and a threat to their economic well-being.[26] The uncertain legal status of undocumented immigrants renders them all the more susceptible to exploitation in the workplace. It is difficult to see how law, whether through bilateral agreement or otherwise, could substantially change this complex social dynamic.

Part I of this article considers various provisions of the Treaty of Guadalupe Hidalgo and NAFTA implicating citizenship rights. Several provisions of the Treaty of Guadalupe Hidalgo purported to protect Mexican citizens. Though U.S. courts have occasionally enforced the Treaty provisions, persons of Mexican descent have never been afforded full membership rights in the United States. NAFTA, though not squarely addressing immigration, does nothing to change the dynamics allowing for a significant undocumented Mexican labor force to participate in the U.S. economy with precious few civil rights. Rather, NAFTA reinforces the immigration status quo between the two nations at a time when economic and other pressures favor change. Part II considers whether, in light of enforcement and related problems exacerbated by the power differential between the United States and Mexico, it matters what an agreement between the two nations might provide in terms of migration.

I. The Tale of Two Treaties

Both the Treaty of Guadalupe Hidalgo and NAFTA failed to address immigration and nationality issues in any meaningful way. Both, however, offer powerful insights about the forces behind United States-Mexico migration, the politics of race in the United States, and the role of law in protecting the rights of minorities in this country.

The parties consummated the two agreements under similar, though different, circumstances. The Treaty of Guadalupe Hidalgo ended a war lost by Mexico and, as some have put it, accomplished the "conquest" of the Southwest[27] by the United States. Mexico obviously had little bargaining power in negotiating the Treaty. The parties agreed to NAFTA not to end a war, but in an effort to improve their economies. Though not nearly as disadvantaged in its relations with the United States as it was in 1848, Mexico, suffering economic woes and facing increasing political instability, needed a free trade agreement much more than either the United States or Canada.[28] As put by one observer,

> [i]nternally, the Mexican government needed desperately to legitimize itself in the face of growing challenges by the opposition and increasing popular dissatisfaction with the sacrifices exacted for the prospect of free trade. Externally, it realized that the nation had to brace itself for the fierce international competition unleashed by the culmination of the cold war. Mexico felt it would fall behind hopelessly if it failed to find new partners and markets.[29]

Clearly, in negotiating both the Treaty of Guadalupe Hidalgo and NAFTA, Mexico possessed much less leverage than the United States.

A. The Treaty of Guadalupe Hidalgo and Immigration and Nationality

Two important provisions of the Treaty of Guadalupe Hidalgo address the citizenship rights of Mexican citizens living in the territory ceded under the Treaty to the United States.[30] Article VIII provides that:

> Mexicans now established in territories previously belonging to Mexico, and which remain for the future within ... the United States ... shall be free to continue where they now reside, or to remove to the Mexican Republic ....
>
> *Those who shall prefer to remain in said territories, may either retain the title and rights of Mexican citizens, or acquire those of citizens of the United States. But, they shall be under the obligation to make their election within one year from the date of the*

> *exchange of ratifications of this treaty; and those who shall remain in said territories, after the expiration of that year, without having declared their intention to retain the character of Mexicans, shall be considered to have elected to become citizens of the United States.*[31]

Article IX further provides that:

> [t]he Mexicans who . . . shall not preserve the character of citizens of the Mexican Republic . . . shall be incorporated into the Union of the United States and be admitted, at the proper time (to be judged by the Congress of the United States) *to the enjoyment of all rights of citizens of the United States according to the principles of the Constitution* . . . .[32]

The two articles of the Treaty together promised Mexican citizens in the surrendered territories the option of U.S. citizenship and guaranteed those who exercised that option the same rights as all other citizens. The liberality of the citizenship provisions provoked controversy in some quarters of the United States. "Many Anglo Texans, for example, resisted the signing of the Treaty of Guadalupe Hidalgo (from the perspective of United States expansionist interests, a highly favorable land cession), because it extended U.S. citizenship to the large Mexican population of the ceded territory."[33] Though it ratified the Treaty without change to the citizenship articles, the United States later experienced great difficulty in honoring the promise of equal citizenship to the new U.S. citizens of Mexican ancestry.

To be fair, Articles VIII and IX of the Treaty resulted in some benefits for Mexican citizens. For example, although most racial minorities were treated as non-whites in a time when U.S. law limited naturalization to "white" immigrants,[34] the court in one important case found itself compelled by the Treaty of Guadalupe Hidalgo to classify Mexican immigrants as "white" for naturalization purposes.[35] In analyzing the significance of Article VIII, the court observed that the citizenship rights applied to "Mexicans (and the term includes all Mexicans, without discrimination as to color)."[36]

Despite its positive impact on formal citizenship rights, the Treaty of Guadalupe Hidalgo failed to guarantee the rights of the new U.S. citizens and their descendants. For example, Anglos, with the help of the federal government invoked a variety of legal (and illegal) mechanisms to strip Chicana/os of their property rights under the Treaty.[37] Similarly, the California Supreme Court rejected a challenge under the Treaty to a foreign miners tax imposed by the state of California.[38] Poverty in unincorporated and impoverished *colonias* populated primarily by Mexican Americans along the United States-Mexico border today serve as stark reminders of the failure of the Treaty's promise to achieve full membership rights for persons of Mexican ancestry.[39]

Richard Delgado succinctly summarized the enforcement record of the Treaty of Guadalupe Hidalgo:

> [t]he Treaty . . . purported to guarantee to Mexicans . . . full citizenship and civil rights. . . . The treaty, modeled after ones drawn up between the U.S. and various Indian tribes, was given similar treatment: The Mexicans' "[l]and and property were stolen, rights were denied, language and culture suppressed, opportunities for employment, education, and political representation were thwarted."[40]

To put it mildly, the Treaty of Guadalupe Hidalgo suffered significant enforcement difficulties.[41] The U.S. government ultimately failed to protect the rights guaranteed under the Treaty to Mexican citizens who became U.S. citizens.

B. NAFTA's Avoidance of Immigration

NAFTA implicated issues of deep domestic concern in the United States. Organized labor feared that, if companies relocated operations to Mexico, jobs of "American workers" would be lost to low wage Mexican workers.[42] Some environmentalists feared that free trade would damage the environment if production facilities in this country moved across the border to Mexico with its less stringent environmental controls.[43] Unlike immigration, however, the NAFTA parties attempted to quell controversy by addressing these issues in side agreements.[44]

NAFTA failed to comprehensively address immigration. Despite the fact that from an economic perspective labor migration and trade are a little different,[45] domestic political concerns prevented the United States from negotiating for more liberal migration from Mexico.[46] The only significant migration provision in the treaty recognized each nation's sovereign right to take measures "to ensure border security and to protect the domestic labor force and permanent employment in their territories."[47] This permitted the development of freer trade between the United States, Mexico, and Canada, combined with U.S. implementation of stricter border controls along its southern border.[48] NAFTA contrasted starkly with more expansive integration agreements of the times, most notably those forming the European Union, which provide for the migration of labor between member nations.[49]

Despite NAFTA's failure to squarely address the issue, migration concerns influenced the debate over its approval. Some restrictionists in the United States, for example, criticized the agreement for not requiring Mexico to assist U.S. efforts to combat illegal immigration.[50] In sharp contrast, prominent Mexican intellectual Jorge Castañeda complained that NAFTA failed to allow for labor mobility: "The governments are opening borders to goods and capital flows, while labor, Mexico's main export, is barred from entry."[51]

NAFTA proponents on the northern side of the border contended that, even if the agreement failed to squarely address immigration, it ultimately might decrease undocumented immigration from the south. When free trade improves the Mexican economy, so the theory went, economic improvement would reduce a major "push" behind Mexican migration to the United States.[52] Though "the NAFTA text stayed well clear of the explosive issues raised by illegal immigration from Mexico to the United States," many understood that the free trade accord might indirectly reduce immigration.[53]

Political roadblocks, including differences of race, barred the contemplation of any agreement facilitating labor migration between the United States and Mexico.[54] NAFTA's failure to address immigration is consistent with the longstanding refusal of the United States to allow for the admission of economic migrants[55] and efforts under the U.S. immigration laws to restrict the migration of the poor.[56] Fears of mass migration unquestionably strike fear into the hearts of many in the United States. Differences of class, culture, language,[57] and physical appearance all contribute to the perception that Mexican citizens are of a different "race."[58] Such differences contribute to calls for restrictionist measures.[59] As commentators have observed, cultural differences between the United States and Mexico cause difficulty in commercial relations.[60] One can expect even greater controversy when the discussion turns to the migration of persons—not capital, income, products, and services—who differ from the Anglo norm in this country.

The perspective of the Mexican government, of course, is very different. Long relying on the migration of its citizens to the United States as a safety valve that prevented serious political unrest, Mexico also sees northern migration as a source of income because migrants send money earned in the United States to their families in Mexico.[61] In addition, concerned with the safety of its citizens, the Mexican government consistently has complained that the U.S. Border Patrol abuses Mexican migrants[62] and focuses deportation efforts disproportionately on Mexican citizens.[63] Despite these concerns, the pressing political and economic need for a free trade agreement[64] could not help but cause the Mexican government to quickly abandon any hopes of dealing with immigration in NAFTA.

Even with NAFTA's silence on the subject, however, immigration was central to United States-Mexico relations at the end of the twentieth century. Many prominent commentators have emphasized the importance of the United States and Mexico working together to resolve immigration issues.[65] In the future, one might see migration between the two nations addressed in a bilateral agreement between the United States and Mexican governments.[66] Unfortunately, racial and other differences made it politically infeasible for the United States at this historical moment to negotiate an accord facilitating labor migration between the two nations.

II. Does It Matter Whether a Treaty Between the United States and Mexico Governs Migration?

Assume that the United States and Mexico filled in the immigration gap left by the Treaty of Guadalupe Hidalgo and NAFTA and agreed to permit free migration of labor between the two nations. Assume also that part of the hypothetical accord required that the parties enforce the same laws—minimum wage, safe working conditions, non-discrimination—applied to the member countries' own citizens. Would free migration positively affect the work-lives of Mexican immigrants in the United States?

There is reason to believe that the best made agreement would not meaningfully change the status quo. Indeed, one might speculate that it would worsen matters for Mexican citizens working in the United States. An open border presumably would increase migration by Mexican workers into the United States, although the magnitude of any immigrant flow is difficult to predict. Due to family ties and social networks developed over generations, two powerful factors in the current Mexican migration to the United States,[67] one would expect continued job segregation as family and social networks steered immigrants to certain jobs. One also would expect many of the migrants to be unskilled.[68] By increasing the supply of unskilled labor in certain jobs, increased migration would place downward pressure on wages.[69] This is precisely what occurred in agriculture with the temporary Mexican labor programs that existed in the United States from World War II through the 1960s.[70] Such a result would be consistent with the fact that both the Treaty of Guadalupe Hidalgo and NAFTA adversely affected agricultural labor, with its large Mexican immigrant and Mexican American component, in the United States.[71]

Nor could we be confident that, regardless of any agreement, the United States could ensure that employers do not exploit Mexican labor.[72] Not-so-distant history suggests the contrary. In the 1950s, the United States and Mexico entered into agreements allowing for the creation of the Bracero Program, a temporary worker program that ostensibly protected the wages and working conditions of Mexican workers.[73] The United States failed to enforce worker protections and, consequently, agricultural growers frequently paid substandard wages to Mexican farmworkers.[74] The Bracero Program also drove down wages for all agricultural workers.[75] As Mario Barrera commented:

> [t]he benefits of the bracero program were disproportionately appropriated by the large growers ... The various adverse effects—which were not supposed to

happen but did—were borne by others. Domestic workers were displaced from jobs; farm wages in California showed a downward trend; housing for workers on the farms deteriorated; and unions experienced even greater difficulties organizing in the countryside.[76]

To worsen the prognosis for change through a migration agreement between the United States and Mexico, U.S. laws designed to protect minority citizens from discrimination and workplace exploitation have been far from effective.[77] The U.S. government long has experienced difficulties enforcing laws protecting racial minorities, whether they be U.S. or foreign citizens. For example, as George Martínez has documented, courts generally have failed to protect the civil rights of Mexican Americans and Mexican immigrants.[78] As commentators have observed, the undocumented, particularly vulnerable due to their uncertain immigration status, need increased protections to prevent exploitation.[79] Whether the law could ever effectively prevent such exploitation is open to debate.

Moreover, facially neutral laws may have unintended racial consequences. For example, the law imposing sanctions on employers of undocumented immigrants has not proven effective[80] and, at the same time, has resulted in national origin discrimination against persons of Latin American and Asian ancestry.[81] Such discrimination occurs despite the fact that it is prohibited by law.[82]

Failure of the United States to abide by the idyllic migration agreement would be consistent with its inability to honor the Treaty of Guadalupe Hidalgo.[83] This history is characteristic of this nation's checkered record of complying with treaty obligations. The United States, for example, infamously violated treaties with Indian tribes.[84] Similarly, the United States has been less than conscientious in adhering to human rights treaties, as demonstrated by the U.S. government's forced return to Haiti of persons fleeing that nation's political violence in the 1990s.[85] More generally, the United States has a spotty record in ensuring that the immigration laws conform to international law.[86]

Finally, Mexico, with its relatively weak bargaining posture,[87] could not be expected to be in a position to ensure that the U.S. government keeps its word with respect to any migration agreement. Mexico's lack of leverage in its dealings with the United States can be seen, for example, in NAFTA's investment provisions, which decidedly favor U.S. interests and may negatively affect Mexican citizens as well as Latina/os in this country.[88] Similarly, the agreement's dispute resolution mechanisms imitate U.S. legal traditions and ignore Mexico's rich, though different, legal culture.[89] Mexico's limited bargaining power in negotiating NAFTA ultimately suggests that it might be unable to pressure the United States to enforce any protections for Mexican citizens in a migration agreement.

The evidence is not all one-sided, however. In the European Union, for example, law has been utilized to combat discrimination against foreign workers in certain cases.[90] Similarly, although dispute resolution under NAFTA has not been perfect, it has worked in some instances.[91]

In sum, the mere fact that the United States might be obligated under an agreement to ensure that employers do not exploit Mexican immigrants does not necessarily mean that this will become a reality. This is true even if Congress passed a plethora of laws designed to implement the accord's mandate. In the end, it is far from certain that a pact liberalizing migration between the United States and Mexico would change the status quo—the existence of a large, easily exploitable labor force of Mexican citizens in the United States with little bargaining power. To facilitate meaningful change, the nations would need to confront the social and economic forces that maintain the current system.

Conclusion

This essay has attempted to outline some of the migration and citizenship issues implicated by the Treaty of Guadalupe Hidalgo and NAFTA. Though immigration emerged as an issue of critical importance to both the United States and Mexico at the end of the twentieth century, it is not likely to be fully resolved through law, either by treaties or otherwise. Economic, social, and historical forces dictate migration patterns. Although business interests treasure the cheap labor provided by the Mexican people, public opinion in the United States strongly opposes legal recognition of migrants of a different race, culture, and class. This dynamic ultimately inures to the benefit of employers able to recruit a vulnerable, easily exploitable low wage labor force of undocumented workers. Even if political obstacles to a migration agreement between the United States and Mexico were overcome and the United States passed laws designed to bar the exploitation of foreign workers, there is little reason to believe that such laws alone would improve the wages and conditions of Mexican citizens laboring in the United States.

This analysis ultimately suggests that, if change in the migration patterns between the United States and Mexico is desired, it is necessary to address the underlying causes, rather that attempt to modify them through law alone. Economic disparities between the United States and Mexico increase migration pressures. Ties between Mexican citizens and family members in the United States also contribute to the steady flow of migrants to this country. Both factors are unlikely to change in the short run. Indeed, it may not be possible to eliminate migration pressures, in light of the substantial—and growing—Mexican American population in the United States with family in Mexico. In any event, what is critical to remember is that law is only one tool for managing migration between the United States and Mexico. Those serious about decreasing migration from Mexico in the long run must consider other means as well. Promoting economic development in Mexico, thereby creating economic incentives to remain there, is one possiblity. A very different alternative would be to simply allow freer migration under the law in recognition that social and economic forces always will determine migration between the United States and Mexico. Whether the public in the United States will expressly acknowledge the inevitability of a Mexican presence in this country, however, remains far from certain.

Notes

[1] *See* The North American Free Trade Agreement, Dec. 17, 1992, U.S.-Can.-Mex., 32 I.L.M. 296 (1994) [hereinafter NAFTA]. Because NAFTA is a congressional-executive agreement rather than a "treaty" under Article II, section 2 of the U.S. Constitution (which would subject it to the approval of two-thirds of the U.S. Senate), its constitutionality has been questioned. *See generally* Bruce Ackerman & David Golove, *Is NAFTA Constitutional?*, 108 HARV. L. REV. 801 (1995) (analyzing arguments about NAFTA's constitutionality).

[2] *See, e.g.*, ROSS PEROT & PAT CHOATE, SAVE YOUR JOB, SAVE OUR COUNTRY: WHY NAFTA MUST BE STOPPED—NOW! (1993) (criticizing NAFTA with principal focus on alleged evils of entering trade agreement with Mexico).

[3] Congress did so, however, only after the addition of environmental and labor side agreements calmed domestic resistance to NAFTA. *See infra* text accompanying notes 42-44.

[4] *See* Kevin R. Johnson, *An Essay on Immigration Politics, Popular Democracy, and California's Proposition 187: The Political Relevance and Legal Irrelevance of Race*, 70 WASH. L. REV. 629, 650-61 (1995) (analyzing racial undertones to the initiative campaign).

[5] *See* League of United Latin American Citizens v. Wilson, 908 F. Supp. 755, 763 (C.D. Cal. 1995) (observing that California voters passed initiative by a 59-41% margin).

[6] *See* U.S. Comm. on Immigration Reform, Becoming an American: Immigration and Immigrant Policy, Executive Summary 34 (Comm. Print 1997) (observing increased resources permitting Operations Hold the Line in Texas, Gatekeeper in California, and Safeguard in Arizona). *See generally* TIMOTHY J. DUNN, MILITARIZATION OF THE U.S.-MEXICO BORDER, 1978-1992 (1996) (documenting great increase in border enforcement).

[7] *See generally* JUAN RAMÓN GARCÍA, OPERATION WETBACK: THE MASS DEPORTATION OF MEXICAN WORKERS IN 1954 (1980) (analyzing enforcement campaign).

[8] *See, e.g.*, U.S. COMM. ON CIVIL RIGHTS, FEDERAL IMMIGRATION LAW ENFORCEMENT IN THE SOUTHWEST: CIVIL RIGHTS IMPACTS IN BORDER COMMUNITIES (1997) (reporting on violence and other civil rights violations by Border Patrol); MEXICAN NAT'L HUMAN RIGHTS COMM., REPORT ON HUMAN RIGHTS VIOLATIONS OF MEXICAN MIGRATORY WORKERS ON ROUTE TO THE NORTHERN BORDER AND UPON ENTERING THE UNITED STATES BORDER STRIP (1991) (same).

[9] *See* Antiterrorism and Effective Death Penalty Act of 1996, Pub. L. No. 104-132, 110 Stat. 1214 (1996); Illegal Immigration Reform and Immigrant Responsibility Act of 1996, Pub. L. No. 104-208, 110 Stat. 3009 (1996). See Lenni B. Benson, *Back to the Future: Congress Attacks the Right of Judicial Review of Immigration Proceedings*, 29 CONN. L. REV. 1411 (1997), for analysis of how these laws eliminated judicial review of a myriad of immigration decisions.

[10] *See* Personal Responsibility and Work Opportunity Reconciliation Act of 1996, Pub. L. No. 104-193, 400-451, 110 Stat. 2105, 2260-77 (1996); *see also* Michael Scaperlanda, *Who is My Neighbor?: An Essay on Immigrants, Welfare Reform, and the Constitution*, 29 CONN. L. REV. 1887 (1997) (criticizing welfare reform legislation as inconsistent with Constitution and Judeo-Christian values).

[11] *See generally* Kevin R. Johnson, *Race, The Immigration Laws, and Domestic Race Relations: A "Magic Mirror" into the Heart of Darkness*, 73 IND. L.J. 1111 (1998) (analyzing how facially neutral immigration laws disparately impact racial minorities, including Mexican citizens).

[12] *See* Treaty of Peace, Friendship, Limits and Settlement with the Republic of Mexico Feb. 2, 1848, U.S.-Mex., 9 Stat. 922 [hereinafter Treaty].

[13] *See infra* text accompanying notes 30-41 (analyzing significance of Articles VIII and IX of Treaty of Guadalupe Hidalgo).

[14] *See, e.g.*, RODOLFO ACUÑA, OCCUPIED AMERICA 18-20, 112-18 (3d ed. 1988) (discussing U.S. violation of treaty); RICHARD GRISWOLD DEL CASTILLO, THE TREATY OF GUADALUPE HIDALGO: A LEGACY OF CONFLICT (1990) (analyzing history of treaty enforcement); Guadalupe T. Luna, *Chicana/o Land Tenure In the Agrarian Domain: On the Edge of a Naked Knife*, 3 MICH. J. RACE & L. (forthcoming 1998) [hereinafter Luna, *Land Tenure*] (documenting Chicana/o dispossession from lands in violation of treaty); Guadalupe T. Luna, *"Agricultural Underdogs" and International Agreements: The Legal Context of Agricultural Workers Within the Rural Economy*, 26 N.M. L. REV. 9, 13-21 (1996) [hereinafter Luna, *Agricultural Underdogs*] (studying how treaty's violation contributed to Chicana/o poverty); George A. Martínez, *Legal Indeterminacy, Judicial Discretion and the Mexican American Litigation Experience: 1930-1980*, 27 U.C. DAVIS L. REV. 555, 566-69 (1994) (analyzing judicial decisions involving property rights of Mexican Americans under treaty); *see also* Christopher David Ruiz Cameron, *One Hundred Fifty Years of Solitude: A Law Professor Critiques the Dominance of Historical Scholarship on the Treaty of Guadalupe Hidalgo*, 5 SW. J.L. & TRADE IN THE AMERICAS 83 (1998) (providing empirical analysis of land grant cases under the Treaty decided by U.S. Supreme Court); Christine A. Klein, *Treaties of Conquest: Property Rights, Indian Treaties, and the Treaty of Guadalupe Hidalgo*, 26 N.M. L. REV. 201 (1996) (comparing deprivation of property rights under Treaty with similar deprivations under Indian treaties). The Treaty's impact has ripple effects lasting to this day. *See, e.g.*, MARY ROMERO, MAID IN THE U.S.A. 8-10 (1992) (analyzing how violation of Treaty resulted in poverty of Chicana/os in Southwest, internal migration between states, and many Chicanas entering urban labor markets as domestic service workers).

[15] *See infra* text accompanying notes 37-41 (analyzing deficiencies in Treaty enforcement); *see also* Richard Griswold del Castillo, *The U.S.-Mexican War: Contemporary Implications for Mexican American Civil and International Rights*, in CULTURE Y CULTURA: CONSEQUENCES OF THE U.S.-MEXICAN WAR, 1846-1848, at 76 (1998) (considering modern civil rights implications of Treaty of Guadalupe Hidalgo).

[16] *See* GRISWOLD DEL CASTILLO, *supra* note 14, at 59-61; *see also* Remarks of Arturo Gándara. "Understanding the Treaty of Guadalupe Hidalgo on Its 150th Anniversary" Conference, Southwestern University School of Law, Feb. 6, 1998 (analyzing legal significance of Gadsden Purchase).

[17] *See* 1 CHARLES GORDON, STANLEY MAILMAN, & STEPHEN YALE-LOEHR, IMMIGRATION LAW & PROCEDURE §§ 2.02 - 2.04, at 2-6 to 2-7 (1996) (summarizing history of federal immigration regulation during this period); James F. Smith, *A Nation That Welcomes Immigrants? An Historical Examination of United States Immigration Policy*, 1 U.C. DAVIS J. INT'L L. & POL'Y 227, 228-31 (1995) (same). Before comprehensive federal regulation, individual states restricted migration in a variety of ways. *See generally* Gerald L. Neuman, *The Lost Century of American Immigration Law (1776-1875)*, 93 COLUM. L. REV. 1833 (1993) (documenting this history).

[18] *See* Kevin R. Johnson, *Free Trade and Closed Borders: NAFTA and Mexican Immigration to the United States*, 27 U.C. DAVIS L. REV. 937, 943-56 (1994). For analysis of the parallels between the Treaty of Guadalupe Hidalgo and NAFTA with respect to dispute resolution; see George A. Martínez, *Dispute Resolution and the Treaty of Guadalupe Hidalgo: Parallels and Possible Lessons for Dispute Resolution Under NAFTA*, 5 SW. J.L. & TRADE IN THE AMERICAS 147 (1998).

[19] *See* Jorge A. Vargas, *Dual Nationality for Mexicans? A Comparative Legal Analysis of the Dual Nationality Proposal and Its Eventual Political and Socio-Economic Implications*, 18 CHICANO-LATINO L. REV. 1 (1996); *see also Congress OKs Letting Expatriates Retain Citizenship Benefits*, CHI. TRIB., Dec. 14, 1997, at C16 (reporting that Mexican Congress unanimously approved expansion of dual nationality to citizens living outside country). *See generally* Peter J. Spiro, *Dual Nationality and the Meaning at Citizenship*, 46 EMORY L.J. 1411 (1997) (contending that a move toward tolerance of dual nationality under U.S. law was appropriate and should not cause concern).

[20] *See* Rachel F. Moran, *Foreword—Demography and Distrust: The Latino Challenge to Civil Rights and Immigration Policy in the 1990s and Beyond*, 8 LA RAZA L.J. 1, 13-24 (1995).

[21] *See* Johnson, *supra* note 18, at 956-59 (outlining reasons why U.S. refused to put immigration on the NAFTA bargaining table).

[22] David López, *Dispute Resolution Under Mercosur from 1991 to 1996: Implications for the Formation of a Free Trade Area of the Americas*, 3 NAFTA: LAW & BUS. REV. OF AMERICAS 3, 7-8 (1997).

[23] I define "exploitation" in this context narrowly to mean that employers of Mexican citizens would be required to comply with generally applicable wage and other labor protections. Consequently, Mexican workers would have the same legal protections as all other workers, including U.S. citizens, in the United States.

[24] *See infra* text accompanying notes 67-91 (analyzing lessons of history in this regard).

[25] *See, e.g.*, KITTY CALAVITA, INSIDE THE STATE: THE BRACERO PROGRAM, IMMIGRATION AND THE I.N.S. (1992) (documenting how growers benefited from Bracero Program allowing Mexican workers to come to nation temporarily); *see also infra* text accompanying notes 72-76 (analyzing how growers gained from cheap labor provided by Bracero Program).

[26] *See, e.g.*, PETER BRIMELOW, ALIEN NATION (1995) (presenting racial, cultural, political, economic, and other arguments for drastic reductions in current levels of immigration).

[27] ACUÑA, *supra* note 14, at 12-15.

[28] *See* Enrique R. Carrasco & Randall Thomas, *Encouraging Relational Investment and Controlling Portfolio Investment in Developing Countries in the Aftermath of the Mexican Financial Crisis*, 34 COLUM. J. TRANSNAT'L L. 539 (1996) (analyzing investment strategies in developing nations in light of Mexican financial crisis of 1990s).

[29] Angel R. Ocquendo, *NAFTA's Procedural Narrow-Mindedness: The Panel Review of Antidumping and Countervailing Duty Determination Under Chapter 19*, 11 CONN. J. INT'L L. 61, 63 (1995); *see* Sergio García-Rodríguez, *Mexico's New Institutional Framework for Antitrust Enforcement*, 44 DEPAUL L. REV. 1149, 1155-57 (1995) (articulating pressures on Mexican leadership to reach free trade accord with U.S.).

[30] *See generally* GRISWOLD DEL CASTILLO, *supra* note 14, at 62-86 (discussing Articles VIII and IX of the Treaty and their implementation).

[31] Treaty of Guadalupe Hidalgo, *supra* note 12, art. VIII (emphasis added).

[32] *Id.*, art. IX (emphasis added). Article IX was interpreted as not requiring Congressional action formally bestowing Mexican citizens, who did not retain Mexican citizenship, with U.S. citizenship. *See*

People v. De La Guerra, 40 Cal. 311, 341-44 (1870) (holding that Treaty of Guadalupe Hidalgo directly conferred citizenship rights and rejecting claim that person of Mexican ancestry in California was not U.S. citizen, and thus was ineligible to serve as judge, because Congress failed to specifically afford citizenship).

[33] Jane E. Larson, *Free Markets Deep in the Heart of Texas*, 84 GEO. L.J. 179, 224-25 (1995) (footnote omitted). *See generally* DAVID MONTEJANO, ANGLOS AND MEXICANS IN THE MAKING OF TEXAS, 1836-1986 (1987) (analyzing history of racial subordination of persons of Mexican ancestry in Texas).

[34] *See generally* IAN F. HANEY LÓPEZ, WHITE BY LAW (1996) (analyzing significance of racial prerequisite for naturalization, which remained in place from 1790 until 1952).

[35] *See In re* Rodríguez, 81 F. 337, 350-51 (W.D. Tex. 1897); *see also* George A. Martínez, *The Legal Construction of Race: Mexican Americans and Whiteness*, 2 HARV. LATINO L. REV. 321, 326-27 (1997) (analyzing significance of *Rodríguez* in demonstrating that race "can be constructed through the political process. Through the give and take of treaty making, Mexicans became 'white' "). Interestingly, two Anglo politicians filed suit attempting to bar Rodríguez from citizenship (and the franchise) and "hoped to prove that [he], a dark Mexican who freely admitted he was probably of Indian descent, was unfit for citizenship." NEIL FOLEY, THE WHITE SCOURGE: MEXICANS, BLACKS AND POOR WHITES IN TEXAS COTTON CULTURE 107 (1997).

[36] *In re* Rodríguez, 81 F. at 352. In making this statement, the court implicitly recognized that "whiteness" was not simply a question of skin color, but a product of the complex interaction of social forces. *See generally* MICHAEL OMI & HOWARD WINANT, RACIAL FORMATION IN THE UNITED STATES (1986) (analyzing forces shaping racial formation in this country). The statement also acknowledges the diversity of physical appearance among persons of Mexican ancestry. *See* Kevin R. Johnson, *"Melting Pot" or "Ring of Fire"?: Assimilation and the Mexican-American Experience*, 85 CAL. L. REV. 1259, 1290-99 (1997) (analyzing significance of diversity of physical appearance in Mexican American community in U.S.).

[37] *See* Luna, *Land Tenure*, *supra* note 14 (offering examples and reviewing case law); *see, e.g.*, United States v. Ortiz, 176 U.S. 422 (1900) (reversing lower court's confirmation of Mexican land grant); Chávez v. United States, 175 U.S. 552 (1899) (affirming lower court's refusal to confirm land grant).

[38] *See* People v. Naglee, 1 Cal. 232, 248-51 (1850). The California legislature later repealed the tax, apparently because of enforcement difficulties. *See* Charles J. McClain, Jr., *The Chinese Struggle for Civil Rights in Nineteenth-Century America: The First Phase, 1850-1870*, 72 CAL. L. REV. 529, 536 n.33 (1984).

[39] *See generally* Larson, *supra* note 33 (studying plight of *colonias* along border in Texas); Luna, *Agricultural Underdogs*, *supra* note 14 (same).

[40] Richard Delgado, *Derrick Bell and the Ideology of Racial Reform: Will We Ever Be Saved?*, 97 YALE L.J. 923, 940 (1988) (footnotes omitted).

[41] *See supra* note 14 (citing authorities to this effect); *see also* Martínez, *supra* note 18 (outlining difficulties experienced by persons of Mexican ancestry with mechanisms for resolving disputes under Treaty of Guadalupe Hidalgo).

The history surrounding the Treaty of Guadalupe Hidalgo reveals the interrelationship of the subordination of different racial minorities in the United States. *See* Kevin R. Johnson, *Racial Hierarchy, Asian Americans and Latinos as "Foreigners," and Social Change: Is Law the Way to Go?*, 76 OR. L. REV. 347, 358-62 (1998) (contending that subordination of various racial minorities is interrelated); George A. Martínez, *African-Americans, Latinos, and the Construction of Race: Toward on Epistemic Coalition*, 19 UCLA Chicano-Latino L. REV. (forthcoming 1998) (offering philosophical argument for this position). The U.S.-Mexican War resulted from American expansionist desires, including a hope by some to protect the institution of slavery in the United States. *See* ACUÑA, *supra* note 14, at 5-31. Thus, an effort to save slavery (and the subordination of African Americans in the United States) served as part of a chain of events contributing to the subordination of Chicana/os in the Southwest.

[42] *See* Roy J. Adams & Parbudyal Singh, *Early Experience with NAFTA's Labour Side Accord*, 18 COMP. LAB. L. 161, 161-64 (1997) (summarizing organized labor's opposition in U.S., Mexico, and Canada to labor side agreement).

[43] *See* William P. Alford, *The North American Free Trade Agreement and the Need for Candor*, 34 HARV. INT'L L.J. 293, 296 (1993) (stating that, in opposing NAFTA, "[w]ith fingers pointed at the tragically low state of Mexican environmental protection, particularly in the maquiladora-dominated industrial

zones that line parts of the U.S. border, some environmental groups have painted grim pictures of what they see as growing pressure to lower, or at least not increase, U.S. environmental standards in order to remain competitive with Mexican industry.") (footnote omitted).

[44] *See* North American Agreement on Labor Cooperation, Sept. 13, 1993, U.S.-Can.-Mex., 32 I.L.M. 1499 (1993); North American Agreement on Environmental Cooperation, Sept. 13, 1993, U.S.-Can.-Mex., 32 I.L.M. 1480 (1993). Critics claim that the side agreements have done little to alleviate the concerns that resulted in their addition to the NAFTA package. *See* María Teresa Guerra & Anna L. Torriente, *The NAALC and the Labor Laws of Mexico and the United States*, 14 ARIZ. J. INT'L & COMP. L. 503 (1997); Ileana M. Porras, *The Puzzling Relationship Between Trade and Environment: NAFTA, Competitiveness, and the Pursuit of Environmental Welfare Objectives*, 3 IND. J. GLOBAL LEG. STUD. 65 (1995); *see also* Richard W. Stevenson, *Union Misgivings on NAFTA are Clinton's Latest Worry*, N.Y. TIMES, Nov. 5, 1997, at A8 (observing concerns expressed with addressing important labor and environmental issues in side agreements to NAFTA, rather than in core of trade accord).

[45] *See generally* JULIAN L. SIMON, THE ECONOMIC CONSEQUENCES OF IMMIGRATION (1989) (offering economic arguments for less restrictive U.S. immigration policies); Howard F. Chang, *Liberalized Immigration as Free Trade: Economic Welfare and the Optimal Immigration Policy*, 145 U. PA. L. REV. 1147 (1997) (criticizing U.S. immigration law and policy from economic perspective).

[46] *See* Johnson, *supra* note 18, at 957-59. NAFTA included some narrow immigration provisions providing for temporary entry of noncitizens into the United States for business purposes. *See* Ellen G. Yost, *NAFTA—Temporary Entry Provisions—Immigration Dimensions*, 22 CAN.-U.S. L.J. 211 (1996) (summarizing provisions). Thus, NAFTA in effect eases travel restrictions for upper class Mexican citizens.

[47] NAFTA, *supra* note 1, art. 1601, 32 I.L.M. at 664 ("[T]his Chapter reflects the preferential trading relationship between the Parties, the desirability of facilitating temporary entry on a reciprocal basis and of establishing transparent criteria and procedures for temporary entry, and the need to ensure border security and to protect the domestic labor force and permanent employment in their respective territories."). For a study of NAFTA's migration provisions based on several years of experience with the agreement, see Noemi Gal-Or, *Labor Mobility Under NAFTA: Regulatory Policy Spearheading the Social Supplemental to the International Trade Regime*, 15 ARIZ. J. INT'L & COMP. L. 365 (1998).

[48] *See supra* text accompanying notes 6-11 (outlining increased border enforcement after NAFTA's approval). The dichotomous treatment of migration of people and goods between the United States and Mexico permitted by NAFTA can also be seen in electricity transfers between the nations. While migration of persons is subject to heavy regulation, transfer of electricity, which has environmental consequences, is not regulated at all. *See* Arturo Gándara, *United States-Mexico Electricity Transfers: Of Alien Electrons and the Migration of Undocumented Environmental Burdens*, 16 ENERGY L.J. 1 (1995) (arguing for regulation of electricity transfers between U.S. and Mexico because of associated environmental burdens).

[49] *See* Johnson, *supra* note 18, at 971-74; *see also* John A. Scanlan, *A View From the United States—Social, Economic, and Legal Change, Persistence of the State, and Immigration Policy in the Coming Century*, 2 IND. J. GLOBAL LEG. STUDIES 79, 129 (1994) (opining that history of European Union, and gradual loosening of migration restrictions between member nations, "may provide a glimmer of hope" of more liberal migration between U.S. and Mexico); *cf.* Boris Kozolchyk, *NAFTA in the Grand and Small Scheme of Things*, 13 ARIZ. J. INT'L & COMP. L. 135, 146 (1996) (seeing NAFTA as part of movement toward integration of international economy and positing that "[i]t is quite possible that the free trade formula embodied . . . in NAFTA, can be the key to a more peaceful and prosperous future for the whole of mankind").

The parties to the European Union (EU) may have found it easier to enter a comprehensive integration agreement because of the relative equality of the member nations, all with developed economies and relative similarities among their populations. Nonetheless, the easing of migration restrictions in the EU has not been problem-free. *See, e.g.*, Jacqueline Bhabha, *European Harmonisation of Asylum Policy: A Flawed Process*, 35 VA. J. INT'L L. 101 (1994) (criticizing development of EU's asylum policy); *Immigration: Frontier Wars*, ECONOMIST, Jan. 10, 1998, at 42 (describing threat to integration of immigration policies in EU due to influx of refugees).

[50] *See, e.g.*, Alan C. Nelson, *NAFTA: Immigration Issues Must Be Addressed*, 27 U.C. DAVIS L. REV. 987, 987 (1994).

[51] *See* Jorge G. Castañeda & Carlos Heredia, *Another NAFTA: What a Good Agreement Should Offer*, in THE CASE AGAINST "FREE TRADE" 86 (1993). This, of course, is consistent with U.S. immigration law and policy, which historically has discriminated against Mexican citizens. *See* Johnson, *supra* note 11 (analyzing discrimination in U.S. immigration law and policy against racial minorities, including Mexican citizens).

[52] *See, e.g.,* Robert T. Matsui, *Free Trade and Democratic Values: NAFTA's Effect on Human Rights*, 27 U.C. DAVIS L. REV. 791, 791 (1994); Dave McCurdy, *The Future of U.S. Immigration Law*, 20 J. LEGIS. 3, 16-17 (1994); *see also* FREDERICK M. ABBOTT, LAW AND POLICY OF ECONOMIC INTEGRATION 17-18 (1995) (stating that stemming illegal immigration from Mexico was "secondary" objective of U.S. in negotiating NAFTA).

[53] GARY CLYDE HUFBAUER & JEFFREY J. SCHOTT, NAFTA: AN ASSESSMENT 25 (rev. ed. 1993); *see* Gary Hufbauer & Jacqueline McFadyen, *Judging NAFTA*, 23 CAN.-U.S. L.J. 11, 22 (1997) ("[A]s a political concept, NAFTA has everything to do with illegal migration. [Mexican] President Carlos Salinas asked rhetorically, 'Do you want our tomatoes or our tomato pickers?' "). Some observers contend that the increased trade between the United States and Mexico facilitated by NAFTA has indirectly increased migration pressures. *See* Douglas S. Massey, *March of Folly: U.S. Immigration Policy After NAFTA*, AM. PROSPECT, Mar.-Apr. 1998, at 22.

[54] *See* Francis Lee Ansley, *North American Free Trade Agreement: The Public Debate*, 22 GA. J. INT'L & COMP. L. 329, 370 (1992) (stating in context of public debate over NAFTA that "[i]t is the politics of racism and prejudice that keeps the issue of broadening the legal participation of the Mexican labor force and access to U.S. labor markets off the table of negotiations on a free trade accord.") (quoting María Jiménez, Immigration Law Enforcement Monitoring Project).

[55] *See* Francis A. Gabor, *Reflections on the Freedom of Movement in Light of the Dismantled 'Iron Curtain'*, 65 TUL. L. REV. 849, 866-68 (1991) (stating that U.S. immigration law fails to address migration of "economic refugees" and contending that such migration should be permitted in certain circumstances).

[56] *See* Kevin R. Johnson, *Public Benefits and Immigration: The Intersection of Immigration Status, Ethnicity, Gender, and Class*, 42 UCLA L. REV. 1509, 1519-28 (1995).

[57] English-only laws, seen with increasing frequency in the 1990s, have been one of the responses to language difference. For analysis of how these laws disparately impact persons of Mexican ancestry, as well as all Latina/os, see Steven W. Bender, *Direct Democracy and Distrust: The Relationship Between Language Law Rhetoric and the Language Vigilantism Experience*, 2 HARV. LATINO L. REV. 145 (1997), and Christopher David Ruiz Cameron, *How the García Cousins Lost Their Accents: Understanding the Language of Title VII Decisions Approving English-Only Rules as the Product of Racial Dualism, Latino Invisibility, and Legal Indeterminacy*, 85 CAL. L. REV. 1347 (1997).

[58] *See* Ian F. Haney López, *Race and Erasure: The Salience of Race to LatCrit Theory*, 85 CAL. L. REV. 1143 (1997) (analyzing racialization of Mexican Americans in U.S. through lens of Supreme Court decision of Hernandez v. Texas, 347 U.S. 475 (1954)); Martínez, *supra* note 14, at 573 ("Mexican Americans have been faced with exclusion from public facilities, neighborhoods, and with racial slurs in a manner similar to the experience of African-Americans."); *see also* Kevin R. Johnson, *Some Thoughts on the Future of Latino Legal Scholarship*, 2 HARV. LATINO L. REV. 101, 117-29 (1997) (analyzing how all Latina/os, citizens and immigrants alike, are classified as "foreigners" in U.S. society); Louis A. Martínez, *En Aquel Entonces: Popular Literature as the Mirror of Political and Cultural Conflict*, 5 SW. J.L. & TRADE IN THE AMERICAS 177 (1998) (analyzing how Mexican women are de-humanized through reliance on racial difference in nineteenth century ballad).

[59] *See supra* notes 9-10 (listing some of these measures).

[60] *See, e.g.,* Stephen Zamora, *The Americanization of Mexican Law: Non-Trade Issues in the North American Free Trade Agreement*, 24 LAW & POL'Y INT'L BUS. 391 (1993) (analyzing significance of cultural differences between two nations in the context of NAFTA); *see also* James F. Smith, *Confronting Differences in the United States and Mexican Legal Systems in the Era of NAFTA*, 1 U.S.-MEXICO L.J. 85 (1993) (contrasting U.S. and Mexican legal systems).

[61] *See* Johnson, *supra* note 18, at 941-42 & n.16.

[62] *See supra* note 8 (citing report of Mexican government documenting abuses).

[63] See Johnson, *supra* note 4, at 652 & n.107 (discussing claims of Mexican officials that Proposition 187 campaign was racist and xenophobic). Evidence supports this contention. *See* U.S. DEP'T OF JUSTICE, 1995 STATISTICAL YEARBOOK OF THE IMMIGRATION AND NATURALIZATION SERVICE 163, 185 (1997) (noting that 68.5% of all noncitizens deported in fiscal year 1995 were Mexican citizens).

[64] *See supra* text accompanying notes 28-29 (outlining pressures on Mexican government to enter free trade agreement with U.S.).

[65] *See, e.g.,* BINATIONAL STUDY ON MIGRATION 65 (1997) (pre-publication draft) (recommending creation of institutionalized mechanisms for U.S. and Mexico to explore mutually agreeable immigration policies); *see also* KEVIN F. MCCARTHY & GEORGES VERNEZ, IMMIGRATION IN A CHANGING ECONOMY 291 (Rand, 1997) (claiming U.S. and Mexico "must realize the special role Mexican immigration plays in the lives of both countries"); SIDNEY WEINTRAUB, NAFTA: WHAT COMES NEXT? 55 (1994) (observing that, "[a]lthough not included in NAFTA, the subject of immigration is a salient element in the economic and social integration of Mexico and the United States").

[66] An expert on U.S.-Mexico relations, Jorge Castañeda, specifically expressed this as a future possibility. *See* Remarks of Dr. Jorge G. Castañeda, "Understanding the Treaty of Guadalupe Hidalgo on Its 150th Anniversary" conference, Southwestern University School of Law, Feb. 6, 1998.

[67] *See* WAYNE A. CORNELIUS, MEXICAN MIGRATION TO THE UNITED STATES: THE LIMITS OF GOVERNMENT INTERVENTION 2-5 (Working Papers in U.S.-Mexican Studies No. 5 1981).

[68] *See* GEORGE J. BORJAS, FRIENDS OR STRANGERS: THE IMPACT OF IMMIGRANTS ON THE U.S. ECONOMY 115-33 (1990) (expressing concern with low skill levels of latest cohort of immigrants).

[69] *See* PHILIP L. MARTIN & DAVID A. MARTIN, THE ENDLESS QUEST: HELPING AMERICA'S FARM WORKERS 174-77 (1994) (contending that only by limiting undocumented immigration will U.S. be able to improve wages for farm labor); *see also* VERNON M. BRIGGS, JR., MASS IMMIGRATION AND THE NATIONAL INTEREST 190-221 (2d ed. 1996) (analyzing negative impact of "mass migration" on U.S. labor market).

[70] *See* CALAVITA, *supra* note 25, at 70-71.

[71] *See* Luna, *Agricultural Underdogs, supra* note 14, at 13-21, 41-44.

[72] *See generally* GERALD N. ROSENBERG, THE HOLLOW HOPE: CAN COURTS BRING ABOUT SOCIAL CHANGE? (1991) (analyzing limits of law in bringing about significant social change); GIRARDEAU A. SPANN, RACE AGAINST THE COURT (1993) (same). The prevalence of exploitation of immigrants in the garment industry specifically suggests the difficulties of enforcing worker protection laws. *See* Laura Ho et al., *(Dis)Assembling Rights of Women Workers Along the Global Assembly Line: Human Rights and the Garment Industry*, 31 HARV. C.R.-C.L. L. REV. 383 (1996). Moreover, it is not certain that these laws benefit the persons who they are designed to protect. Some, for example, contend that the minimum wage law hurts low wage workers and racial minorities. *See, e.g.,* Daniel Shaviro, *The Minimum Wage, the Earned Income Tax Credit, and Optimal Subsidy Policy*, 64 U. CHI. L. REV. 405 (1997); Harry Hutchison, *Toward a Critical Race Reformist Conception of Minimum Wage Regimes: Exploding the Power of Myth, Fantasy, and Hierarchy*, 34 HARV. J. ON LEGIS. 93 (1997). Indeed, law arguably serves in many situations to maintain Anglo hegemony over minorities. *See* Kenneth B. Nunn, *Law as a Eurocentric Enterprise*, 15 LAW & INEQ. 323 (1997).

Besides the fact that a liberal migration agreement might not be enforceable, the United States, as it did with the Treaty of Guadalupe Hidalgo, see *supra* text note 14 (citing authorities to this effect), could undermine the Treaty's protections in implementing legislation or judicial decisions.

[73] *See* SELECT COMM'N ON IMMIGRATION AND REFUGEE POLICY, STAFF REPORT OF THE SELECT COMMISSION ON IMMIGRATION AND REFUGEE POLICY 469-77 (1981) [hereinafter SCIRP STAFF REP.].

[74] *See* CALAVITA, *supra* note 25, at 29, 45-46, 64-66, 70-71; ERNESTO GALARZA, MERCHANTS OF LABOR: THE MEXICAN BRACERO STORY 183-98 (1964).

[75] *See* GALARZA, *supra* note 74, at 199-218; SCIRP STAFF REP., *supra* note 73, at 475-76. Moreover, efforts by the Mexican government in negotiating predecessors to the Bracero Program to exclude the use of temporary workers in Texas because of that state's history of racial discrimination, proved impossible to enforce. *See* CALAVITA, *supra* note 25, at 20, 23-24, 29-30, 33-36, 45-46; GALARZA, *supra* note 74, at 48-51.

[76]MARIO BARRERA, RACE AND CLASS IN THE SOUTHWEST 118 (1979) (citation omitted); *see* JULIAN SAMORA, LOS MOJADOS: THE WETBACK STORY 81 (1971) (stating that Bracero Program was ideal for growers because only single individuals were admitted, there was no need to house families, wages and considerations favorable to business were established, and that "the only persons who were in a disadvantaged position were domestic agricultural workers (U.S. citizens) willing to work (but for decent wages) and the Mexican nationals.").

[77]*See, e.g.*, Charles R. Lawrence III, *The Id, the Ego, and Equal Protection: Reckoning with Unconscious Racism*, 39 STAN. L. REV. 317 (1987) (criticizing discriminatory intent requirement for establishing violation of Equal Protection Clause of 14th Amendment); Alan D. Freeman, *Legitimizing Racial Discrimination Through Antidiscrimination Law: A Critical Review of Supreme Court Doctrine*, 62 MINN. L. REV. 1049 (1978) (contending that resort to antidiscrimination laws perpetuates, not eradicates, racial discrimination).

[78]*See* Martínez, *supra* note 14; *see also* Kevin R. Johnson, *Civil Rights and Immigration: Challenges for the Latino Community in the Twenty-First Century*, 8 LA RAZA L.J. 42, 45-56 (1995) (reviewing limits of litigation for Latina/os and contending that such strategies must be combined with efforts at political mobilization).

[79]*See, e.g.*, Peter Margulies, *Stranger and Afraid: Undocumented Workers and Federal Employment Law*, 38 DEPAUL L. REV. 553 (1989); María L. Ontiveros, *To Help Those Most in Need: Undocumented Workers' Rights and Remedies Under Title VII*, 20 N.Y.U. REV. L. & SOC. CHANGE 607 (1993-94).

[80]*See* Cecelia M. Espenoza, *The Illusory Provisions of Sanctions: The Immigration Reform and Control Act of 1986*, 8 GEO. IMMIGR. L.J. 343, 369-80 (1994) (surveying data revealing that employer sanctions under Immigration Reform and Control Act of 1986 have failed to reduce undocumented workforce in United States).

[81]*See* U.S. GEN. ACCT. OFF., IMMIGR. REFORM: EMPLOYER SANCTIONS AND THE QUESTION OF DISCRIMINATION 5-7 (1990) (reporting that "survey results indicate that national origin discrimination resulting from [employer sanctions under the Immigration Reform and Control Act] constitutes 'a serious pattern of discrimination' " and "that the national origin discriminatory practices reported do establish a widespread pattern of discrimination"); U.S. COMM'N ON CIVIL RIGHTS, THE IMMIGR. REFORM AND CONTROL ACT: ASSESSING THE EVALUATION PROCESS at iv (1989) (finding "no doubt that the employer sanctions have caused many employers to implement discriminatory hiring practices").

[82]*See* Immigration & Nationality Act § 274B, 8 U.S.C. § 1324b (1994 & Supp. II 1997).

[83]*See supra* note 14 (citing authorities).

[84]*See generally* ROBERT A. WILLIAMS, JR., LINKING ARMS TOGETHER: AMERICAN INDIAN TREATY VISIONS OF LAW AND PEACE, 1600-1800 (1997); ROBERT A. WILLIAMS, JR., THE AMERICAN INDIAN IN WESTERN LEGAL THOUGHT: THE DISCOURSES OF CONQUEST (1990).

[85]*See* Sale v. Haitian Centers Council, 509 U.S. 155 (1993) (upholding return of Haitians fleeing political violence without determining whether they might be entitled to refuge in U.S. under international law); *cf. The Chinese Exclusion Case* (Chae Chan Ping v. United States), 130 U.S. 581, 589-603 (1889) (holding that law excluding immigration of Chinese persons trumped treaty with China barring such discrimination). Professor Harold Koh has forcefully argued that the U.S. treatment of Haitian refugees violated international law. *See* Harold Hongju Koh, *The "Haiti Paradigm" in United States Human Rights Policy*, 103 YALE L.J. 2391 (1994); *see also* Carlos Manuel Vázquez, *The "Self Executing" Character of the Refugee Protocol's Nonrefoulement Obligation*, 7 GEO. IMMIGR. L.J. 39 (1993) (contending that relevant treaty was self executing and therefore prohibited Haitian interdiction and repatriation policy). The Court's treatment of Haitian refugees reflects a larger problem of inconsistency in the U.S. courts' approach to the application of international human rights treaties. *Compare* INS v. Cardoza-Fonseca, 480 U.S. 421, 436-42 (1987) (interpreting U.S. asylum law through reference to international law), *with Sale*, 509 U.S. at 177-87 (construing U.S. law as consistent with international law by narrowly construing international law).

[86]*See* Joan Fitzpatrick & William McKay Bennett, *A Lion in the Path? The Influence of International Law on the Immigration Policy of the United States*, 70 WASH. L. REV. 589 (1995) (contending that U.S. immigration law and policy violates international law in important ways); *see also* Berta Esperanza Hernández-Truyol & Kimberly A. Johns, *Global Rights, Local Wrongs, and Legal Fixes: An International*

Human Rights Critique of Immigration and Welfare Reform, 71 S. CAL. L. REV. 547 (1998) (analyzing how recent welfare and immigration legislation conflict with international law).

[87] *See supra* text accompanying notes 28-29 (observing how Mexico's relatively weak bargaining position affected NAFTA's various provisions).

[88] *See* José E. Álvarez, *Critical Theory and the North America Free Trade Agreement's Chapter Eleven*, 28 U. MIAMI INTER-AM. L. REV. 303 (1996-97) (observing that the U.S. direct investment in Mexico facilitated by NAFTA may result in increasing Mexican migration to the United States, which may affect Latina/os already in the country); *see also* Jorge A. Vargas, *NAFTA, the Chiapas Rebellion, and the Emergence of Mexican Ethnic Law*, 25 CAL. W. INT'L L.J. 1 (1994) (analyzing significance of NAFTA in provoking rebellion of indigenous people in Mexico because of agreement's feared negative economic impacts); *cf.* Amy L. Chua, *The Privatization-Nationalization Cycle: The Link Between Markets and Ethnicity in Developing Countries*, 95 COLUM. L. REV. 223, 303 (1995) (analyzing trend toward privatization in various developing nations and contending that "contrary to received wisdom, market solutions in developing countries appear actually to aggravate ethnic hatreds, which in turn subvert market solutions"). In addition, NAFTA, by encouraging development of *maquiladoras* along the border, may impose disproportionate environmental consequences on Mexican Americans in the region. *See* Xavier Carlos Vásquez, *The North American Free Trade Agreement and Environmental Racism*, 34 HARV. INT'L L.J. 357 (1993); *see also* Francisco T. Valdés, *Under Construction LatCrit Consciousness, Community, and Theory*, 185 CAL. L. REV. 1087, 1121-22 (1997) (analyzing how new Latina/o communities and identities transcend national borders); *cf.* Elizabeth M. Iglesias, *Human Rights in International Economic Law: Locating Latinas/os in the Linkage Debates*, 28 U. MIAMI INTER-AM. L. REV. 361, 362 (1996-97)("[G]lobal capitalism and the interstate system are undergoing fundamental restructuring and this restructuring has already had and will continue to have profound impact on the lives of Latinas/os both in the United States and in Latin America.") (footnotes omitted).

[89] *See* Martínez, *supra* note 18.

[90] *See* JOSEPHINE STEINER, EEC LAW 179-81 (3d ed. 1992) (analyzing caselaw addressing prohibition of discrimination on the grounds of nationality of worker).

[91] *See* David López, *Dispute Resolution Under NAFTA: Lessons from the Early Experience*, 32 TEX. INT'L L.J 163, 208 (1997). *But cf.* Martínez, *supra* note 18 (analyzing how NAFTA's dispute resolution provisions favor U.S. over Mexican national interests).

Dispute Resolution and the Treaty of Guadalupe Hidalgo

PARALLELS AND POSSIBLE LESSONS FOR DISPUTE RESOLUTION UNDER NAFTA

George A. Martínez
SOUTHERN METHODIST UNIVERSITY

I. Introduction

It has been 150 years since the United States and Mexico entered into the Treaty of Guadalupe Hidalgo (hereinafter Treaty).[1] In 1848, the Treaty ended the war between the United States and Mexico. The Treaty purported to protect certain rights of Mexican citizens in the areas ceded to the United States. Over the years, Mexican Americans have sought to litigate their rights that were supposedly protected by the Treaty.

Subsequently, in 1993, the United States and Mexico entered into another important treaty—the North American Free Trade Agreement (hereinafter NAFTA).[2] NAFTA created considerable controversy in the United States.[3] It governs trade between the NAFTA parties: Canada, Mexico and the United States.[4] The NAFTA parties trade hundreds of billions of dollars worth of goods a year.[5] Thus, one can expect that many trade disputes will arise under NAFTA.[6] As a result, NAFTA has provided procedures for dispute resolution.

This article seeks to briefly discuss the experience of Mexicans and their Mexican American heirs in litigating their rights under the Treaty of Guadalupe Hidalgo. It seeks to ask whether there may be any parallels and possible lessons to be learned from the litigation experience of Mexican claimants under the earlier Treaty for the NAFTA parties—especially Mexico—as the NAFTA parties engage in dispute resolution.

Part II of this article sets out the background of the Treaty, including a brief review of the United States-Mexican War. It describes the terms of the Treaty and observes that Mexico had unequal bargaining power when it negotiated the Treaty with the United States. It describes how the Treaty sought to protect the rights of the former Mexican citizens in the conquered territories but was ultimately unable to do so. In seeking to litigate their rights under the Treaty, the dispute resolution process generally failed to protect Mexican claimants and their heirs. Through a variety of legal devices, the promises of the Treaty were devalued. In particular, implementing legislation undermined the property rights protections in the Treaty. It did so by, among other things, requiring that Mexican claimants assume the burden of proof in proving the validity of their titles and negotiate a maze of legal requirements in a foreign legal system and in a language that was foreign to them. The implementing legislation also established what might be viewed as an alternative dispute resolution to resolve claims, *e.g.*, the office of the surveyor general. These alternative tribunals sometimes created difficulties for the Mexican claimants. Similarly, the Treaty failed to protect full membership rights in American society to persons of Mexican ancestry. For all these reasons, the promises of the Treaty were minimized and devalued.

Part III of the article explores parallels between the NAFTA dispute resolution process and the dispute settlement process of the Treaty of Guadalupe Hidalgo. In this regard it notes that just as with the earlier Treaty, Mexico negotiated the NAFTA from a very weak bargaining position. As a result, just as the United States had virtually dictated the terms of the Treaty of Guadalupe Hidalgo, the United States imposed conditions on Mexico in the NAFTA. In the dispute resolution context, part III explains that this means that the United States imposed on Mexico, especially in the NAFTA Chapter 19 areas of antidumping and countervailing duties, procedural rules based on United States procedural law. By so doing, the NAFTA dispute resolution process may generate a number of difficulties for Mexico that parallel problems that Mexican claimants experienced in litigating their rights under the earlier Treaty. Among these are difficulties arising from language, the unique burdens that are experienced by one who must litigate in a foreign legal system *i.e.*, the NAFTA dispute resolution process, which is based on Anglo-Saxon notions of procedure, and misunderstandings of Mexican law by North American panelists. In the course of the discussion, part III also points out that in constructing the NAFTA dispute settlement procedures, Mexico was treated in ways that parallel the dominant society's treatment of Mexican Americans in the years since the Treaty of Guadalupe Hidalgo. Part III also explains that the NAFTA dispute resolution procedures may be viewed as alternative dispute resolution. It argues that Mexico will likely experience difficulties in the NAFTA alternative dispute resolution regime in light of its position as a relatively weak disputant. This generates another parallel: Mexican claimants experienced difficulties arising out of the alternative dispute resolution-like system established under the Treaty of Guadalupe Hidalgo. Given all of this, part III concludes that there is reason to think that the NAFTA dispute resolution process may put Mexico at a disadvantage just as the earlier Treaty of Guadalupe Hidalgo dispute settlement process placed Mexican claimants and their heirs at a disadvantage. In this regard, part III notes that an analysis of the early results of the NAFTA dispute resolution process shows that Mexico has fared the least well of the three NAFTA countries.

II. The Treaty of Guadalupe Hidalgo

In the 1800s, many in the United States believed it was America's destiny to expand westward so as to govern the entire continent.[7] Writing in 1845, journalist John O'Sullivan explained: "[T]he American claim is by the right of our manifest destiny to overspread and to possess the whole of the continent which Providence has given us for the development of the great experiment of liberty and federative self-government entrusted to us."[8]

In accordance with this notion of "manifest destiny," in 1846, the United States went to war against Mexico in an effort to incorporate the western territories of California and New Mexico and certain Texas borderlands.[9] At the war's end in 1848, the Treaty of Guadalupe Hidalgo required Mexico to cede about half of its then existing territory.[10] Much of the American West and Southwest was acquired by the United States in the 529,000 square mile cession by the Republic of Mexico.[11] Thus, the United States conquered Mexico in 1848. The Treaty of Guadalupe Hidalgo completed that conquest and, therefore, completed the conquest of the Southwest.[12]

In agreeing to the Treaty of Guadalupe Hidalgo, Mexico—a conquered nation—obviously had much less bargaining power than the United States. The Mexican government was under tremendous political and financial pressure to sign the Treaty.[13] Mexican officials viewed the Treaty as a final opportunity to preserve Mexico.[14] With the American Army just outside of Mexico City, they believed that if the war continued, all of Mexico would have been acquired by the United States.[15] In addition, British money brokers, who had made large loans to Mexico, were pushing Mexican officials to end the war and pay off Mexico's debts.[16] Under these circumstances, "the United States virtually dictated the terms of the [Treaty]."[17] So one-sided was the Treaty in favor of the United States that the American political party, the Whigs, who were opponents of the war, concluded that the Treaty was morally bankrupt.[18] In particular, the Whigs argued that it was unethical to require a defeated country to "sell" its territory.[19] Despite this, Mexico sought to provide certain rights for Mexican citizens in the territories ceded under the Treaty to the United States.[20]

Article VIII of the Treaty provided that:

> Mexicans now established in territories previously belonging to Mexico, and which remain for the future within . . . the United States . . . shall be free to continue where they now reside, or to remove . . . to the Mexican Republic. . . .
>
> Those who shall prefer to remain in said territories, may either retain the title and rights of Mexican citizens, or acquire those of citizens of the United States. But they shall be under the obligation to make their election within one year from the date of the exchange of ratifications of this treaty; and those who shall remain in the said territories after the expiration of that year, without having declared their intention to retain the character of Mexicans, shall be considered to have elected to become citizens of the United States.[21]

Article VIII also provides that:

> In the said territories, property of every kind, now belonging to Mexicans not established there, shall be inviolably respected. The present owners, the heirs of these, and all Mexicans who may hereafter acquire said property by contract, shall enjoy with respect to it guaranties equally ample as if the same belonged to citizens of the United States.[22]

Finally, Article IX provides that:

> Mexicans who . . . shall not preserve the character of citizens of the Mexican republic . . . shall be incorporated into the Union of the United States, and be admitted . . . to the enjoyment of all the rights of citizens of the United States, according to the principles of the constitution; and in the mean time shall be maintained and protected in the free enjoyment of their liberty and property, and secured in the free exercise of their religion without restriction.[23]

Since Mexico did not have much bargaining power when it entered into the Treaty, it would have been surprising if it had been successful in its effort to protect the former Mexican citizens in the conquered territories. And, indeed, the Treaty of Guadalupe Hidalgo was unable in significant ways to protect the rights of the new American citizens and their Mexican American descendants.[24] For example, scholars have documented how Mexican Americans were generally unable to protect their property rights arising under Spanish and Mexican land grants.[25] For instance, in New Mexico approximately three-fourths of the land claims were found to be invalid by the American courts.[26]

Indeed, American tribunals basically ignored the provisions of the Treaty in deciding Mexican property claims.[27] In this regard, Congress has often "superceded treaty pledges by later enacted statutes."[28] The courts have justified this practice by acknowledging the equal status of treaty and federal statute and applying the more recent law where there is a conflict.[29] The equality of treaty and federal statute undermined the Treaty provisions regarding the rights to property.[30] In this connection, the property rights provisions of the Treaty are not viewed as "self-executing."[31] As a result, they were not effective until Congress had passed laws to implement the Treaty.[32] Accordingly, the courts relied on the implementing legislation—and not the Treaty—in deciding Hispanic land claims.[33]

That legislation imposed a number of significant obstacles on the Mexican American claimants.[34] For example, the legislation placed on Mexican claimants the burden of proving that they had a right to the land.[35] It also required the Mexican landowners to make their way through a complex set of legal requirements in a foreign legal system and in a language that was foreign to them.[36] In this regard, language difficulties particularly worked to the disadvantage of the Mexican claimants, resulting in the loss of claims.[37] Mexican claimants also lost out because American tribunals would ignore, misunderstand, or distort Mexican law in determining the validity of claims.[38]

The implementing legislation devalued the Treaty's promises in other significant ways. For example, the Treaty's guarantee that property rights would be respected was limited by legislation in California to a period of two years.[39] Under the California Land Settlement Act of 1851, if one failed to assert a land claim within two years, the claimed property would be deemed to be in the public domain.[40]

The implementing legislation also established what might be regarded as alternative dispute resolution to resolve claims. Thus, under the California Land Settlement Act, claims were to be submitted to a special three-person commission.[41] Similarly, Congress established the position of surveyor general to resolve Hispanic land claims in the territory of New Mexico.[42] "The surveyor general was directed to investigate land claims and to issue recommendations to Congress whether to confirm or reject such claims."[43] These alternative tribunals sometimes created difficulties for the Mexican claimants. For example, the surveyor general lacked sufficient resources to determine title to millions of square miles of territory.[44] Moreover, most of the surveyors general lacked legal training and were not in a position to resolve difficult questions of law regarding the validity of the Hispanic land grants.[45] In addition, Congress failed to act in a timely manner upon the surveyor general's recommendations.[46]

Similarly, the Treaty failed to protect full membership rights in American society to persons of Mexican ancestry. In this regard, white identity traditionally has been a source of privilege and protection.[47] Indeed, during the time of slavery in this country, because whites could not be enslaved, the color line between black and white protected one in a very important way: whiteness prevented one from being transformed into property.[48] The status of being white has therefore been an important asset and has usually provided one with valuable privileges, and benefits.[49]

Given this, one might have thought that the Treaty would have provided for full membership rights since the Treaty operated to construct the race of Mexican Americans as legally white. A Texas federal court addressed in an immigration context the question of whether Mexicans were white in *In re Rodríguez*.[50] At that time, the federal naturalization laws required that an alien be white in order to become a citizen of the United States.[51] There, the court stated that Mexicans would probably be considered non-white from an anthropological perspective.[52] The court noted, however, that the United States had entered into the Treaty of Guadalupe Hidalgo with Mexico. That Treaty expressly allows Mexicans to become citizens of the United States.[53] Under these circumstances, the court concluded that Congress intended that Mexicans were entitled to become citizens. Thus, the court held that Mexicans were white within the meaning of the naturalization laws.[54] Through the social and political process of treaty making, then, Mexican Americans became "white."[55]

Since the law recognized Mexican Americans as white, one might have expected that social action would have reflected the Mexican American's privileged legal status as white. Legal recognition of Mexican Americans as white, however, did not provide Mexican Americans with full membership rights. Far from deriving protection from the Treaty and their legal definition as white, Mexican Americans faced discrimination throughout the American Southwest very similar to that experienced by African Americans.[56] Thus, Mexican Americans were excluded from public facilities and neighborhoods and were the targets of racial slurs.[57] Mexican Americans typically lived in one section of town because they were not allowed to purchase or lease housing anywhere except in the "Mexican Colony," irrespective of their social standing.[58] Similarly, Mexican Americans were segregated in public schools.[59] Mexican Americans also faced significant discrimination in the area of employment.[60] Moreover, police officers often discriminated against Mexican Americans.[61] When Mexican Americans and Mexican immigrants attempted to assert their civil rights under laws designed to protect them, the courts generally failed to protect them.[62]

Interestingly, at the time the Treaty was being negotiated, some in Mexico opposed ratification of the Treaty based on the ground that the Mexican citizens in the ceded territories would not be protected.[63] In particular, Manuel Crescencio Rejon argued that American racism would cause them to be treated unjustly.[64] He wrote: "[t]he North Americans hate us, their orators deprecate us even in speeches in which they recognize the justice of our cause, and they consider us unable to form a single nation or society with them."[65] These concerns proved to be prophetic. Through these and other legal devices, the promises of the Treaty were minimized and devalued. As a result, the Mexicans' and their Mexican American heirs' rights were denied and their property lost.[66]

III. The NAFTA and the Treaty of Guadalupe Hidalgo

This section of the article seeks to explore parallels between the NAFTA dispute resolution process and the dispute settlement process of the Treaty of Guadalupe Hidalgo. In this regard, it argues that Mexico negotiated both treaties from a very weak bargaining position. In doing so, the NAFTA dispute resolution process may generate a number of difficulties for Mexico that parallel problems that Mexican claimants experienced in litigating their rights under the earlier Treaty. For example, Mexico may experience problems in dealing with a foreign procedural system, *i.e.*, the NAFTA dispute settlement process which is based on Anglo-Saxon notions. Mexico may also experience difficulties arising out of the fact that the NAFTA dispute resolution procedures constitute alternative dispute resolution. In the course of the discussion, this section points out that in constructing the NAFTA dispute resolution procedures, Mexico was treated in ways that parallel the dominant society's treatment of Mexican Americans in the years since the Treaty of Guadalupe Hidalgo.

A. Unequal Bargaining Power for Mexico

The United States and Mexico entered into NAFTA in the 1990s.[67] Similar to the Treaty of Guadalupe Hidalgo, Mexico negotiated the NAFTA from a very weak bargaining position.[68] Mexico was under great internal and external pressures to enter into the NAFTA.[69]

With respect to internal pressures, the Mexican government needed to justify its programs against the criticism of its opponents.[70] As to external pressures, Mexico believed that it would suffer serious problems in the global economy if it failed to find new markets.[71] On the other hand, the United States had the greatest bargaining power in the NAFTA negotiations.[72] The NAFTA was simply not as important to the United States' economy as it was to Mexico's.[73] The American economy is twenty-five times the size of Mexico's.[74] This difference in the relative economic importance of the agreement insured that the United States had greater bargaining power in the NAFTA negotiations.[75] Under these circumstances, just as the United States had virtually dictated the terms of Treaty of Guadalupe Hidalgo,[76] the United States imposed conditions on the weaker party, Mexico. In negotiating the Treaty, Mexico was reluctant to press its interests and too willing to make concessions.[77]

B. Parallels Arising Out of NAFTA's Imposition of an Anglo/Saxon Procedural System on Mexico and the Problem of Dealing with a Foreign Procedural System

In the dispute resolution context, Mexico's weak bargaining position resulted in the United States imposing on Mexico, especially in the areas of antidumping and countervailing duties, procedural rules based on United States procedural law.[78] The NAFTA provides for four major dispute resolution devices.[79] Chapter 20 provides a way to resolve general disputes regarding the interpretation or application of the NAFTA.[80] The Chapter 19 dispute resolution mechanism applies only to antidumping and countervailing duty disputes between the NAFTA parties.[81] "'Dumping' is an unfair trade practice, whereby products of one country are exported to another country at below cost or at less than the domestic price of the products."[82] 'Antidumping' or 'countervailing' duties are duties that are imposed by the importing country to compensate for the unfair price of the exported products.[83] Each of the NAFTA parties has its own statutes that outlaw the dumping of imported goods and establish a way to place countervailing duties on imported goods that are priced too low.[84] All of these laws remain valid under the NAFTA.[85] The NAFTA, however, provides that decisions by National Tribunals on antidumping and countervailing duty disputes are subject to review by binational panels.[86] Beyond the Chapter 19 and 20 procedures, the North American Agreement on Environmental Cooperation (the "Environmental Side Agreement") provides dispute settlement procedures that may be employed to resolve controversies involving environmental laws.[87] Similarly, the North American Agreement on Labor Cooperation (the "Labor Side Agreement") provides a dispute settlement process for certain types of labor controversies.[88]

The NAFTA Chapter 19 panel review procedure provides a striking illustration of how the United States imposed an American procedural superstructure on Mexico. The Chapter 19 panel review procedure reproduces the details of American procedure.[89] For instance, the Chapter 19 panel rules copy, often verbatim, many aspects of the American federal procedure.[90] The panel rules provide for an opening pleading stage and a later phase of briefing and an oral hearing that is based on American federal trial and appellate practice.[91] In addition, in describing the objective of the Chapter 19 panel procedural rules, the panel procedures mirror the American system.[92] Thus, Rule 2 of the Chapter 19 rules says that "the purpose of these rules is to secure the just, speedy, and inexpensive review of final determinations."[93] This provision imitates Rule 1 of the Federal Rules of

Civil Procedure, which provides that the rules "shall be construed and administered to secure the just, speedy and inexpensive determination of every action."[94]

There are many other similarities between the Chapter 19 Rules and the American Federal Rules of Civil Procedure. For example, section 3 of Panel Rule 55, governing the signings of pleadings, duplicates Federal Rule 11.[95] In addition, the format of the pleadings[96] and motions[97] in the Chapter 19 and American procedural systems are very similar.[98] Moreover, the briefs permitted in the Chapter 19 panel reviews mirror those employed in the American federal appellate practice.[99] The panel review oral hearing finds its counterpart in the oral proceedings that are held in the American federal courts of appeal.[100] Thus, the Chapter 19 panel rules have duplicated the procedural details of the American federal procedural system.

Beyond imitating the American procedural details, the Chapter 19 procedural rules also reflect American conceptions of procedure.[101] In this regard, the Chapter 19 panel review procedure is focused on a single hearing, in which the lawyers advance their perspectives on the facts and applicable legal principles.[102] Significantly, centering on a single event is a key aspect of the American common law tradition.[103] In addition, the Chapter 19 panel review procedure also incorporates the traditional American common law idea of a distinct and drawn-out opening pleading stage.[104] The Chapter 19 panel procedure also embraces the traditional reactive or passive role of the American common law judge by relegating a passive role to the Chapter 19 panel.[105] Thus, the American common law tradition forms the conceptual basis for the Chapter 19 panel review process.

In so doing, the panel review procedure ignores or renders invisible the Mexican point of view.[106] Perhaps the best illustration of this point is that the rules provide that English or French may be employed when a panel reviews a Canadian judgment.[107] In addition, the rules provide that if the proceedings implicate legal issues that are of "general public interest or importance" or are conducted, at least in part, in both English and French, there must be simultaneous translation in both English and French.[108] Clearly, the rules should have provided for the use of Spanish as well.[109] Almost all of Mexico's citizens speak Spanish, and few speak fluent English.[110] Despite this, the NAFTA does not expressly provide for the use of Spanish in panel reviews of Mexican judgments.[111]

The omission or invisibility of the Mexican perspective as shown in the failure to provide for Spanish in the NAFTA finds an important parallel in the fact that since the Treaty of Guadalupe Hidalgo, the perspective of Mexican Americans has been rendered virtually invisible. One of the identifying characteristics of being a Mexican American or a Latino in the United States is being ignored as if one does not exist.[112] Latinos have been virtually absent from the leading venues of mainstream American society, including civil rights discourse,[113] historical accounts,[114] leading periodicals,[115] and popular culture.[116] Kevin Johnson described this invisibility by referring to Latinos as "Los Olvidados," or "the Forgotten Ones."[117]

In any event, this failure to consider the Spanish language could have adverse consequences for Mexico in NAFTA dispute resolution. As we observed in the Treaty of Guadalupe Hidalgo context, one of the factors that helped generate adverse litigation results for the former Mexican citizens and their heirs involved problems in dealing with an English language legal system in the American courts.[118]

Beyond this, the fact that Mexico would have to deal with a foreign procedural system in the NAFTA context should raise concern for Mexico's prospects in NAFTA dispute resolution. As discussed, the NAFTA panel review procedure basically reproduces

U.S. procedural law.[119] Mexico, however, has a legal system that is distinct from that of the United States.[120] Since Mexico is a civil law jurisdiction, its legal system is more similar to those found in "continental Europe than that of the United States."[121] The Mexican conception of procedure is fundamentally different from the American common law system.[122] In contrast to the American system, Mexican civil procedure is not centered on a single, formal oral hearing.[123] Under Mexican law, there is no trial of a case.[124] Instead, the parties present evidence at a number of hearings.[125] A series of hearings reduces the possibility of surprise.[126] Since there is no limit on the number of hearings, new information can always be examined at later hearings.[127] The series of hearings also encourages settlement.[128] In not focusing on a single concentrated event, the Mexican procedural system is firmly based in the tradition of the civil law.[129] One commentator has described the civil law tradition as follows:

> There is no such thing as a trial in our sense; there is no single, concentrated event. The typical civil proceeding in a civil law country is actually a series of isolated meetings of and written communications between counsel and the judge, in which evidence is introduced, testimony is given, procedural motions and rulings are made, and so on.[130]

Thus, the Mexican civil procedure arises from a different and distinct legal tradition than that of the United States.

The civil law procedural system differs from the common law system in other ways. For example, discovery is less important in the civil law tradition.[131] In addition, civil law judges seem to be more active than traditional common law judges.[132] For instance, Mexican judges take a major role in questioning witnesses.[133] Because the judge is more active in the civil tradition, the parties are not as independent.[134] The civil law tradition also has a different notion of an appeal from that found in the common law system.[135] Given all of this, it is clear that Mexico has a distinct civil procedure, stemming from the civil law tradition. Thus, the Mexican legal system is foreign to that of the United States. Accordingly, Mexico is required, under NAFTA, to litigate in a foreign procedural superstructure.

The United States Supreme Court has expressed concern about the fairness of requiring parties to litigate in a foreign system. In *Asahi Metal Industry Co. v. Superior Court*,[136] Gary Zurcher, a resident of California, was hurt when his motorcycle tire exploded while he was traveling on a California highway.[137] He filed a lawsuit in a California state court against the Taiwanese manufacturer of the tube, Cheng Shin.[138] Cheng Shin then sought indemnification from Asahi Metal, the Japanese entity that supplied the tube valve assemblies to the Taiwanese company.[139] Asahi Metal moved to dismiss for lack of jurisdiction.[140] In concluding that the Due Process Clause of the United States Constitution did not permit the exercise of personal jurisdiction over Asahi Metal, the Court expressed serious concerns about the fairness of requiring parties to submit their disputes to a foreign nation's judicial system.[141] The Court observed that there are "unique burdens placed upon one who must defend oneself in a foreign legal system."[142] In light of this heavy burden, the Court concluded that the exercise of personal jurisdiction by a California court over Asahi would be unreasonable and unfair.

Among the burdens that an outsider could experience in attempting to proceed in a foreign legal system is the danger of oppression. The strangeness and complexity of a legal system creates the danger of oppression.[143] The danger is that those who are more familiar with the legal system will be able to use the system to their advantage.[144] Those with superior knowledge of the legal system will be able to maneuver others into situations where the legal system will benefit them at the expense of others who are less familiar with the system.[145] This amounts to oppression.

Given the reasoning in *Asahi* and the problem of oppression, it would seem that Mexico would also face "unique burdens" in being required to litigate in the NAFTA dispute resolution process—a foreign procedural system. In this regard, one of the obstacles that Mexican claimants faced in litigating claims under the Treaty of Guadalupe Hidalgo was having to litigate in the foreign American legal system.[146] Thus, there is reason to question whether the results of the NAFTA dispute resolution process will be reasonable and fair to Mexico.

In this connection, NAFTA's imposition of a foreign procedural structure on Mexico, in effect, forces Mexico to assimilate into the dominant United States legal system. There are parallels here with respect to the dominant American society's treatment of Mexican Americans in the years since the Treaty of Guadalupe Hidalgo. It is widely thought that Mexican Americans and other Latinos should assimilate into the American mainstream.[147] They are said to have a duty to learn English, surrender the culture of their origins, and become "American."[148] Certain groups have sought to enforce, through law, this purported obligation to assimilate.[149] For example, the English-only advocates seek to eliminate the use of Spanish,[150] and immigration restrictionists[151] seek to curtail immigration of Latinos on the ground that they wrongfully refuse to assimilate.[152] Thus, in the years since the Treaty of Guadalupe Hidalgo, the dominant American society has sought to force Mexican Americans to assimilate Anglo-Saxon ideals just as the NAFTA seeks to force Mexico to assimilate into an Anglo-Saxon procedural system.

A certain conception of historical development rooted in the nineteenth century has generated this push toward assimilation. According to this conception, progress requires assimilating smaller cultures into larger cultures.[153] Thus, for both leftists and liberals in the last century the major nations were the vehicles of positive change.[154] For example, John Stuart Mill wrote:

> Experience proves it is possible for one nationality to merge and be absorbed into another: and when it was originally an inferior and more backward portion of the human race absorption is greatly to its advantage. Nobody can suppose that it is not more beneficial to a Breton, or a Basque of French Navarre, to be brought into the current of the ideas and feelings of a highly civilized and cultivated people—to be a member of the French Nationality, admitted on equal terms to all the privileges of French citizenship—than to sulk on his own rocks, the half-savage relic of past times, revolving in his own little mental orbit, without participation or interest in the general movement of the world.[155]

In this view, smaller countries were underdeveloped and could only become modern by giving up their native culture and assimilating into the larger nation.[156] Significantly, this view provided not only a justification for assimilating minorities into the larger state, but also for colonizing other people elsewhere.[157] This conception of historical development is based on a key assumption—that "progress and civilization require[d] assimilating 'backward' minorities to 'energetic' majorities."[158] This nineteenth-century assumption, however, has gradually been rejected.[159] For example, the contention that the Czechs could not take part in modernity except by being absorbed into Germany has been shown to be mistaken.[160] Similarly, other groups—the Flemish, Québécois, and Basques—also have been able to resist assimilation and nevertheless exist as thriving modern cultures.[161]

Despite this, this outmoded conception of history seems to have been at work in the NAFTA negotiation process and probably led to the NAFTA dispute resolution procedures incorporating Anglo-Saxon procedural notions. The presumption of the superiority of an Anglo-American world view over the Mexican world view operated in the NAFTA negotiations.[162] Several Mexican negotiators have stated that during the NAFTA negotiations process the North American negotiators devalued Mexican perspectives as being rooted in a backward legal system.[163] The American negotiators made it clear that they presumed the "inadequacy of Mexican law and legal institutions."[164] Indeed, the NAFTA negotiation process was seen as an opportunity for the United States to "Americanize" Mexico, *i.e.*, to promote a legal, political, and economic system in Mexico that more closely resembles that of the United States.[165] Thus, the NAFTA negotiations process may be viewed as an attempt to force Mexico to assimilate Anglo-Saxon ideals—*e.g.*, Anglo-Saxon procedural notions—based on the outmoded assumption that such assimilation is necessary in order to allow "progress," *i.e.*, Mexican participation in the modern world. In this regard, there is a striking parallel between the NAFTA negotiation process and the Treaty of Guadalupe Hidalgo negotiation process. Just as in the NAFTA negotiation process, American officials assumed an attitude of moral superiority in negotiating the Treaty of Guadalupe Hidalgo.[166] They viewed the forcible incorporation or assimilation of almost one-half of Mexico's territory "as fulfilling the Manifest Destiny of the United States to spread the benefits of democracy to the lesser peoples of the continent."[167]

In this connection, the differences between the American and Mexican legal systems could generate other problems. In the earlier Treaty of Guadalupe Hidalgo, difficulties in understanding Mexican law caused Mexican claimants to lose out.[168] Similar difficulties in understanding Mexican law may generate problems for Mexico in NAFTA dispute resolution. The potential for such problems is illustrated in litigating a Chapter 19 dispute, where Mexican lawyers may cite principles of Mexican law.[169] This generates the difficulty of presenting an argument that can be understood by North American panelists.[170] For example, consider the fundamental Mexican legal principle of *motivación* and *fundamentacion*.[171] This principle is one of the key aspects of Mexican constitutional law, and its meaning is well taught to Mexican law students.[172] Since North American panelists do not possess a Mexican legal education, it would be very hard for them to comprehend and correctly apply this key Mexican legal principle.[173] Thus, Mexico could face difficulties in the NAFTA dispute resolution process arising out of such misunderstandings.

That it is plausible that such confusion regarding Mexican law could occur is confirmed by recent experience regarding the Canada-U.S. Free Trade Agreement dispute settlement mechanism, which served as the model for NAFTA dispute resolution. In the recent *Softwood Lumber III*[174] case, serious concerns were expressed regarding the ability of Canadian panelists to understand American law, despite the fact that Canada belongs to the common law tradition.[175] Writing in dissent, the American panelist, Judge Malcolm Wilkey, former Chief Judge of the Court of Appeals for the D.C. Circuit, found that the Canadian panelists had misunderstood American law and that this represented a threat to the dispute settlement system.[176] He observed that the lack of training of Canadian panelists in United States administrative law presents a problem for the dispute resolution system.[177] In addition, he stated that Canadians do not understand the place of legislative history in the American legal system or the principles on which American case law should be interpreted.[178] Obviously, if Canadian panelists are unable to understand American law despite their common law training, then it seems unlikely that North

American panelists will be able to understand Mexican law in light of the fact that Mexican law stems from a different and distinct civil law tradition.

C. A Parallel Arising Out of Disadvantages for Mexico Stemming from Alternative Dispute Resolution

The NAFTA dispute resolution procedures may also be viewed as alternative dispute resolution.[179] There are three fundamental kinds of alternative dispute resolution that are used in an international setting: (1) mediation; (2) non-binding arbitration; and (3) binding arbitration.[180] NAFTA uses all three types of alternative dispute resolution in one circumstance or another.[181] Mediation procedure involves an effort by the parties to negotiate a settlement of their claims.[182] Either party can ask for a mediator to resolve the dispute.[183] The mediation process is governed by certain time limitations.[184] Usually "the mediation provisions of trade agreements provide for some sort of permanent commission" whose members may act as mediators.[185] "Chapter 20 of NAFTA establishes such a commission."[186]

As for nonbinding arbitration,[187] it differs from mediation in that there is a third party who renders an opinion and states that one of the parties is at fault.[188] The parties, however, do not agree to be bound by the arbitrator's report.[189] Under the NAFTA, nonbinding arbitration is the method for settling almost all controversies that cannot be disposed of by mediation.[190]

With respect to binding arbitration, the parties agree to be bound by the arbitrator's report and decision regarding a legal obligation.[191] Under the NAFTA, some categories of disputes that involve binding arbitration are: investment, antidumping and countervailing duty controversies between a NAFTA party and citizens of another party.[192]

In light of Mexico's relatively weak position with respect to the United States, the fact that the NAFTA's dispute resolution process involves forms of alternative dispute resolution is significant. Scholars have recently argued that alternative dispute resolution—*e.g.*, mediation and arbitration—with its deformalized procedures poses special risks for weaker disputants.[193] These scholars link fairness to formality. The fundamental notion is that the public and formal ideals of most societies are highminded and dedicated to equality.[194] In a formal context, the average person will often act on these ideals.[195] In an informal context, however, the same person may not feel constrained to behave in accordance with the community's formal ideals.[196] As a result, traditional, formal in-court adjudication is less likely to be influenced by bias than informal alternative dispute resolution.[197] In such informal situations, there is a danger that decision making may be more inclined to be unfair with weaker disputants.[198] Thus, weaker disputants should select a more formal setting for dispute resolution. Given this, Mexico, as a relatively weak disputant, must be concerned that the NAFTA alternative dispute resolution process may be biased against Mexico. This generates another parallel: Mexican claimants experienced difficulties arising out of the alternative dispute resolution-like regime established under the Treaty of Guadalupe Hidalgo.[199]

D. The Early Results of the NAFTA Dispute Resolution Process

Given all of the above, it seems that there are reasons to conclude that the NAFTA dispute resolution process may put Mexico at a disadvantage just as the earlier Treaty of Guadalupe Hidalgo dispute resolution process placed Mexican claimants at a disadvantage. A review of the early results of the NAFTA dispute resolution process provides some evidence to support this conclusion. A major study analyzing the early results of the NAFTA dispute resolution process shows that Mexico has fared the least well of the three NAFTA countries.[200] As of December 1996, Mexico had "experienced some relatively significant unfavorable rulings . . . but had no substantial favorable ruling to offset" these setbacks.[201] A couple of examples will suffice to illustrate this point. Consider the cement case,[202] a Chapter 19 antidumping case. The dispute arose when the United States promulgated a final material injury order regarding the export of Mexican cement.[203] In response, Mexico initiated proceedings under the General Agreement on Tariffs and Trade (GATT).[204] In 1992, a GATT panel decided that the American findings of material injury was mistaken and that antidumping duties that had been placed on Mexican cement should be returned.[205] Despite this, the United States refused to comply with the panel's decision.[206] In 1995, the United States insisted that it was proper to impose an antidumping duty on Mexican cement.[207] In response, Mexico's leading cement company asked for a NAFTA Chapter 19 panel to be established.[208] In 1996, Mexico sustained a significant loss when the NAFTA panel unanimously concluded that the antidumping duties on Mexican cement were fully justified.[209]

Similarly, the "Cut-Length Steel Plate" case, another antidumping case involved a Chapter 19 NAFTA panel.[210] In 1994, the Mexican government issued a final dumping and injury determination and imposed large countervailing duties on Bethlehem Steel Corporation (46.18%) and USX Corporation (76%).[211] Subsequently, the two United States companies invoked the Chapter 19 review process.[212] In a lengthy opinion and by a slim majority, the NAFTA panel issued a decision against Mexico.[213] The panel ordered Mexico to refund antidumping duties that had been placed on the American companies.[214] The "panel, a majority of whose members were not trained in Mexican law,"[215] determined that Mexico had "failed to comply with basic [Mexican] constitutional and other applicable legal principles" in conducting the antidumping investigation.[216] Under these circumstances, it is hardly surprising that Mexican officials have been troubled by outcomes of the first Chapter 19 panel discussions involving Mexico.[217]

These early results of the NAFTA dispute resolution process have implications for determining the success of the NAFTA procedural system. One reason international trade agreements incorporate dispute settlement mechanisms is to try and prevent pre-agreement bargaining power from becoming post-agreement bargaining power.[218] Thus, one way to judge the success of the NAFTA dispute resolution procedures is to evaluate whether they have prevented the pre-agreement bargaining power of the United States from becoming post-agreement bargaining power. In other words, have the NAFTA dispute resolution procedures helped equalize post-agreement bargaining power between the United States and Mexico? Since Mexico to date has achieved no significant victories in the NAFTA dispute settlement process, there is some reason to be concerned that the NAFTA dispute resolution procedures may not have been successful in preventing the United States' pre-agreement bargaining power from becoming post-agreement bargaining power.

That the United States may have retained its pre-bargaining strength may also be indicated in the United States' willingness to disregard the NAFTA to satisfy internal political needs. For example, in 1996, Mexico requested Chapter 20 consultations concerning the United States' decision not to permit Mexican trucking businesses additional access to American border states as expressly provided for by NAFTA.[219] Previously, Secretary of Transportation Federico Peña had announced that the United States would not adhere to this NAFTA requirement.[220] The American decision to ignore the NAFTA was viewed as the result of pressure from the American trucking industry.[221] Similarly, Mexico sought to consult with the United States regarding the enactment of the Cuban-Liberty and Democratic Solidarity Act of 1996 (the Helms-Burton Act).[222] This Act may constitute a breach of NAFTA because it establishes a private right of action against foreign businesses, including Mexican businesses, who knowingly profit from property taken by the Castro government.[223] The Helms-Burton Act is seen as the product of political pressure of Cuban-Americans during an election year.[224] These events suggest that the United States may be willing to violate or ignore NAFTA given sufficient pressure from domestic political interests.[225]

IV. Conclusion

This article has sought to explore parallels between the dispute resolution process of the Treaty of Guadalupe Hidalgo and the NAFTA dispute settlement process. In this regard it has argued that Mexico negotiated both treaties from a weak position. In so doing, the NAFTA dispute resolution process may generate a number of the difficulties for Mexico that parallel problems that Mexican claimants experienced in litigating their rights under the earlier Treaty. For example, Mexico may experience problems in dealing with a foreign procedural system, *i.e.*, the NAFTA dispute settlement procedures. Among these problems are difficulties arising from language, from misunderstandings of Mexican law by North American panelists, and the unique burdens that are experienced by one who must litigate in a foreign legal system. The article also has argued that the NAFTA dispute resolution procedures may be viewed as alternative dispute resolution. It has contended that Mexico is likely to experience difficulties in such alternative dispute resolution in light of its relatively weak position. Given all of this, there is reason to believe that the NAFTA dispute resolution process may put Mexico at a disadvantage just as the earlier Treaty of Guadalupe Hidalgo dispute settlement process placed Mexican claimants and their heirs at a disadvantage. In this regard, an analysis of the early results of the NAFTA dispute resolution process demonstrates that Mexico has fared the least well of the three NAFTA countries.

Notes

[1] *See* Treaty of Peace, Friendship, Limits and Settlement with the Republic of Mexico, Feb. 2, 1848, U.S.-Mex.-Can., 9 Stat. 922 [hereinafter Treaty of Guadalupe Hidalgo].

[2] *See* The North American Free Trade Agreement, Dec. 17, 1992, U.S.-Can.-Mex., 32 I.L.M. 296, 33 I.L.M. 649 (1994); *see also* Joseph J. Norton, *The NAFTA "Process" in Context, in* NAFTA AND BEYOND: A NEW FRAMEWORK FOR DOING BUSINESS IN THE AMERICAS 7 (1995) ("NAFTA is a landmark in U.S. trade and economic policy in the Americas and provides a reference point for future U.S. bilateral and multilateral trade negotiations and arrangements"); Boris Kozolchyk, *NAFTA in the Grand and Small Scheme of Things*, 13 ARIZ. J. INT'L & COMP. L. 135, 146 (1996) (NAFTA is part of a movement toward integration of international economy).

[3] *See, e.g.*, C. O'Neal Taylor, *Fast Track, Trade Policy and Free Trade Agreements: Why the NAFTA Turned into a Battle*, 28 GEO. WASH. J. INT'L L. & ECON. 1, 2 (1994) ("One of the hardest fought trade battles in decades was waged over the ratification of the North American Free Trade Agreement"); Frances L. Ansley, *North American Free Trade Agreement: The Public Debate*, 22 GA. J. INT'L & COMP. L. 329 (1992). For example, some worried that American companies would transfer manufacturing jobs from the United States to Mexico to take advantage of presumed lower costs of production. *See* Stephen

Zamora, *The Americanization of Mexican Law: Non-Trade Issues in the North American Free Trade Agreement*, 24 LAW & POL'Y INT'L BUS. 391, 401 (1993); ROSS PEROT & PAT CHOATE, SAVE YOUR JOB, SAVE OUR COUNTRY: WHY NAFTA MUST BE STOPPED—NOW! (1993).

[4] See David López, *Dispute Resolution under NAFTA: Lessons from the Early Experience*, 32 TEX. INT'L L.J. 163, 164 (1997).

[5] See id.

[6] See id.

[7] See Christine A. Klein, *Treaties of Conquest: Property Rights, Indian Treaties, and the Treaty of Guadalupe Hidalgo*, 26 N.M. L. REV. 201, 208 (1996).

[8] RICHARD WHITE, "IT'S YOUR MISFORTUNE AND NONE OF MY OWN:" A HISTORY OF THE AMERICAN WEST 73 (1991).

[9] See Klein, *supra* note 7, at 208; *see also* HAROLD HONGJU KOH, THE NATIONAL SECURITY CONSTITUTION, SHARING POWER AFTER THE IRAN-CONTRA AFFAIR 84 (1990) (describing President Polk's term in office, during which the Mexican War occurred as "an almost frantic period of territorial conquest"); J. J. Bowden, *Spanish and Mexican Land Grants in the Southwest*, 8 LAND & WATER L. REV. 467, 467 (1973) ("Contrary to the avowed policy of the United States not to prosecute a war for the purpose of securing additional territory, President James K. Polk, following the outbreak of hostilities with Mexico, formulated a plan for the speedy military conquest and possession of New Mexico and California in order to insure their acquisition by the United States when peace was made.") (footnotes omitted).

[10] See Klein, *supra* note 7, at 201. *See also* Bowden, *supra* note 9, at 468-70; CHARLES F. WILKINSON, THE AMERICAN WEST: A NARRATIVE BIBLIOGRAPHY AND A STUDY IN REGIONALISM 7, 23 (1989).

[11] See Klein, *supra* note 7, at 201. *See also* Bowden, *supra* note 9, at 468-70.

[12] See RODOLFO ACUÑA, OCCUPIED AMERICA: THE CHICANO STRUGGLE TOWARD LIBERATION 9-33 (1972); Kevin R. Johnson, *An Essay on Immigration, Citizenship, and U.S./Mexico Relations: The Tale of Two Treaties*, 5 SW. J. L. & TRADE AM.; *see also* PATRICIA NELSON LIMERICK, THE LEGACY OF CONQUEST, THE UNBROKEN PAST OF THE AMERICAN WEST 26-28 (1987) ("Conquest forms the historical bedrock of the whole nation, and the American West is a preeminent case study in conquest and its consequences") *Id.* at 28; Louis A. Martínez, *En Aquel Entonces Y Ahora: Popular Literature as the Mirror of Political and Cultural Conflict*, 5 SW. J. L. & TRADE AM. 77, 77 (1998) (the Treaty of Guadalupe Hidalgo "was spawned in era in which the zeitgeist shaped ideological formations that include notions that certain territories and people require and beseech domination").

[13] See RICHARD GRISWOLD DEL CASTILLO, THE TREATY OF GUADALUPE HIDALGO: A LEGACY OF CONFLICT 40-42 (1990).

[14] See id. at 40.

[15] See id. at 28-29, 51 ("The recurring theme in the writings of treaty advocates was that by ending the war, the treaty saved Mexico from possible obliteration as a nation.").

[16] See id. at 40-41.

[17] Id. at xii.

[18] See id. at 26. The Treaty of Guadalupe Hidalgo "has been criticized as `one of the harshest in modern history.'" Malcolm Ebright, *New Mexican Land Grants: The Legal Background*, in LANDS, WATER AND CULTURE: NEW PERSPECTIVES ON HISPANIC LAND GRANTS 28 (Charles L. Briggs & John R. Van Ness eds., 1987) (quoting LUIS G. ZORRILLA, HISTORIA DE LAS RELACIONES ENTRE MEXICO Y LOS ESTADOS UNIDOS DE AMERICA: 1800-1958 218 [Mexico 1965]).

[19] See DEL CASTILLO, supra note 13, at 26. The Whigs also opposed the Treaty because they thought the annexation of territory "would increase the slavocracy's power in Congress." *Id* at 44.

[20] See id. at 62-86.

[21] Treaty of Guadalupe Hidalgo, *supra* note 1, at art. III.

[22] Id. Interestingly, there is some authority for the proposition that general principles of international law hold that private property rights should be unchanged following a conquest. *See, e.g.*, Ely's Administrator v. United States, 171 U.S. 220, 223 (1898) ("[I]n harmony with the rules of international law . . . the change of sovereignty should work no change in respect to rights and titles").

[23] Treaty of Guadalupe Hidalgo, *supra* note 1, at art. IX.

[24] See Johnson, *supra* note 12.

[25] See Klein, *supra* note 7, at 218. *See also* Bowden, *supra* note 9, at 472, 497.

[26] See Klein, *supra* note 7, at 218.

[27] See *id.*

[28] *Id.* at 217. Some Mexican defenders of the Treaty apparently misunderstood this aspect of American law. For example, Bernardo Couto argued that "the rights of former Mexican citizens would be protected because, in American law 'every treaty has a superiority and preference under civil legislation.'" DEL CASTILLO, *supra* note 13, at 51.

[29] See Klein, *supra* note 7, at 217. Interestingly, Louis Henkin contends that such equality cannot be supported on the basis of Article VI of the Constitution. *See* LOUIS HENKIN, FOREIGN AFFAIRS AND THE CONSTITUTION 156-57, 163-64 (1972).

[30] See Klein, *supra* note 7, at 217.

[31] See *id.* For more on the notion of self-executing treaties, *see generally* Carlos Manuel Vásquez, *The Four Doctrines of Self-Executing Treaties* 89 AM J. INT'L. L. 695 (1995).

[32] See Klein, *supra* note 7, at 217; *see also* Váquez, *supra* note 31, at 695 ("At a general level, a self-executing treaty may be defined as a treaty that may be enforced in the courts without prior legislation by Congress, and a non-self-executing treaty, conversely, as a treaty that may not be enforced in the courts without prior legislative 'implementation' "). Interestingly, "under Mexican law, international treaties signed by the President and approved by the Mexican Senate are" self-executing, without the need to implement them through legislation. Robert E. Lutz, *Law, Procedure and Culture in Mexico under the NAFTA: The Perspective of a Nafta Panelist*, 3 SW. J.L. & TRADE AM. 391, 401 (1996).

[33] See Klein, *supra* note 7, at 218.

[34] See *id.*

[35] See *id.*

[36] See *id.*

[37] See Guadalupe Luna, *Chicana/o Land Tenure in the Agrarian Domain: On the Edge of a Naked Knife*, 3 MICH. J. RACE & LAW (1998).

[38] See *id.* ("In the analysis of the property rights, the new legal regime selectively ignored Mexican law. It indulged new legal interpretations that contradicted long established [Mexican] law determining a grant's validity in the antecedent government.")

[39] See Klein, *supra* note 7, at 220. *See* "An Act to ascertain and settle the private Land claims in the State of California," Act of Congress of March 3, 1851, ch. XLI, 9 STAT. 631 (1851)[hereinafter California Land Settlement Act].

[40] See Klein, *supra* note 7, at 220; California Land Settlement Act, *supra* note 39 at § 13.

[41] See Klein, *supra* note 7, at 220; *see also* United States v. Ritchie, 58 U.S. 525, 533 (1854) (the board of commissioners was not a court, under the constitution, invested with judicial powers).

[42] See Klein, *supra* note 7, at 225. *See also* Bowden, *supra* note 9, at 474 ("the primary responsibility for the adjustment of private land claims in New Mexico was vested in the Surveyor General").

[43] Klein, *supra* note 7, at 225.

[44] See *id.* *See also* DEL CASTILLO, *supra* note 13, at 78 (discussing claimants' difficulties with the surveyor general's office).

[45] See Bowden, *supra* note 9, at 474. *See also* DEL CASTILLO, *supra* note 13, at 79 ("The process of reviewing the New Mexico claims gave no assurance that the Treaty of Guadalupe Hidalgo, or indeed the rule of law, outweighed the political influence of those behind the scenes").

[46] See Klein, *supra* note 7, at 225. *See also* Bowden, *supra* note 9, at 472 ("the history of the effort to solve the land grant problem in. . . the area ceded to the United States by Mexico—the 'Southwest'—is one filled with disinterest, indecision and delay") (footnote omitted).

[47] See Cheryl Harris, *Whiteness As Property*, 106 HARV. L. REV. 1709, 1721 (1993). For more on the analysis of whiteness, *see generally* CRITICAL WHITE STUDIES: LOOKING BEHIND THE MIRROR (Richard Delgado & Jean Stefancic eds., 1997); BELL HOOKS, YEARNING: RACE, GENDER, AND CULTURAL POLITICS (1990); RUTH FRANKENBERG, WHITE WOMEN, RACE MATTERS: THE SOCIAL CONSTRUCTION OF WHITENESS (1993); IAN F. HANEY LÓPEZ, WHITE BY LAW: THE LEGAL CONSTRUCTION OF RACE (1996); Barbara J. Flagg, *"Was Blind, But Now I See:" White Race Consciousness and the Requirement of Discriminatory Intent*, 91 MICH. L. REV. 953 (1993).

[48] *See* Harris, *supra* note 47, at 1721.

[49] *See id.* at 1713; *see also* Stephanie M. Wildman & Adrienne D. Davis, *Language and Silence: Making Systems of Privilege Visible*, 35 SANTA CLARA L. REV. 881, 893-94 (1995) (defining white privilege as "an invisible package of unearned assets" which is "like an invisible weightless knapsack of special provisions, assurance, tools, maps, guides, codebooks, passports, visas, clothes, compass, emergency gear, and blank checks") (citing Peggy McIntosh, *Unpacking the Invisible Knapsack: White Privilege*, in CREATION SPIRITUALITY 33 [Jan./Feb 1992]).

[50] 81 F. 337 (W.D. Tex. 1897).

[51] *See* Kevin R. Johnson, *Racial Restrictions on Naturalization: The Recurring Intersection of Race and Gender in Immigration and Citizenship Law*, 11 BERKELEY WOMEN'S L.J. 142, 143 (1996) (reviewing IAN FIDENCIO HANEY LÓPEZ, WHITE BY LAW: THE LEGAL CONSTRUCTION OF RACE [1996]—from 1790 to 1952 only white immigrants could naturalize as citizens).

[52] *See In Re* Rodríguez, 81 F. 337 at 349.

[53] *See id.* at 350-52.

[54] *See id.* at 354-55.

[55] The *Rodríguez* case provides support for the proposition that race is socially constructed. *See* George A. Martínez, *African-Americans, Latinos and the Construction of Race: Toward an Epistemic Coalition*, 19 UCLA CHICANO-LATINO L. REV. (1997). For more analysis of Mexican Americans and whiteness, *see* George A. Martínez, *The Legal Construction of Race: Mexican Americans and Whiteness*, 2 HARV. LATINO L. REV. 321 (1997).

[56] *See generally*, George A. Martínez, *Legal Indeterminacy, Judicial Discretion and the Mexican American Litigation Experience: 1930-1980*, 27 U.C. DAVIS L. REV. 555 (1994). *See also* Paul Brest & Miranda Oshige, *Affirmative Action for Whom?*, 47 STAN. L. REV. 855, 888 (1995) ("Latinos have encountered prejudice and systematic discrimination in virtually all realms, including housing, employment and education").

[57] *See* Martínez, *supra* note 56, at 573.

[58] *See* PAULINE R. KIBBE, LATIN AMERICANS IN TEXAS 123-24 (1946).

[59] *See* Martínez, *supra* note 56, at 584. *See also* GUADALUPE SAN MIGUEL JR., "LET ALL OF THEM TAKE HEED": MEXICAN AMERICANS AND THE CAMPAIGN FOR EDUCATIONAL EQUALITY IN TEXAS, 1910-1981, 54-55 ("School officials and board members, reflecting the specific desires of the general population, did not want Mexican students to attend school with Anglo children regardless of their social standing, economic status, language capability, or place of residence"); Richard Delgado, *Rodrigo's Twelfth Chronicle: The Problem of the Shanty*, 85 GEO. L. J. 667, 673 (1997) ("School authorities sent Mexican kids to schools that were different from—and inferior to—the ones attended by Anglo children"); Michael A. Olivas, *Torching Zozobra: The Problem with Linda Chávez*, RECONSTRUCTION, Vol. 2, No. 2, 48, 51 (1993) (noting that Mexican Americans were isolated in underfunded schools).

[60] *See, e.g.*, CAREY MCWILLIAMS, NORTH FROM MEXICO 195-97 (1948).

[61] *See* U.S. COMM'N ON CIVIL RIGHTS, MEXICAN AMERICANS AND THE ADMINISTRATION OF JUSTICE IN THE SOUTHWEST 2, 13 (1970).

[62] *See generally* Martínez, *supra* note 56; Kevin R. Johnson, *Civil Rights and Immigration: Challenges for the Latino Community in the Twenty-First Century*, 8 LA RAZA L.J. 42, 45-56 (1995) (reviewing limits of litigation for Latinos and contending that such strategies must be combined with efforts at political mobilization).

[63] *See* DEL CASTILLO, *supra* note 13, at 49-50.

[64] *See id.* at 50.

[65] *Id.*

[66] *See* Richard Delgado, *Derrick Bell and the Ideology of Racial Reform: Will We Ever Be Saved?* 97 YALE L.J. 923, 940 (1988) (The Treaty of Guadalupe Hidalgo "purported to guarantee to Mexicans caught on the U.S. side of the border full citizenship and civil rights, as well as protection of their culture and language. The Treaty, modeled after ones drawn up between the U.S. and various Indian tribes, was given similar treatment: the Mexicans' '[l]and and property were stolen, rights were denied, language and culture suppressed, opportunities for employment, education and political representation were thwarted.'") *quoting* A. RENDÓN, CHICANO MANIFESTO 71 (1971) (footnotes omitted).

⁶⁷ *See* North American Free Trade Agreement, *supra* note 2. *See also* Zamora, *supra* note 3, at 402 ("The NAFTA negotiations took place over a twelve month period, from August 1991, until the announcement by U.S., Mexican and Canadian trade negotiators on August 12, 1992, that negotiations on the agreement had been completed") (footnote omitted).

⁶⁸ *See* Angel R. Oquendo, *NAFTA's Procedural Narrow-Mindedness: The Panel Review of Antidumping and Countervailing Duty Determinations under Chapter Nineteen*, 11 CONN. J. INT'L. L. 61, 63 (1995).

⁶⁹ *See id.* at 63. *See also* Zamora, *supra* note 3, at 394 (Mexico was willing to enter into the NAFTA because "the political leadership of Mexico—President Carlos Salinas de Gortari and the leaders of the Partido Revolucionario Institucional . . . [felt] that there [was] no viable alternative").

⁷⁰ *See* Oquendo, *supra* note 68, at 63. *See also* Zamora, *supra* note 3, at 395 (the political leadership of Mexico "realizes that it can preserve a measure of its political monopoly only if the economy prospers and only if jobs and salaries increase. In the judgment of President Salinas and his advisors, this can only happen by increasing its trade and investment with the United States").

⁷¹ *See* Oquendo, *supra* note 68, at 63.

⁷² *See* O. Thomas Johnson, Jr., *Alternative Dispute Resolution in the International Context: The North American Free Trade Agreement*, 46 SMU L. REV. 2175, 2177 (1993).

⁷³ *See id.*

⁷⁴ *See id.*

⁷⁵ *See id.*

⁷⁶ *See* DEL CASTILLO, *supra* note 13, at xii.

⁷⁷ *See* Oquendo, *supra* note 68, at 63-64.

⁷⁸ *See id.* at 85.

⁷⁹ *See* David López, *Dispute Resolution under a Free Trade Area of the Americas: The Shape of Things to Come*, 28 U. MIAMI INTER-AM. L. REV. 597, 605 (1997). For additional analysis of the NAFTA dispute resolution provisions, see Jeffrey P. Bialos & Deborah E. Siegel, *Dispute Resolution Under the NAFTA: The Newer and Improved Model*, 27 INT'L LAW. 603 (1993); Jack I. Garvey, *Trade Law and Quality of Life—Dispute Resolution under the NAFTA Side Accords on Labor and the Environment*, 89 AM. J. INT'L L. 439 (1995).

⁸⁰ *See* López, *supra* note 79, at 605. For recent work on Chapter 20 dispute resolution, *see generally* John C. Thomure, Jr., *Star Chamber Accountability: Appellate Review of NAFTA Chapter 20 Panel Decisions*, 28 U. MIAMI INTER-AM. L. REV 629, 634-35 (1997).

⁸¹ *See* López, *supra* note 4, at 173.

⁸² *Id. citing* DOMINICK SALVATORE, INTERNATIONAL ECONOMICS 212 (1983).

⁸³ *See* López, *supra* note 4, at 173.

⁸⁴ *See* Johnson, *supra* note 72, at 2184. *See also* López, *supra* note 4, at 173 ("Mexico, Canada, and the United States all have in place domestic statutes that create mechanisms for investigating allegations of dumping and for implementing appropriate countervailing duties").

⁸⁵ *See* Johnson, *supra* note 72, at 2184.

⁸⁶ *See id.* at 2185. Interestingly, some have questioned the constitutionality of having these disputes decided by supranational panels possessing binding authority. *See e.g.*, Robert P. Deyling, *Free Trade Agreements and the Federal Courts: Emerging Issues*, 27 ST. MARY'S L.J. 353, 376-81 (1996); Demetrios G. Metropoulos, *Constitutional Dimensions of the North American Free Trade Agreement*, 27 CORNELL INT'L L.J. 141, 159-68 (1994).

⁸⁷ *See* López, *supra* note 4, at 185. For recent work on the Environmental Side Agreement, see Ileana M. Porras, *The Puzzling Relationship Between Trade and Environment: NAFTA, Competitiveness, and the Pursuit of Environmental Welfare Objectives*, 3 IND. J. GLOBAL LEG. STUD. 65 (1995).

⁸⁸ *See* López, *supra* note 4, at 607-08. For recent analysis of the Labor Side Agreement, see Maria Teresa Guerra & Anna L. Torriente, *The NAALC and the Labor Laws of Mexico and the United States*, 14 ARIZ. J. INT'L & COMP. L. 503 (1997); Laura Okin Pomeroy, Note, *The Labor Side Agreement Under NAFTA: Analysis of Its Failure to Include Strong Enforcement Provisions and Recommendations for Future Labor Agreements Negotiated with Developing Countries* 29 GEO. WASH. INT'L L. & ECON. 769 (1996).

⁸⁹ *See* Oquendo, *supra* note 68, at 80.

⁹⁰ *See id.* at 81.

[91] *See id.*

[92] *See id.* at 82.

[93] North American Free Trade Agreement: Rules for Article 1904 Binational Panel Reviews, 59 Fed. Reg. 8686, rule 2 [hereinafter 1904 Panel Rules].

[94] FED. R. CIV. P. 1.

[95] *Cf.* 1904 Panel Rules, *supra* note 93, rule 55(3) ("Every pleading filed on behalf of a participant in a panel review shall be signed by counsel for the participant or, where the participant is not represented by counsel, by the participant") with FED. R. CIV. P. 11 ("Every pleading, written motion, and other paper [of a party represented by an attorney] shall be signed by at least one attorney of record in the attorney's individual name, or if the party is not represented by an attorney, shall be signed by the party. Each paper shall state the signor's address . . .").

[96] *Cf.* 1904 Panel Rules, *supra* note 93, at rule 39(2) ("Every complaint . . . shall contain the following information(:) . . . the precise nature of the Complaint . . . [and] a statement describing the interested person's entitlement to file a Complaint") with FED. R. CIV. P. 8(a) ("A pleading" shall contain "a short and plain statement of the claim showing that the pleader is entitled to relief").

[97] *Cf.* 1904 Panel Rules, *supra* note 93, at rule 61 (3)(a) ("Every notice of Motion . . . shall contain . . . a statement of the grounds to be argued.") with FED. R. CIV. P. 8(a) (The motion "shall state the grounds therefore").

[98] *See* Oquendo, *supra* note 68, at 82.

[99] *See id.* at 83.

[100] *See id.* at 84.

[101] *See id.* at 85.

[102] *See id.*

[103] *See id.*

[104] *See id.* at 86.

[105] *See id.* at 87.

[106] *See id.* at 80.

[107] *See* 1904 Panel Rules, *supra* note 93, rule 29.

[108] *Id.* at rules 30 and 31.

[109] *See* Oquendo, *supra* note 68, at 79.

[110] *See id.*

[111] *See id.*

[112] *See* Christopher Ruiz Cameron, *How the García Cousins Lost Their Accents: Understanding the Language of Title VII Decisions Approving Speak-English-Only Rules as the Product of Racial Dualism, Latino Invisibility, and Legal Indeterminacy,* 85 CAL. L. REV. (1997); Juan F. Perea, *Los Olvidados: On the Making of Invisible People,* 70 N.Y.U. L. REV. 965, 966 (1995) (Latinos are invisible features of the American landscape); LA RAZA: FORGOTTEN AMERICANS (Julian Samora ed., 1966); GEORGE I. SÁNCHEZ, FORGOTTEN PEOPLE: A STUDY OF NEW MEXICANS (1967) (analyzing the history of "forgotten people" of northern New Mexico).

[113] *See, e.g.,* Rachel Moran, *Foreword—Demography and Distrust: The Latino Challenge to Civil Rights and Immigration Policy in the 1990s and Beyond,* 8 LA RAZA L. J. 1, 10 (1995) (Although the Black/White race paradigm "has elevated race and ethnicity to a position of central importance in defining equality of opportunity. . . race and ethnicity have proven to be somewhat artificial organizing principles for Latinos because they have different racial origins and come from a range of countries."); Deborah Ramírez, *Multicultural Empowerment: It's Not Just Black and White Anymore,* 47 STAN. L. REV. 957, 958 (1995) ("When courts and legislatures first created race-conscious remedies in the 1960s, the United States was seen as a black and white society. . . [B]lacks were, for all practical purposes, the only racial minority group of significant size") (footnote omitted).

[114] *See, e.g.,* DEL CASTILLO, *supra* note 13, at 113 (discussing an influential college textbook that emphasized political and military aspects of United States—Mexican War and Treaty of Guadalupe Hidalgo, but ignored their effects on "the 100,000 Mexican citizens annexed in the bargain," who "remained invisible in this national history").

[115] *See, e.g.,* Kevin R. Johnson, *Some Thoughts on the Future of Latino Scholarship,* 2 HARV. LATINO L. REV. 101, 107-108 (1997) ("In Los Angeles, the area east of downtown—from East Los Angeles to

Montebello to the San Gabriel Valley—where a great many Latino[/as] live, often is invisible in the eyes of the regional newspaper of record, the Los Angeles Times") (footnote omitted).

[116] See Cameron, *supra* note 112.

[117] See Kevin R. Johnson, *Los Olvidados: Images of the Immigrant, Political Power of Noncitizens, and Immigration Law and Enforcement*, 1993 B.Y.U. L. REV. 1139. The growing critical Latino theory movement has focused attention on Latino invisibility. For important foundational readings on this and related subjects, *see* THE LATINO CONDITION: A CRITICAL READER (Richard Delgado & Jean Stefancic eds., 1998).

[118] See *supra* notes 36-37, and accompanying text.

[119] See *supra* notes 89-105 and accompanying text.

[120] See Oquendo, *supra* note 68, at 65; James F. Smith, *Confronting Differences in the United States and Mexican Legal Systems in the Era of NAFTA*, 1 U.S.-MEX. L.J. 85, 86-87 (1993) ("United States and Mexican legal traditions . . . are so markedly different").

[121] See Oquendo, *supra* note 68, at 65. *See also* Homer E. Moyer, Jr., *Chapter 19 of the NAFTA: Binational Panels as the Trade Courts of Last Resort*, 27 INT'L LAW. 707, 714 (1993) ("Unlike both Canada and the United States, Mexico is a civil law country, not a common law country"); *see also* Smith, *supra* note 120, at 87 ("Mexico's private law system, including torts, property, commerce, and inheritance, traces its origin to the Roman civil law").

[122] See Oquendo, *supra* note 68, at 91. For general analysis of the Mexican legal system, *see* JAMES E. HERGET & JORGE CAMIL, AN INTRODUCTION TO THE MEXICO LEGAL SYSTEM (1978); William J. Bridge, et. al., *Mexico's Legal System*, in AN INTRODUCTION TO DOING BUSINESS IN MEXICO (William E. Mooz Jr. ed. 1995); Jorge A. Vargas, *Mexico's Legal Revolution: An Appraisal of Its Recent Constitutional Changes*, 1988-1995, 25 GA. J. INT'L & COMP. L. 497 (1996).

[123] See Oquendo, *supra* note 68, at 91.

[124] See *id.* at 91-92.

[125] See *id.* at 91.

[126] See *id.* at 92.

[127] See *id.*

[128] See *id.*

[129] See *id.* at 93.

[130] JOHN MERRYMAN, THE CIVIL LAW TRADITION: AN INTRODUCTION TO THE LEGAL SYSTEMS OF WESTERN EUROPE AND LATIN AMERICA 112 (2d. ed. 1985). *See also* Fernando Orrantia, *Conceptual Differences between the Civil Law System and the Common Law System*, 19 SW. U. L. REV. 1161 (1990).

[131] See Oquendo, *supra* note 68, at 99.

[132] See *id.*

[133] See *id.* at 100-01.

[134] See *id.* at 105.

[135] See *id.* at 106.

[136] See 480 U.S. 102 (1987). For an analysis of the *Asahi* decision, *see* Earl M. Maltz, *Unraveling the Conundrum of the Law of Personal Jurisdiction: A Comment on Asahi Metal Industry Co. v. Superior Court of California*, 1987 DUKE L.J. 669.

[137] See *Asahi*, 480 U.S. at 106.

[138] See *id.*

[139] See *id.*

[140] See *id.*

[141] See *id.* at 116.

[142] *Id.* at 114. Other jurisdictions have recognized the burdens that outsiders face in a foreign legal system. Thus, historically some jurisdictions have sought to ameliorate the foreignness of a legal system. For example, in ancient English legal practice, "[t]rials *de medietate linguae*,' literally 'trials of the half tongue' or trials in which one party was an alien whose native language was not English. James C. Oldham, *The Origins of the Special Jury*, 50 U. CHI. L. REV. 137, 167 n.157 (1983); *See* Deborah A. Ram'rez, *The Mixed Jury and the Ancient Custom of Trial by Jury "De Mediate Linguae:" A History and A Proposal for Change*, 74 B.U. L. REV. 777, 783-96 (1994). *See generally* MARIANNE CONSTABLE, THE

LAW OF THE OTHER: THE MIXED JURY AND CHANGING CONCEPTIONS OF CITIZENSHIP, LAW, AND KNOWLEDGE (1994) (discussing history of mixed juries). "Such trials would be conducted before a jury with one half of the jury composed of noncitizens [sic] and one half citizens." Kevin R. Johnson, *Why Alienage Jurisdiction? Historical Foundations and Modern Justifications for Federal Jurisdiction over Disputes Involving Non-citizens*, 21 YALE J. INT'L L. 1, 8 (1996) (citing Oldham, *supra* at 167-71. Clearly, the existence of mixed juries represented an effort to take into account the difficulties that outsiders face in a foreign legal system).

[143] *See* William H. Simon, *The Ideology of Advocacy*, in THE STRUCTURE OF PROCEDURE 48, 56 (Robert M. Cover & Owen M. Fiss 1979).

[144] *See id.*

[145] *See id.*

[146] *See supra* notes 36-38 and accompanying text.

[147] *See* George A. Martínez, *Latinos, Assimilation and the Law: A Philosophical Perspective*, (unpublished manuscript); Kevin R. Johnson, *Civil Rights and Immigration: Challenges for the Latino Community in the Twenty-First Century*, 8 LA RAZA L.J. 42, 79 (1995). *See also* Rachel F. Moran, *Neither Black Nor White*, 2 HARV. LATINO L. REV. 61, 81 (1997) ("Under the immigration paradigm, Latinos receive the message that they are supposed to assimilate like White, ethnic immigrants"); Enid Trucios-Haynes, *Race and Latino/a Identity: Quienes Somos? Who Are We?*, 3 MICH. J. RACE & LAW (1998) (discussing assimilation theory and Latinos).

[148] *See* Martínez, *supra* note 147; Johnson, *supra* note 147, at 79.

[149] *See* Martínez, *supra* note 147.

[150] *See* Cameron, *supra* note 112 (analyzing impact of speak-English-only workplace rules on Latinos); BILL PIATT, ¿ONLY ENGLISH? LAW AND LANGUAGE POLICY IN THE UNITED STATES (1990); Steven W. Bender, *Direct Democracy and Distrust: The Relationship Between Language Law Rhetoric and the Language Vigilantism Experience*, 2 HARV. LATINO L. REV. 145 (1997) (discussing language vigilantism against the use of Spanish); Antonio J. Califa, *Declaring English the Official Language: Prejudice Spoken Here*, 24 HARV. C.R.-C.L. L. REV. 293 (1989).

[151] *See generally* PETER BRIMELOW, ALIEN NATION: COMMON SENSE ABOUT AMERICA'S IMMIGRATION DISASTER (1995) (arguing that failure of Latinos to assimilate into dominant Anglo-Saxon culture justifies drastic restrictions on immigration).

[152] *See* Martínez, *supra* note 147.

[153] *See* THE RIGHTS OF MINORITY CULTURES 5 (Will Kymlicka ed., 1995).

[154] *See id.*

[155] *Id.* citing John Stuart Mill, *Considerations on Representative Government* (1861), in UTILITARIANISM ON LIBERTY, CONSIDERATIONS ON REPRESENTATIVE GOVERNMENT 395 (H.B. Acton ed. 1972).

[156] *See* THE RIGHTS OF MINORITY CULTURES, *supra* note 153 at 5-6.

[157] *See id.* at 6.

[158] *Id.* (footnote omitted).

[159] *See id.* at 6.

[160] *See id.*

[161] *See id.*

[162] *See* Zamora, *supra* note 3, at 444. Psychologist Manuel Ramírez has described the presumption of superiority of a European or Anglo-American world view: "from the perspective of the European world view, peoples and cultures identified with traditional values and belief systems are assumed to be psychologically underdeveloped and in need of Europeanization or westernization. MANUEL RAMÍREZ III, PSYCHOLOGY OF THE AMERICAS: MESTIZO PERSPECTIVES ON PERSONALITY AND MENTAL HEALTH 4 (Arnold P. Goldstein & Leonard Krasner eds., 1983). The European view can be contrasted with the mestizo world view. *See* Zamora, *supra* note 3, at 444. The mestizo perspective is consistent with the cultural attitudes of the Americas and emphasizes cooperation among diverse peoples. *See id.*

[163] *See* Zamora, *supra* note 3, at 445.

[164] *Id.*; *see id.* at 398-434.

[165] *See id.* at 395 ("to be blunt, the United States can use NAFTA to 'Americanize' Mexico . . . While this goal may not be espoused openly, it is an important part of the agenda underlying the

NAFTA negotiations"). Interestingly, some Mexicans opposed the Treaty of Guadalupe Hidalgo on the ground that it would lead to "the Americanization of Mexico." DEL CASTILLO, *supra* note 13, at 50.

[166] *See* DEL CASTILLO, *supra* note 13, at xii.

[167] *Id. See also* Martínez, *En Aquel Entonces*, *supra* note 12 ("modernity is the carrot offered by American society").

[168] *See supra* notes 36-38 and accompanying text.

[169] *See* Jimmie V. Reyna, et al., *Practice before U.S.-Mexico Binational Panels under Chapter Nineteen of NAFTA: A Panel Discussion*, 5 U.S.-MEX. L.J. 73, 74 (1997).

[170] *See id.*

[171] *See id.*

[172] *See id.*

[173] *See id.*

[174] *See In re* Certain Softwood Lumber Products from Canada, No. ECC-94-1904-O1USA, 1994 FTAPD LEXIS 11 (Binational Review) (Aug. 3, 1994)[hereinafter Softwood Lumber III].

[175] *See* Charles M. Gastle & Jean-G. Castel, *Should the North American Free Trade Agreement Dispute Settlement Mechanism in Antidumping and Countervailing Duty Cases be Reformed in the Light of Softwood Lumber III?* 26 LAW & POL'Y INT'L BUS. 823, 826 (1995).

[176] *See id.* at 824, 865.

[177] *See id.* at 866; *Softwood Lumber III*, 1994 FTAPD 11, at * 220.

[178] *See* Gastle & Castel, *supra* note 175, at 868.

[179] *See generally*, Johnson, *supra* note 72. On the American domestic front, the later 1980s and early 1990s have been characterized by "an unprecedented rise of alternative dispute resolution (ADR) in public and private spheres at both the state and federal levels." BARBARA ALLEN BABCOCK & TONI M. MASSARO, CIVIL PROCEDURE: CASES AND PROBLEMS 329 (1997). "This movement toward more informal methods of dispute resolution is one of the most" important developments in modern civil procedure. *Id.*

[180] *See* Johnson, *supra* note 72, at 2178.

[181] *See id.*

[182] *See id. See also* LEONARD L. RISKIN & JAMES E. WESTBROOK, DISPUTE RESOLUTION AND LAWYERS 91 (1987) (mediation is an informal process in which a neutral third party, who lacks authority to impose a solution, helps participants reach their own agreement for resolving a dispute); Lon L. Fuller, *Mediation—Its Forms and Functions*, 44 S. CAL. L. REV. 305, 327 (1971) (the central quality of mediation is "its capacity to reorient the parties toward each other, not by imposing rules on them, but by helping them to achieve a new and shared perception of their relationship").

[183] *See* Johnson, *supra* note 72, at 2178.

[184] *See id.*

[185] *Id.* at 2179.

[186] *Id.*

[187] *See* BABCOCK & MASSARO, *supra* note 179, at 338 ("Although there are many different types of arbitration, they have in common informal procedures that are less adversarial than the civil trial").

[188] *See* Johnson, *supra* note 72, at 2180.

[189] *See id.*

[190] *See id.* at 2181.

[191] *See id.* at 2182.

[192] *See id.* at 2183.

[193] *See* Richard Delgado, *Alternative Dispute Resolution Conflict as Pathology: An Essay for Trina Grillo*, 81 MINN. L. REV. 1391, 1394 (1997). *See also* BABCOCK & MASSARO, *supra* note 179, at 352 ("Another potential drawback of some forms of ADR is that they may favor informal, discretionary decisionmaking [sic] over more formal and bounded methods. This can lead to more impressionistic, idiosyncratic, or standardless decisionmaking [sic], which may result in bias against some litigants or arbitrary outcomes"); GARY B. BORN, INTERNATIONAL COMMERCIAL ARBITRATION IN THE UNITED STATES: COMMENTARY & MATERIALS 7 (1994) (Because arbitration allows for a less rigid procedural structure than does formal litigation, it may permit or even facilitate party misconduct).

[194] *See* Delgado, *supra* note 193 at 1398.

[195] *See id.*

[196] *See id.*

[197] *See id.* at 1398-99. *See also* Carrie Menkel-Meadow, *Pursuing Settlement in an Adversary Culture: A Tale of Innovation Co-opted or "The Law of ADR,"* 19 FLA. ST. U. L. REV. 1, 3-4 (1991) ("courts try to use various forms of [alternative dispute resolution] to reduce caseloads and increase court efficiency at the possible cost of realizing better justice").

[198] *See* Delgado, *supra* note 193, at 1398-99; *see also* Richard Delgado, et al., *Fairness and Formality: Minimizing the Risk of Prejudice in Alternative Dispute Resolution*, 1985 WIS. L. REV. 1359, 1394 ("informal forums greatly disadvantage weaker parties").

[199] *See supra* notes 41-46 and accompanying text.

[200] *See* López, *supra* note 4, at 204.

[201] *Id.*

[202] *See In re* Gray Portland Cement and Clinker from Mexico, No. USA-95-1904-02 (NAFTA Binat'l Panel, Sept. 1996), 1996 FTAPD Lexis 4.

[203] López, *supra* note 4, at 179.

[204] *See id.*

[205] *See id.*

[206] *See id.*

[207] *See id.*

[208] *See id.*

[209] *See In Re* Gray Portland Cement and Clinker from Mexico, No. USA-95-1904-02 (NAFTA Binat'l Panel, Sept. 13, 1996), 1996 FTAPD Lexis 4 at *29-36; Article 1904 Binational Panel Reviews, 61 Fed. Reg. 54,621- 622 (NAFTA Sec., Dept. of Com. 1996); López, *supra* note 4, at 179.

[210] *See In Re* Mexican Antidumping Investigation into Imports of Cut-to-Length Plate Products from the United States, MEX-94-1904-02 (NAFTA Binat'l Panel, Aug. 30, 1995), 1995 FTAPD LEXIS 11, at *1 - *3, *10 - *11; López, *supra* note 4, at 180.

[211] *See* López, *supra* note 4, at 180.

[212] *See id.*

[213] *See id.*

[214] *See id.*

[215] Stephen Zamora, *Allocating Legislative Competence in the Americas: The Early Experience under NAFTA and the Challenge of Hemispheric Integration*, 19 HOUS. J INT'L L. 615, 637 (1997).

[216] *In re* Mexican Antidumping Investigation into Imports of Cut-to-length Plate Products from the United States, MEX-94-1904-02 (NAFTA Binat'l Panel, August 30, 1995, 1995 FTAPD LEXIS 11, *3,); *see also* López, *supra* note 4, at 180.

[217] *See* Gustavo Vega-Canovas, *Disciplining Anti-Dumping in North America: Is NAFTA Chapter Nineteen Serving Its Purpose?*, 14 ARIZ. J. INT'L & COMP. L. 479, 487 (1997).

[218] *See* Johnson, *supra* note 72, at 2177. For example, Canada's Deputy Attorney General made these remarks on dispute settlement during the negotiation of the Canada-United States Trade Agreement:

We have done pretty well [at resolving trade disputes] in the past, but there are two reasons that I would advance have kept us from doing better. The first is what I would call the level playing field reason. This reason recognizes that the negotiating strengths of the two parties are not equal.... [M]echanisms to solve disputes are vital to Canada. The existence of such mechanisms are going to make or break the issue in Canada. Quite apart from the substantive disagreements, any agreement without a satisfactory dispute resolution mechanism will not be acceptable. We cannot have a system that will see differences resolved on the basis of raw power.

T. Bradbrooke Smith, *Comments on Dispute Resolution under a North American Free Trade Agreement*, 12 CAN.-U.S. L.J. 337, 337 (1987).

[219] *See* López, *supra* note 4, at 169.

[220] *See id.*

[221] *See id.* at 206.

[222] *See id.* at 169.

[223] *See id.* at 169-70; *see also* W. Fletcher Fairey, *The Helms-Burton Act: The Effect of International Law on Domestic Implementation*, 46 AM. U.L. REV. 1289, 1323-24 (1997) (explaining how the Helms-Burton Act may violate NAFTA); Luisette Gierbolini, *The Helms-Burton Act: Inconsistency with International Law and Irrationality at Their Maximum*, 6 J. TRANSNAT'L & POL'Y 289, 315-18 (1997) (arguing that the Helms-Burton Act violates NAFTA).

[224] *See* López, *supra* note 4, at 206.

[225] *See id.* This behavior is consistent with the United States erratic history in honoring its treaty obligations. For example, the United States failed to abide by its treaties with Indian tribes. *See* ROBERT A. WILLIAMS, JR., LINKING ARMS TOGETHER: AMERICAN INDIAN TREATY VISIONS OF LAW AND PEACE, 1600-100 (197); ROBERT A. WILLIAMS, JR., THE AMERICAN INDIAN IN WESTERN LEGAL THOUGHT: THE DISCOURSES OF CONQUEST (1990). The United States also had had difficulty abiding by human rights treaties. *See* Sale v. Haitian Centers Council, 509 U.S. 155 (1993) (upholding return of Haitians fleeing political violence without determining whether they might be entitled to relief under international law); Johnson, *supra* note 12.

Border Crossings in the Mexican American War

*Rosemary King**
ARIZONA STATE UNIVERSITY

One seldom opens up a newspaper today without noticing the prevalence of violence erupting in or around international borders, as in the case of the Balkans, central Africa, and the former republics of the Soviet Union. Even in the Americas, the United States-Mexico border has become increasingly militarized. An investigation into the origins of the border is useful in understanding the current conflicts between multiple communities in the United States-Mexico borderlands as we approach the twenty-first century. This paper explores the origin of the border and its manifestations through an application of Benedict Anderson's theory of a nation, set forth in *Imagined Communities,* to various first-hand accounts of the Mexican American War (1846-48) written by U.S. and Mexican citizens. The following three snapshots in time offer a useful case study for such an analysis: General Scott's landing at Vera Cruz, the capture of the San Patricios, and the American occupation of Mexico City. Recognizing the patterns of how communities created the border approximately 150 years ago from the crucible of the Mexican American War may improve our understanding of the contentious United States-Mexico border today: if we recognize how borders are constructed, perhaps we may facilitate better our own crossings.

The War in Context: Manifest Destiny

In the nineteenth century, newly independent nations throughout the Americas had problems populating isolated regions located in outlying border zones. Mexico was no exception. Following the war of independence with Spain in the 1820s, Mexico had difficulty settling its northern provinces of Colorado, New Mexico, Arizona, California, and Texas (Skidmore, 228). In an effort to populate the region, the Mexican government continued a policy initiated by Spain that allowed Americans to settle in the region (Martínez, 11; Eisenhower, 196). The fledgling nation's liberal policy backfired when Texas declared its independence from Mexico, and the United States annexed the state in 1845 (Skidmore, 228). The Mexican government viewed the annexation as a hostile act and severed relations with the United States for two reasons (McAfee, 1).[1] First, Mexican politicians felt U.S. settlers in Texas had taken advantage of Mexican good will efforts allowing them to homestead in the area. Second, Mexicans feared the United States would make further land claims on Mexican territory. These fears were exacerbated by the fact that the western frontier of Texas was not clearly delineated. According to Mexican historian Enrique Krauze, "at the start of its independence, [Mexico] was not even close to

---

*The author wishes to thank the following professors at Arizona State University for their feedback and support on this project: Elizabeth Horan, Cordelia Candelaria, Kathleen Sands, Scott Stevens, and Robert Alvarez.

having a reliable map of its territories and borders" (131). The disputed land between the United States and Mexico ultimately became the site of conflict that sparked the war (Skidmore, 229; Martínez, 12).

During this period, American expansionists interested in laying claim to Mexican territory became increasingly vocal and aggressive. Secretary of State James Buchanan, for instance, recommended U.S. territorial goals be pursued through a policy of "firmness and action accompanied by moderation of language" toward Mexico such that the "[p]ower and true greatness [that] belong to our country ought never waste themselves in words towards a feeble and distracted sister republic" (McAfee, 2-3). Expansionists used the ideology of Manifest Destiny to back claims on Mexican territory, arguing that the United States had a moral duty to spread westward to the Pacific Ocean (Eisenhower, 196). This moral duty took many forms, depending on the particular biases and motives of the source. For example, some argued Americans should share their "superior [political] institutions with those less favored;" some claimed the Mexican people were inferior and needed paternal guidance; others argued "Providence" called on the United States to expand as a nation; finally, still others believed the United States had a duty to "civilize" the wild Mexican frontier (Eisenhower, 198). Regardless of their particular rationale, American expansionists believed "Mexico stood in the way of the American dream of Manifest Destiny" (Eisenhower, xviii). From the Mexican point of view, however, Manifest Destiny was nothing more than a façade designed to hide U.S. territorial goals. Mexican historian Orlando Martínez calls Manifest Destiny "one of the best known euphemisms for bumptious expansionism ever minted" (Selby, 156).[2]

While the ideology of Manifest Destiny was gaining support in the United States, the Mexican government was trying to remain stable and solvent long enough to counter American expansionists. Early in the nineteenth century, Mexico was a fledgling country struggling to claim a national identity.[3] From the time of priest Miguel Hidalgo y Costilla's *grito* for independence from Spain in 1809 until the American invasion in 1846, Mexico had a rapid succession of governments (Robinson, 102). Power struggles occurred among the Creoles (Mexicans of Spanish descent), who fought each other to fill the vacuum of power left when Mexico declared its independence from Spain (Krauze, 119-25). According to Krauze, Spain abandoned Mexico: Spain did not submit to President Iturbide's request to appoint a prince to rule the Mexican Empire [sic], and it did not officially recognize Mexico as a sovereign nation until fifteen years after independence (125). The *gachupines* (Spanish officials who had governed Mexico for three decades) did not take the Creoles under their wing. The republic's attempt at self-rule floundered (Robinson, xiii-xiv, Krauze, 132). Although the Creoles worked hard to establish a stable government and forge a national identity, Mexico had still not become a nation by the start of the Mexican American War. For thirty-seven years, the Mexican government was characterized by violent military coups, mounting national debt, a flight of foreign capital, and increasing class stratification between rich and poor that left the general populace disillusioned with the federal government (Robinson, 14, 102). The fifty military regimes that governed sporadically from 1822–47 prevented many Mexicans from developing a sense of national identity.

During this period, Mexican citizens were less concerned with the nation than with local leaders, such as caciques and caudillos, local *jefes* (chiefs) who ruled individual fiefdoms of their own. "Even though Mexico was no longer a colony or had any place in the supranational order of the Spanish Empire, it was not yet a nation. It was an assemblage of villages, settlements, and provinces isolated from one another, without any conception of politics, even less of nationality, and controlled by the strong men of each locality" (Krauze, 132). On one level, the national government mirrored this trend: strong men fought for control of the presidency, an office not emblematic of Mexico's nationalism but symbolized by the persona of a *patrón*. Santa Anna, for example, assumed the presidency eleven times between 1833–1855 (Krauze, n.p.).[4]

On the eve of war in 1845, the reigning Mexican government collapsed in response to the prolonged and intensive American policy of dollar diplomacy. In essence, the U.S. Congress tried to buy Mexican territory adjacent to the United States throughout the 1820s and 1830s (Martínez, 12). According to the Mexican historian Josefina Zoraida Vázquez, the approach taken by the United States offended many Mexicans (Robinson, 201). One Mexican government official, Luis de Onís, warned as early as 1812 that the U.S. government would do all it could to absorb Mexico's northern provinces (Martínez, 11). By the 1820s, Mexican diplomats assigned to Washington, D.C., echoed de Onís's warning (Martínez, 12). In the 1840s, Polk sent John Sidell to negotiate an agreement whereby Mexico would cede the greater part of the present-day Southwest in exchange for five million dollars and would lose California for twenty-five million dollars (Robinson, xxvii). As the Mexican president Herrera was considering Sidell's proposal, a military coup led by Major General Mariano Paredes y Arrillaga toppled the government, accusing Herrera of "selling out the national soil and honor" (McAfee, 134; Robinson, xxviii).

Once in office, Paredes established himself as the president who would defend all of Mexico's territory (Miller, 12; Robinson, xxviii). For all his rhetoric, Paredes soon realized that Mexico was in a poor position to defend even its own territory because of its depleted coffers, continual political bickering, and ill-equipped army. Furthermore, the revolving door of Mexican government left the populous not only without a clear sense of national identity, but with little motive to unify around a government that they felt had served them poorly for decades. Mariano Otero, Mexico's minister of internal and external relations, summarizes it well:

> Say what one might, patriotism, that noble and chivalrous sentiment which in other countries moves the people and raises them to such a pitch of fervor that they would a thousand times prefer death to permitting the slightest offense against their country, this sentiment cannot exist in a country ... which has been lacerated by thirty-seven years of travail and misery. (Robinson, 14)

By the mid-1840s, the relationship between the United States and Mexico had deteriorated to the point that each nation considered the other a threat to its national territory. In 1846, President Polk ordered General Taylor's troops into Texas, an act that the Mexican government conceived as an invasion of disputed territory (Skidmore, 229) as evidenced by the Mexican president Paredes's following proclamation:

> But the defense of the Mexican territory, which the U.S. invaded, is an urgent necessity, and my responsibility would be immense before the nation if I did not give commands to repel those forces who act like enemies, and I have so commanded. From this day commences a defensive war, and those points of our territory which are invaded or attacked will be energetically defended. (McAfee, 135)

When a skirmish broke out between Mexican and U.S. troops, both nations declared war (Martínez, 13; Skidmore, 229). As the commander in chief, President Polk decided to use military force to resolve the dispute between the nations. In a carefully worded statement to Congress on 11 May 1846, Polk declared that "Mexico had passed the boundary of the U.S., has invaded our territory, and shed American blood on American soil" (McAfee, 149). Even though Polk's statement is dubious at best (given the unclear delineation of the border and the two countries different conceptions of the disputed zone), Congress declared war on Mexico immediately. In terms of borders, however, both the American and Mexican national leaders were in agreement: foreigners crossing into national territory equated to war.

During the Mexican American War, the American military used five separate armies to invade Mexico. General Taylor's army proceeded from Corpus Christi to Monterrey; General Wool's troops marched from San Antonio to Saltillo; General Kerney's division was ordered westward to invade New Mexico and California; Colonel Doniphan's army marched from New Mexico to Chihuahua to Saltillo; and General Scott's troops landed at Vera Cruz and moved westward to Mexico City (Miller, 20). Other than Kerney's westward route, most of the American force traveled southward toward Mexico City, with the objective of forcing the Mexican capital to surrender. When the U.S. Congress declared war, the total strength of the army was approximately 6,500 soldiers with an authorization for enlisting 50,000 additional volunteers (Miller, 21). Generals Santa Anna, Ampudia, and Arista rallied troops to meet the U.S. forces. According to Pedro María Anaya, the Mexican minister of war, the total strength of the Mexican army was approximately 65,000 men in 1845 when all were mustered (McAfee, 145). Anaya pointed out, however, that the army lacked uniforms, food, shelter, guns, and ammunition to effectively combat the U.S. troops (145). In addition to limited resources, the Mexican army was also crippled by infighting among political and military leaders and by poorly trained conscripts with relatively little battlefield experience (Krauze, 142-44, Miller, 13).

The war ended in 1848 when the Mexican army surrendered at Chapultepec Castle and the U.S. army occupied Mexico City. In accordance with the Treaty of Guadalupe Hidalgo, the United States paid Mexico 15 million dollars in exchange for nearly half of Mexico's territory (Krauze, 144, Skidmore, 229). While the U.S. army occupied the Mexican capital, American expansionists crusaded to seize all of Mexico in an aggressive expression of Manifest Destiny (Martínez, 15). Soon members of Polk's cabinet, military leaders, and influential American businessmen began to support the "all Mexico" platform. Manuel de la Peña y Peña, Mexico's interim president overseeing the peace negotiations, was acutely aware of the expansionists' ambitions. In his "Address in Support of the Treaty of Guadalupe Hidalgo" issued to the Mexican congress, Peña y Peña articulates Mexico's debilitated bargaining position: "The negotiations cannot be condemned for not having lessened the loss of territory, and perhaps they even deserve praise for having seen to it that the first territorial demands were not later increased—especially in view of the facts that the capital was lost and the army, which evacuated it . . . was disbanded" (107). Ultimately, the Mexican Congress concurred with Peña y Peña's rationale and agreed to the terms of the treaty because they were wary of further encroachment on their soil (Martínez, 15).

Since the case study of the Batallón de San Patricio is integral to this paper, it is important to note their role as both deserters and heroes. Many U.S. troops deserted the army throughout the war. In fact, the desertion rate during the Mexican American War is the highest of any American foreign war (Miller, 23). In total, anywhere from 9,000 to 10,800 soldiers deserted (Miller, 23-24; Hogan, 113). Reasons for desertion varied from disenchantment with military life, to resentment of the harsh living conditions, to disgruntlement with superiors, to overt discrimination against immigrant soldiers (Smith and Judah, 431-32). In the latter case, discrimination against the Irish in particular ran high because of the massive influx of immigrants in the mid-nineteenth century due to famines in Ireland (Wynn, 2).[5] Furthermore, many of the Irish and German soldiers were Roman Catholic and thus felt allegiance to Mexico, a predominantly Roman Catholic nation (Smith and Judah, 432). Among the deserters were 200 Irishmen who formed a division in the Mexican army called the Batallón de San Patricio (St. Patrick's Battalion) (Miller, 32, Hogan, 112). The San Patricios were lead by John Riley, who deserted from General Taylor's army on 12 April 1846 while it was bivouacked along the Rio Grande (Miller, 29; Wright, 237). Known as "the Irish who had shed their blood in defense of Mexico" (Barcena, v. 3, 300), the San Patricios fought valiantly during the war until they died fighting or were captured by the Americans at the battles of Churubusco and Contreras in 1847 (Miller, 92; Wright, 237; Singletary, 91). Of the seventy-two defectors captured and court-martialed, fifty were hanged (Miller, 101, 104-5). Those who deserted just prior to the U.S. government's declaration of war received "fifty lashes each on their naked backs" and were "branded with the letter D high up on the cheek-bone" (Davis, 224).[6]

The American Military: An Exaggeration of the Imagined Community

In *Imagined Communities,* Anderson traces the origin of the contemporary notion of a nation as an imagined community that developed out of/in relation to the cultural legacies of sacred religious communities and dynastic realms (9-22). From his sociohistorical analysis comes a definition integral to this paper: a nation is "an imagined community—and imagined as both inherently *limited* and *sovereign*" (5-7; my emphasis). An imagined community is not simply the opposite of real; in this definition, an imagined community is a projection, conception, or visualization of a paradigm of a community. For example, individuals living in Michoacán and Jalisco conceive of an imagined community of Mexican citizenship; even though they may never meet one another, they consider Mexicans living in other states fellow citizens who share their general notions of what it means to be a citizen of Mexico. As imagined communities in the nineteenth century evolved into nations as we know them today, borders became increasingly important as a means of delineating the territorial space of one nation from another (Anderson, 7). Borders of nations are characterized as inherently finite (i.e., limited and sovereign) and yet elastic, because they may contract or expand through processes such as the Mexican American War or the Louisiana Purchase (Anderson, 7, 12). The rigid delineation of a limited, finite border, some scholars contend, results in borders becoming sites of conflict in peacetime.[7] There is little doubt that war intensifies border conflict: as nations fight to defend or extend their territory in an effort to impose sovereignty, borders become intensely dynamic and elastic.

Anderson's concept of a nation as an imagined community has two significant implications for borders. First, members of a nation are bounded by a peripheral, physical border, such as the United States-Mexico border that existed at the outbreak of hostilities in 1846. In this case, a border is defined as an international geopolitical boundary whose function is to "delimit one national territory from another, as well as control and regulate the crossing of people and goods" (Rosler, 8). Both U.S. and Mexican soldiers were willing to die to protect the borders of a nation because of its infinite relation backward and forward in time.[8] General Scott's landing at Veracruz and march westward toward Mexico

City demonstrate the elasticity of the peripheral borders of both the United States and Mexico, which stretched to delineate the finite and limited territory of each nation.

Second, members of an imagined community create a hierarchical border when they react simultaneously to emblems of the nation. Let me detail this concept by defining three key terms and offering several concrete examples. Emblems of the nation, such as the American flag or Mexican national anthem, are symbols representing the sovereignty of an imagined community (Anderson, 133, 141-154). Sovereignty is the authority of a nation to exert power over the territory it controls (Anderson, 7). Unisonance is the simultaneous response of many people to emblems of the nation, which is well illustrated by an excerpt from a letter written during the Mexican American War.[9] A newly enlisted American soldier writes, "Here we are from all quarters of our glorious Union, acting in the same concert as if all were children of one state or family" (Hogan, 113).[10] In this case, unisonance cuts across diverse communities, subordinating differences of ethnicity, class, or gender, for example, to the shared status of national citizenship. Furthermore, citizens conceive the "deep, horizontal comradeship" (i.e., patriotism) of unisonance relative to those who do not experience it. For example, a U.S. citizen singing the national anthem may feel patriotic for two reasons: first, other Americans are singing the same words simultaneously; second, Mexican citizens are *not* singing the American national anthem and thus are *not* part of the American imagined community (Anderson, 145).[11] In other words, unisonance binds people in a fraternity while simultaneously excluding those outside the community (Anderson, 7).[12] American soldiers who cheered when the U.S. flag was hoisted over Chapultepec noted the dejection that registered among Mexican citizens; a hierarchical border separating individuals into different imagined communities of conqueror/conquered reinforced U.S. sovereignty in the newly acquired territory.

Anderson's definition of a nation and the resulting implications for borders lend themselves well to the organization of the military, which is an exaggerated form of an imagined community. Military members react—and even project—emblems of the nation. Military personnel wear the same uniforms and march as a unit to one drum beat, two examples of unisonance. In contrast to the U.S. civilian national community, however, the reaction of troops to patriotic emblems is magnified because a soldier must respond to them: during the Mexican American War, for instance, American troops awoke to the trumpeting of reveille, entered platoon formations, and saluted the flag (Smith and Judah, 281-82, 292). Illustrating a significant aspect of an exaggerated community, the enforcement of behavioral codes is harsh, involving severe punishment for those who do not meet prescribed behavioral codes. During the Mexican American War, U.S. soldiers who were caught drunk while on guard duty (a task related to patrolling borders and often associated with guarding the flag) received the following sentence: "to be confined in charge of the guard for thirty days, and to ride a wooden horse from reveille to retreat during the same period of time, with the exception of half an hour for each meal" ("Execution," 1).[13] Finally, the military community codifies emblems of the nation by having members swear to defend the constitution in a legally binding oath.

Furthermore, the military is an exaggerated community in its manifestation of borders. First, I will address the peripheral, physical borders of the military community. The American military community is bounded by finite but elastic territorial claims such as air force bases, army forts, naval stations, or marine camps. Bases are self-contained communities, surrounded by fences, patrolled by military police, and accessible only through gatehouses. The barricades that delineate a military base illustrate its separateness from the civilian population and serve to protect it from would-be intruders. Thus, the military is a community within a community that uses fortified borders to separate it, somewhat ironically, from the citizens it is trained to protect. An important distinction between soldiers and civilians, then, lies in the use of borders. The peripheral borders of the military community are exaggerated in comparison to the national borders surrounding the civilian community. In other words, military installations are surrounded by physical borders, whereas the nation, albeit bounded by a geopolitical line, is not always and everywhere fortified against its neighbors. This statement is particularly true in the context of the Mexican American War: the American military heavily guarded Fort Brown (which ultimately became Brownsville), for example, while a greater part of the border between the United States and Mexico was not guarded.[14]

In addition to the physical borders of a military community, another manifestation of the border exists: the separation between military and civilian members. In contrast to the civilian community, clear markers such as uniforms, dog tags, and identification cards separate military members from other communities. The "deep, horizontal comradeship" that Anderson describes among members of the nation is intensified in the military because members, who often do not know one another prior to enlistment, are ordered to work as a unit to accomplish a mission. In fact, members vow (again in a legally binding contract) to risk their lives accomplishing the mission if necessary—a clear distinction from the imagined civilian community. There are also important distinctions between civilians and soldiers in the way they enter each community. In general, most U.S. citizens are born into the community of the nation and become citizens because of the physical location of their birth on U.S. soil, whereas, entrance into the military occurs through a process of inscription. Membership into the military community is legally binding and supported by a rigid hierarchical structure that clearly delineates membership. As mentioned, punishment for violating behavioral codes in the military is strict. Whereas Americans can renounce citizenship—although they rarely do for a number of reasons—troops must honor their commitment to the military or face criminal prosecution.

In sum, there are two manifestations of the borders surrounding the military: a conspicuously fortified border and numerous conspicuous signs of a less tangible—but no less significant—border separating communities. As an exaggerated form of an imagined community, these borders become intensified when the military carries out the orders of the nation with force. More specifically, as an exaggerated imagined community, the military creates a rigid separation between itself and other communities and protects its borders with force. During the Mexican American War, the U.S. military community crossed the peripheral, physical United States-Mexico border. The U.S. military then manifested hierarchical borders that demarcated the U.S. and Mexican communities as it marched deeper into Mexico. Such borders extended American sovereignty into Mexican territory.

Physically Crossing the United States-Mexico Border

General Scott's landing at Vera Cruz on 9 March 1847 illustrates the intensity and elasticity of the peripheral, physical United States-Mexico border during the war (Eisenhower, 382). Colonel George Turnbull Davis, Scott's aide-de-camp during the invasion, describes crossing the border as an honorable feat in his autobiography.[15] In this passage, General Scott allows General Shields to "occupy the post of honor by having the advance in all active operations of the army" (123). General Scott then orders General Quitman to a position "second in line," which, according to Colonel Davis, causes "a spirit of jealously and unrest" among General Quitman's troops because of their subordinate position (123). Describing the landing at Vera Cruz, Colonel Davis writes, "General [Shields] sprang into the surf up to his armpits, and waded to the shore, that the boast and glory might be his of being the first of General Scott's army that stood on Mexican soil" (123). Colonel Davis's word choice, "boast" and "glory," suggests that stepping onto Mexican soil is a heroic feat of war. Shields is privileged to be the first of ten thousand men to cross into enemy territory (Eisenhower, 254).[16]

Following behind General Shields, Colonel Davis describes the "wild enthusiasm of our forces and their struggles to be among the first to reach the enemy's shores," which becomes for him, "a sight such as no imagination can conceive, and which our future history may never again be witness" (124-25). In relation to time, then, Davis's narrative is both backward- and forward-looking as the oxymoron future history suggests. In other words, Davis knows that invading another nation's territory is significant enough to warrant mention in America's history books (and perhaps Mexico's); moreover, he suggests the scene is so incredible that it may never be repeated in America's future. In applying Anderson's view of time and sacrifice, Davis's implication is that the glory of participating in this border crossing—with its past and future implications for his country—is worth risking his own life and the lives of his fellow soldiers.

General Scott's army surrounded Vera Cruz, using divisions led by Generals Worth, Patterson, and Twiggs. The army divisions cut the supply lines while the navy bombarded the city until the Mexican commander surrendered on 27 March 1847 (Miller, 60). Twenty U.S. troops died and two hundred Mexican soldiers and civilians died in the siege (Miller, 6). After the battle, the first act of the American military community was to raise the flag, an emblem of the nation, effectively creating a deterritorialized, hierarchical border between the U.S. and Mexican communities.[17] Colonel Davis describes the unisonance of the military community at the sight of the flag:

> As the sun was setting on that memorable day, our national flag was unfurled, and as its folds were flaunted in the face of the strongly entrenched and fortified city of Vera Cruz, a shout from American throats, both upon the land and from the sea, greeted by a salvo of guns from our shipping was heard, which fairly made the earth quake, and the waters of the Gulf of Mexico rise and swell with commotion. (125)

Davis's rhetoric personifies the flag and the city. The flag welcomes the Americans to the port city and is "greeted" by the exploding guns. The flag is "flaunted" in the "face" of the Mexican city. Furthermore, Davis notes that the flag flies over the "strongly entrenched and fortified city." The American flag is conceived in opposition to the fortitude of the Mexican city. The flag has significance to Colonel Davis precisely because of the strength of the Mexican military. In Davis's view, American bravado is all the more impressive because the army defeats a worthy adversary, an often made claim in the classical canon of Western literary tradition.[18]

Also, in this passage, the patriotism of the cheering American soldiers coupled with the din of exploding artillery shells stirs nature: land and sea respond to the flag simultaneously with the American soldiers, an image consistent with nascent American identity. Specifically, Davis's passage resonates with images of war and nature in the lyrics of the Star Spangled Banner, composed only three decades before the War. From the American perspective of the national anthem and Davis's account, nature seemingly heeds the call of Manifest Destiny to glorify the conqueror, cow the conquered.

Like the flag, a show of force is another important emblem of the military community that creates a hierarchical border, thereby delineating national communities. For example, Colonel Davis writes a lengthy paragraph describing General Worth's victory march into Vera Cruz. Worth is accompanied by an "imposing escort comprising artillery, cavalry, and the infantry . . . a detachment of naval officers and a detail of sailors and marines" (Davis, 130). When the "national colors are displayed," American flags are simultaneously hoisted at Fort Conception and Fort Santiago (both in Vera Cruz) (Davis, 130). Colonel Davis adds that the flags were then "saluted amid great enthusiasm and rejoicing on the part of both our army and navy" (130-31). Shortly after writing this paragraph, Colonel Davis goes into excruciating detail about the formidable Mexican forts. He catalogues the various pieces of Mexican artillery found in Vera Cruz. The American armament and troops that escort General Worth constitute a show of force that is somehow more impressive to Colonel Davis, given the Mexican army's ability to wage war. Like the description of Vera Cruz as well fortified, Mexican military might bolsters American patriotism because the soldiers have defeated a worthy adversary; Davis "imagines" a hierarchical border between the United States and Mexican communities that is deterritorialized to the extent that it delineates social space within "conquered" territory.

In contrast to the American viewpoint, several first-person accounts by Mexican citizens emphasize the bravery of Mexican soldiers in relation to the American invaders. Carlos María de Bustamante[19] writes the following account in *Historia de la invasión de los anglo-americanos en México*:

> La desolación y el terror se habían apoderado de las familias que no han podido salir; mas no de la tropa de la guardia nacional que estaban muy entusiasmadas, particularmente la última, que cantaba canciones mexicanas, españolas, y francesas, al retumbo de la artillería y resplandor de las llamas, vitoreando a la libertad e independencia, cada vez que el general Morales se presentaba en los puntos para visitarlos. Este general lloraba algunas veces de ternura, al presenciar el valor indomable de tanto joven imberbe que deseaba antes la muerte que la ignominia. (261)

In this account, the rhetoric suggests that the youthful Mexican soldiers respond defiantly to the nearly constant American bombardment of the city by singing and cheering. Whereas Mexican civilians, unable to flee from the city to safety, are shaken by the exploding artillery, the Mexican soldiers are anything but cowed by it. The Mexican soldiers risk their lives by staying within the contested territory of the border. Their courage is particularly noteworthy because this account recalls events on 25 March, effectively the end of the battle, when there was slim chance of a Mexican victory. Moreover, the Mexican soldiers respond in unisonance to the presence of General Morales by identifying themselves as national defenders of "liberty and independence," a *grito* (battle cry) that echoes back to Mexican independence.

Mexico had achieved its independence from Spain in 1821—with a full generation preceding the experiences of these particular soldiers in the Mexican American War. The soldiers' shouts illustrate that the imagined community of a nation has no beginning or ending point in time.[20] While individuals may give the ultimate sacrifice for a nation conceived in an infinite extension of time forward and backward, time in this passage is contracted: Mexican soldiers in the mid-1800s carry on the battle cries of their fathers, who expelled the Spanish from their territory in the first quarter of the century. As a result, Morales cries at witnessing the "insurmountable bravery" of the youth, whose willingness to sacrifice their lives is perhaps more acute because time is contracted from its potentially infinite stretch to the narrow scope of a mere generation.

Mariano Otero, a Mexican congressman during the war, offers additional insight from across the border. In his pamphlet, *Considerations Relating to the Political and Social Situation of the Mexican Republic in the Year 1847*, he captures the bravery of the Mexican soldiers.[21]

> In addition, we have witnessed the youth of Veracuz—a united band of only three or four thousand soldiers—roused to a pitch of fervor by no other considerations than their devotion to the honor of the region which gave them their birth. From within the decrepit walls that surround their city, they have defied an army of twelve or thirteen thousand men and, with honor and equanimity, they have withstood a horrible bombardment, which in eighty or ninety hours of firing dropped onto the plaza more than six thousand shells, causing tremendous havoc and ruin. And when these young men realized that their military leaders were engaged in talked with the enemy aimed at the surrender of the city, they angrily threw their weapons into the sea rather than allow them to fall into the hands of the conqueror. (18-19. Translated by Robinson.)

As in Bustamante's account, the young soldiers are valorized not only in the heroic front they put on in the face of American bombardment, but also in contrast to their very own leadership. Otero suggests that the common soldiers are more heroic than the military leadership because they defy the enemy (much like the singing and cheering in Bustamante's account) by discarding their weapons to deprive U.S. troops from using them. Furthermore, Mexican acts of resistance become signifiers of unisonance among the young soldiers, effectively separating them from their superiors. This passage contrasts with Davis's notion of defeating a worthy adversary. Otero labels the walls of Vera Cruz as "decrepit," describes the wreckage of the plaza, and enumerates how badly the Mexican forces were outnumbered. These details counterpoint, in an indirect sense, Davis's description of the enemy's formidable and well-equipped forts. In Otero's account, the Mexican soldiers are more heroic in relation to an overwhelming adversary: they are what Mariano Azuela termed *los de abajo* (the underdogs). As these examples show, the account suggests a hierarchical border of separation between the military leadership and the common soldiers within the Mexican community.

When the Mexican army surrendered at Vera Cruz, General Scott ordered the city to be transformed into a base camp, or "a more permanent installation built by the combat troops under the supervision of engineers and frequently with Mexicans as laborers" (Smith and Judah, 273). Base camps were ultimately built at Saltillo, Jalapa, Puebla, and Tacubaya (on Scott's route westward) (Smith and Judah, 273). In general, Mexican civilians were allowed freedom of movement within the city, but the U.S. military was everywhere present in the streets, plazas, and public spaces. To defend the city from an attempt by the Mexican military to reconquer it, the Americans fortified the peripheral border around the city well.[22] That a military community would guard and protect its perimeter is not surprising. What is significant, however, is that the borders of those base camps delineated newly acquired U.S. territory within which American sovereignty reigned, much like the contemporary notion of sovereignty associated with the land occupied by an embassy.

San Patricios: Borders Separating Communities

After the U.S. occupation of Vera Cruz, General Scott prepared to march his troops 270 miles for a grand assault on Mexico City, following Cortés's westward route (Smith and Judah, 223). His troops fought several battles, such as those at Jalapa, Cerro Gordo, and Puebla, as they moved toward Mexico City. As American troops marched deeper into Mexico, the Mexican army released leaflets in English to American soldiers, encouraging them to desert. A pamphlet released at Puebla reads: "Come to us! We will welcome you as friends with open arms, take care of your needs, and offer you more than the Yankees can provide" (Zeh, 55). Santa Anna sent handbills to the Americans when they were just ten miles southeast of Mexico City that read as follows: "The Mexican nation ... stretches out to you a friend's hand, [we] offer you the felicity and fertility of [our] territory" (Miller, 77). Another leaflet by General Ampudia, dated 15 September 1846, states: "I offer all individuals that will lay down their arms and separate themselves from the American Army, seeking protection, they will be well received and treated" (Miller, 45). These leaflets echo one consistent theme: enemy soldiers were promised safe passage across the border that separated the two distinct communities. Those who successfully crossed were offered a hero's welcome. Ironically, this border crossing resonates with Shields's landing at Vera Cruz by negating and mirroring it: from Shields's perspective, American heroes such as those at Vera Cruz are those who cross into danger—not the deserters, who cross into a supposed guarantee of safety.

The Mexican leaflets illustrate another significant facet of borders: crossing into enemy camp is a means of transcending national loyalties and identifying instead with all of humanity.[23] The Mexican leaders appeal to the needs of all men: they extended the helping hand of a friend who freely offers food and shelter. Of course, much of the propaganda lured deserters by offering land, rank, and money,[24] although the rhetoric claimed to satisfy basic human needs, which may have had more appeal to the soldiers than claims of citizenship. Ironically, immigrants could swear to defend the constitution as soldiers, but they could not vote in U.S. elections at this time (Wynn, 2). Such political limitations coupled with overt discrimination in America makes one question the extent to which the recent immigrant soldiers identified themselves as U.S. citizens. In fact, the immigrants may have had a greater affiliation to a religious claim of Catholicism than to a national claim of citizenship. Mexicans charged that Yankees did not provide for (e.g., meet the basic needs of) the Irish immigrant soldiers, who were predominantly Catholic. In these leaflets, the term *Yankee* refers to the Protestants of the Atlantic seaboard who prized, among other values, self-reliance and individualism. By implication, the Mexican Catholics offer to "take care of [the] needs" of the immigrant soldiers: Catholics help Catholics. Moreover, the fertile land of Mexico itself (not the government or military of Mexico) is available to immigrant soldiers willing to desert: abundant, fecund fields await cultivation. Ironically, the appeal echoes that of American expansion westward with its optimism of new growth and life, a nineteenth century promise that may have initially motivated many of the immigrant soldiers to sail to America.

In August of 1847, Scott's divisions fought the Battles of Contreras and Churubusco; the fall of these two cities marked the last obstacle American troops faced before entering Mexico City (Smith and Judah, 237, 244). The Americans won the battle and captured approximately three thousand prisoners after intense fighting (Wright, 238). José Fernando Ramírez, a member of the Mexican congress, notes in a letter the exact moment of the American attack and the fate of the San Patricios. From his home in Mexico City, he writes to a friend: "I was about to continue this, but the ringing of alarm bells in the cathedral warns us of an attack by the enemy. It is three o'clock in the afternoon. God help us! A few moments ago I was frightened and horrified by the news of the terrible slaughter of our luckless Irish soldiers who fell into the enemy's hands" (160). Ramírez captures the urgency of the moment—even noting the time of day—with his exclamation and records his gut reaction: he is stunned by the murder of the San Patricios. Since the land had fallen into enemy hands, it was subject to U.S. control so that the San Patricios were now considered deserters—they were now on the wrong side of the border. In this case, the concept of desertion illustrates the intensity of borders during war. In a sense, desertion takes on meaning because a border between the U.S. and Mexican communities exists: if there had been no community to leave or border to cross, it would have been impossible for the Americans to label the San Patricios as traitors and for the Mexicans to call them heroes.

Shortly after the battles. a U.S. military tribunal court-martialed the San Patricios for desertion in two separate trials. Twenty-seven of the San Patricios were sentenced to hang at San Angel and thirty were sentenced to hang at Tacubaya (Miller, 92, 105). Of the remaining fifteen, fourteen were sentenced to flogging and branding. One San Patricio was pardoned (Miller, 103).[25] The case of the pardoned soldier illustrates an interesting hierarchy of values within the American military community. General Scott pardoned the elderly San Patricio primarily because his son was loyal to the U.S. flag; the pardon implies that Scott knew it must have been a difficult decision for the son to place national claims above familial ones, to remain loyal to the United States when his father was not. As if rewarding the son, General Scott pardoned the father, thus inverting the relationship again: familial claims superseded national ones. The son's loyalty and unisonance with "the colors" (i.e., the flag) saved his father's life.[26]

After the sentencing, Colonel William Selby Harney was ordered to hang twenty-nine San Patricios on 13 September 1847.[27] Colonel Harney coordinated the execution with the American attack on Chapultepec Castle just three miles away. According to the *American Star*, a bilingual newspaper published in Mexico during the war, Harney placed nooses around the necks of the San Patricios as they waited on the gallows and "told them that they should live long enough to see the American flag hoisted upon the battlements of that fortress and no longer" ("Execution," 1). Several hours later, the siege ended. When the American flag unfurled, the order was given, and the San Patricios died. From Colonel Harney's perspective, the flag signaled a U.S. military victory over the last enemy stronghold in Mexico City. He delimited the American and Mexican military communities by using a simplistic and absolute criterion: the Americans control Chapultepec Castle and the Mexicans do not; that is, the Americans won and the Mexicans lost. In this case, the territory within the newly prescribed border delineated a "fixed and unrelenting standard of citizenship and belonging" (Castronovo, 196). The betwixt-and-between status of the San Patricios violated the protocol of a fixed win/lose scenario, and, as a result, the soldiers were eliminated from the space altogether. Borders thus take on weighty significance in war—there are no ambiguous positions. Since the border separates alliances to nations for which soldiers have pledged to die, they cannot straddle the line: to do so is to risk one's life, a gamble heightened by the fluidity of the peripheral and hierarchical borders of war.

An American artilleryman named James Reilly commented on Harney's theatrics.[28] His narrative illustrates another dimension of the flag as an emblem capable of creating unisonance. He writes, "As soon as the flag was seen floating in the breeze they were launched into eternity by him [Harney] with as much sang froid as a military martinet could put on. What must have been the feelings of those men when they saw that flag—for they knew their time had come! But on the other hand, a cheer came from them which made the valley ring" (Miller, 107-8).[29] Reilly noted the effect of the sight of the American flag on both the executioner and the executed. Harney became a wooden toy soldier devoid of emotion who, in a demonstration of pure discipline, carried out his orders when he saw the ethereal symbol of his nation. Conversely, the San Patricios burst into an emotional cheer when they saw the flag. The American soldiers most likely observed the event with a sober discipline akin to that of Harney. As if defying such discipline, the San Patricios cried out.[30] At the climactic moment of this public spectacle, the American troops reaffirmed their membership in the military community, whereas Harney confirmed the San Patricios' status as outsiders by executing them.

The fate of the San Patricios illustrates another facet of borders because their execution took place on Mexican soil. One American soldier writes, "These executions, which would have been proper at any time, were [so] particularly now, as we were in the midst of the enemy's country" (Miller, 108). Like Reilly's comment that "their time had come," the rhetoric of the present moment is acute in this passage: the allegiance of the San Patricios at this exact point in time and at this precise territorial location conflicts with the American rules of war. In a general sense, the hanging serves as a deterrent: it shows every member of the military what happens to those who cross the border to the other side.[31] On another level, executing the San Patricios on Mexican territory shows American sovereignty: U.S. military justice is carried out on these Mexican heroes even here—just three miles from the capital city. Finally, it also represents a tragic irony: the San Patricios will be hanged on the very territory they fought to defend.

According to one Mexican source, some American soldiers refused to participate in the execution of the San Patricios.[32] Bustamante writes

> [E]nemigos una horda de poblanos guías de este ejército, que se esmera en desarrollar su inmoralidad, y como descendientes legítimos de los antiguos tlaxcaltecas, conservan todavía el odio que mostraron en la toma de México al servicio de Hernán Cortés: Quién creyera que mandados ahorcar y sellar la frente de los soldados llamados de San Patricio, y resistiéndose a obedecer esta orden atroz los soldados angloamericanos, los poblanos la ejecutaran muy gustosos para comprobar su adhesión a los que han escogido por señores? (1)

This passage is significant because of the definition of traitor. Bustamante defines traitors by distinguishing between those who help carry out the "atrocious order" to execute the San Patricios and those who do not. Mexicans who participate in the execution are traitors to the country much as those traitors who had helped Cortés in taking Mexico City. The Mexicans who refuse to participate are not traitors: to use Bustamante's term, they are moral. The moral Mexican citizens are compared to the American soldiers who also refuse to participate in the execution—as opposed to the immoral ones who do—in order to prove their own servility. As a result, Bustamante's definition of traitor creates a paradigm that groups moral Mexican and Americans together, an act that ignores national claims of citizenship by positing morality as the highest end.[33]

Bustamante's definition of traitor develops by way of analogy to what he claims to be a history in which Mexicans (actually their ancestors) abet conquerors. He associates those Mexicans aiding the American army with the ancient Indian tribes who allied with Cortés to attack the Aztec empire. The historical allusion is all the more striking because General Scott followed Cortés's westward march from Vera Cruz to Mexico City. Bustamante rebukes Mexicans for their willingness to be enslaved to American masters, who exert sovereignty over Mexican soil. Thus, executing the San Patricios is a demonstration of U.S. sovereignty, so that those who willingly help establish such sovereignty are traitors to Mexico.

Also relevant to this passage is Bustamante's background as a soldier who fought for Mexico's independence from Spain. The Tlaxcalans helped Cortés defeat Montezuma, which resulted in the fall of the Aztec empire and gave birth to three centuries of Spanish rule over Mexico. It is not surprising that the author would be angry, as the tone of his writing suggests, with those Mexicans who help the Americans. Moreover, at the time of writing, the Americans were on the verge of conquering Mexico City, the site of Cortés's final victory.

Mexico City: Sovereignty and Manifest Destiny

Within miles of Mexico City, General Scott set up headquarters in Tacubaya because his troops needed to rest from the long march westward (Smith and Judah, 247). Realizing Santa Anna's army was equally fatigued and perhaps unable to defend the capital, Scott demanded capitulation. Santa Anna signed Scott's proposed armistice, but violations by both sides caused tension almost immediately (Smith and Judah, 250). Less than one month after arriving at Tacubaya, Scott attacked Molino del Rey and Chapultepec Castle. Both fortifications fell quickly, although not without heroic efforts from the Mexican military. As a case in point, the *Niños Héroes* (Child Heroes) jumped over the wall of Chapultepec Castle with the Mexican flag (i.e., an emblem of the nation) rather than allow it to fall into American hands (Krauze, 7). Shortly thereafter, the American military defeated the forces at Chapultepec and captured Mexico City on 13 September 1847 (Eisenhower, 383).

Offering the Mexican perspective on the fall of the capital, Alcaraz et al. in *La guerra entre México y los Estados Unidos* write:

> En la noche del 15 presentaba México el contraste más espantoso. Por una parte, los mexicanos, encerrados en sus casas, se entregaban á la consternación y al desaliento, mientras que por otra, la soldadesca triunfante, llena de júbilo, y escitada por licores embriagantes, sentía deslizarse las horas entre la risa y la algazara. Con la aurora terminó el espanto de los unos y la insultante alegría de los otros; y el Sol que años antes vio á México libertada por sus heroicos hijos, alumbró un pueblo esclavo y resignado ya con su ignominia. . . . Las brigadas [mejicanos] marchaban en silencio; la tristeza reinaba en todos los corazones. Se alejaban con sentimiento de la ciudad que habían defendido, considerando que el Sol del día siguiente alumbraría la entrada triunfante de los enemigos, quienes iban a ver cumplida la amenaza que todos habíamos despreciado, como hija de un delirio del orgullo. (333, 335)

This passage is significant for various reasons. First, it shows the clear hierarchical demarcation between the Mexicans locked up in their homes and the Americans who occupy public spaces. This is the same hierarchical border that American soldiers described in response to emblems of the nation. Second, the conduct of the American soldiers is not only insulting to the Mexican community, it also suggests that the Americans can now act without censure: they have national sovereignty, and, on an individual level, the soldiers are in control because they can do as they wish. Third, the Mexican military marches silently in a unisonance of defeat: the Americans have conquered the capital, a threat the Mexicans thought impossible. Finally, the sun, which no longer illuminates the Mexican community but shines on an American one, evokes powerful symbols of Manifest Destiny when understood in relation to time. This passage may suggest that, as the sun rises on Mexico in the future, the Sun will light the way for the American nation, leaving the Mexican nation in the darkness of their own humiliation.

In contrast to the somber passage above, Chauncey Forward Sargent,[35] a nineteen-year-old American private from Pennsylvania, describes the event in his diary. On 29 March 1847, he writes, "Our troops entered (Mexico) City, the Stars and Stripes were run up in the city and castle. The fleet fired the National [sic] saluted the bands playing Hail Columbia and we returned to camp to the tune Yankee Doodle" (Sargent, 7). American troops poured into Mexico City. Colonel Davis describes the American troops with "bands enlivening the enthusiasms of the scene with our national anthems" (237). When General Quitman entered the Mexican national palace in Mexico City, his first act was to raise the American flag. Colonel Davis writes: "The Stars and Stripes were then run up from the plaza, which produced the same effect upon the [Mexican] inmates of all the buildings fronting the grand plaza, as flaunting a red flag in the face of a wild and infuriated bull" (238). He goes on to describe the effect of flying the American flag on U.S. troops as "an enthusiasm and demonstration of pride and victory that it is idle for me to attempt to depict" (238). In these particular accounts, George and Davis describe the effect of the flag on the American troops: simultaneously, members of the American military react similarly in expressing their patriotism. Moreover, their intense unisonance is contrasted with its effect on the Mexican community, which, according to Davis, is as "wild and infuriated" as a bull, a particularly symbolic animal in Latin America. From the perspective of the writer, the unisonance that unites each of the two communities also constitutes a hierarchical, deterritorialized border between them.

Once in full control of the capital, General Scott appointed General Quitman to the post of civil and military governor of Mexico City. Colonel Davis describes the ceremony in relation to the grandeur of the Mexican National Palace. From the U.S. perspective, Colonel Davis describes General Scott's staff as "all . . . in full-dress" and escorted by a "magnificent corps of U.S. Dragoons." The flag was displayed atop the National Palace as the general passed through "the great body of his generals, their staffs, and many of his field officers" (238-39). Colonel Davis writes a lengthy passage describing the interior of the National Palace, which Quitmen will occupy. He notes that the palace "had been the private apartment of Santa Anna as the President of the Republic of Mexico" and goes on about the magnificent portraits of Mexican conquerors (239-341). American leaders now operate from the site formerly occupied by Mexican military leaders implying the Mexican National Palace is now within the borders of—and in control of—the American military community. Furthermore, the glory of the American military is intensified because it is conceived relative to the luxuriant National Palace; the Americans are all the more heroic because they have conquered a worthy adversary. In contrast to the aforementioned passage by Mexican scholars, Davis concludes that the U.S. military occupies the public space of the plaza and the private space of elite members of the Mexican military.

Although, no doubt, the palace was highly polished for the American ceremonial assumption of command, there is a discrepancy between Davis's description of the ceremony on 14 December and José Fernando Ramírez's letter dated 30 September. Ramírez writes:

> The Palace and almost all public buildings have been savagely ransacked and destroyed. I think it only right to say, however, that our disgraceful rabble were the ones who began it all. When the enemy's troops entered the Palace, the doors had already been broken down and the building had been plundered. Three days later the embroidered velvet canopy was sold for *four pesos* at the Palace entrance. The Government records and other items were sold for two reales. (161; Ramírez's emphasis)

In this passage, Ramírez is ashamed of the acts of his countrymen, describing them as a "disgraceful rabble" who plunder their own National Palace for personal gain. Breaking the doors and ransacking buildings further suggests a sense of disrespect for the buildings that symbolize government (and perhaps nation). In other words, he points to a hierarchy of values that places monetary worth above a sense of propriety and respect for the government, a prospect that is particularly troubling to Ramírez because the goods fetch low prices. Gone, in contrast with the other passages, is the sense of defiance associated with Mexican soldiers' resisting American sovereignty by cheering for independence or throwing their weapons into the Gulf of Mexico. This passage highlights divisiveness within the Mexican community after the fall of the capital.

In another passage, Ramírez blames the fall of Mexico on "partisan hatreds" within the country (121). In a letter to a friend of 25 April 1847, he states that history records cases in which nations drew together in a "feeling of nationality" to repel foreign invaders but that in Mexico's case the opposite has occurred on two distinct occasions:

> In our privileged country quite the contrary has happened on the only two occasions there have been to prove the truth of the maxim: namely, the Spanish conquest under Cortés, and the Yankee conquest under Scott. And to make the terrible comparison complete, both set foot upon the shores of Veracruz during Holy Week. The reason for the difference is clear. A sensible, patriotic people unites and offers a solid front at the first hint of the common peril. A people that is neither sensible nor patriotic grows weak, thus smoothing out difficulties for the invader, who wins without opposition. (121)

Although Ramírez's frustration is evident in his word choice, which describes his own community as "neither sensible nor patriotic," he seems particularly disturbed by Scott's march to Mexico City, which parallels that of Cortés. Ramírez criticizes the inability of the Mexican community to unite in defending the nation, a rhetoric of blame that is a communal mea culpa of sorts. Furthermore, his mention of the timing of the two invasions during Holy Week evokes the traditional historical tools, such as dates, times, and places. In other words, Mexico is reliving a chapter from the sixteenth century which, like the Mexican American War, also ended with foreign occupation. Ramírez argues that history records many incidents in which nations united to withstand invasion. In the case of the Mexican American War, according to his logic, Mexico does not warrant mention because of its double failure to repel Spanish and American invaders.

After the pomp and circumstance of entering Mexico City, General Scott set about occupying the capital city in a methodical manner. He declared martial law over the Mexican and American communities alike to establish their peaceful coexistence within the city until negotiators finalized the Treaty of Guadalupe Hidalgo (Eisenhower, 346). Throughout Mexico, the other four U.S. armies of invasion were consolidating their power as well. Scott bluntly summarizes the U.S. plan to occupy the entire country in the first sentence of General Order 376: "This army is about to spread itself over and to occupy the Republic of Mexico until the latter shall sue for peace on terms acceptable to the Government of the United States" (Wright, 239). Scott goes on to list all areas under American sovereignty, such as Vera Cruz, Puebla, Tamaulipas, the Calfornias [sic], New Mexico, Chihuahua, Coahuila, and New León (Wright, 239).

During the U.S. occupation of Mexico City, American soldiers settled into a routine that involved patrolling the perimeter of the city while on duty (Smith and Judah, 313). Off duty, the Americans toured the country, visiting places such as the National Museum in Mexico City, the pyramids, and chapel at Cholula. Colonel Davis describes one excursion, comparing the American exploits to Cortés's. In this passage, he describes Cholula as "the theatre of that Spanish conqueror's most memorable military exploit" (184). He notes how "fearful" the Aztecs must have been because they were "wholly unacquainted with firearms and their uses" (184). Colonel Davis applauds the Spaniards' decision to destroy the Aztec pyramid, "their principal idol temple," and erect on the site a Catholic church; Cortés rightly silenced the Aztec "pagan songs" and decimated these "monuments of heathen-worship" (185). Most revealing in this passage, however, is how the Americans leave the ruins.

> The band . . . was ordered by him [General Twigg] to play in succession our three popular national anthems: "Hail Columbia," "Yankee Doodle," and "The Star Spangled Banner," and from the highest elevation of that famed Mexican pyramid the general's orders were executed in an inimitable style, the symphony of which inspired all our hearts with a renewed remembrance and love of country and our homes—a touching and appropriate close to one of the best-spent days, when in camp, that I had thus far experienced during that campaign. (186)

The band plays patriotic music from atop the highest point of the ancient Aztec empire. As with the earlier explication of the "Star Spangled Banner," American military members sing patriotically in an act that resonates with the very lyrics of the "Marine Hymn"—they physically occupy "the Halls of Montezuma." Just as Cortés built a church over the Aztecs' place of worship, the American forces appropriate the site, albeit to a lesser degree, playing U.S. national anthems where Aztec "pagan songs" were once sung.

It is also significant that Colonel Davis experiences a sense of nostalgia for country and home when leaving the ruins. Outsiders often valorize ruins of ancient people as indigenous vestiges of a glorious past that have fallen in preparation for a new transformation (Pratt, 130). Colonel Davis romanticizes the plight of the Aztecs, noting that they bravely faced guns for the first time in battle against Cortés. Furthermore, Davis thinks of home because he conceives the Aztec ruins as the foundation for what his country has to offer Mexico (184-85). Davis writes later in his journal: "The flag of our country was floating over that land from the sea-coast to its very centre. . . . The time is not far distant when . . . the United States must in some manner and form control or direct her destinies to save Mexico [from] disappearing from the galaxy of recognized civilized nations" (292-93). Here the American flag becomes a territorial extension of American sovereignty that reflects Scott's route, the one Davis himself had taken, from Vera Cruz to Mexico City. According to Davis, the flag represents U.S. sovereignty over all of Mexico in the present moment. He goes on, however, to speculate on the future, using the rhetoric of Manifest Destiny that speaks to America's moral duty to ensure that Mexico is aligned properly with a supernal configuration of nations. The relation to time here is an unmistakable thread in the discourse of the nation, stretching from the ancient pyramids of the Aztecs to a future cosmos of recognized civilizations that outshine all else. If the United States does not save Mexico in the foreseeable future, Davis reasons, it will disappear from the galaxy permanently.

Ramifications and Manifestations of Borders

This study begins with an investigation into the origins of the current United States-Mexico geopolitical border and ends by raising more questions about the border. The case studies of the U.S. military community invading Vera Cruz, executing the San Patricios, and occupying Mexico City show repeated representations of borders: peripheral borders demarcate American sovereignty within conquered territory within which are created hierarchical borders separating Americans from Mexicans. In attacking and defending these borders, both U.S. and Mexican soldiers repeatedly risk their lives for the nation, an imagined community that transcends time. Although almost 150 years have passed since the Mexican American War, the United States-Mexico border is more militarized than it has ever been; thus, the manner in which the U.S. military established borders in the nineteenth century may still be relevant today. Certainly, the American military will not invade Mexico any time soon. On a more subtle level, however, Mexico—and many other nations for that matter—has already been invaded through the process of neocolonialism vis-à-vis global capitalism. Over the past 30 years, the United States has developed—and currently dominates—a world economic system through "*military*, political, and economic" intervention (Sassen, 214; my emphasis). As a result, the border has become increasingly deterritorialized through the long arms of international finance that now reach well beyond the *maquiladoras* (assembly plants) of the United States-Mexico border region.

The U.S. military manifestations of the border during the Mexican American War offer some parallels with the contemporary deterritorialization of the border. As Michael Kearney points out, the process of economic globalization is a power struggle to control markets in an arena that has become exceedingly detached from any grounding within national territory (552-53). Might NAFTA's authorization for American businesses to operate in Mexico be a form of testing the elasticity of the United States-Mexico border? In other words, does NAFTA expand the landscape of the American business world by opening up new markets? As U.S. businesses compete to cross the border (albeit for different reasons than those of the military), are they not rewarded economically if they succeed in exploiting a new market? Might the emblems of the nation extend to capitalism, as demonstrated over the past 50 years of steady purchases by the Mexican middle class of products labeled "Made in the "U.S.A."? As Mexicans grow more dependent on American products and jobs in American-owned/managed *maquiladoras*, is not a hierarchical border created between "those who have" and "those who have not"? Is there a border separating the poverty-stricken barrios in Mexico and the upper-class residential neighborhoods in the United States, even as the two communities abut one another? Is the American business community's extension of the border through economic expansion simply a more insidious expression of the American military's invasion of Mexico? As the United States gains increasing financial leverage in Mexico, does it gain a form of economic sovereignty over the nation as well? Finally, what is the future concept of the nation for which Americans or Mexicans are willing to die?

I raise these provocative questions because there are more parallels between the borders established by the American military and the American business community than may have been recognized in the past. The origins of the border reveal much about the current status of the border. Perhaps one of the biggest objections to such speculations may be the argument that the military used force to back American sovereignty on Mexican soil. In response, I argue that the market forces of capitalism are capable of causing just as much violence and of exerting just as much force.

Notes

[1] See Ward McAfee and J. Cordell Robinson's *The Origins of the Mexican War* for examples of several primary sources written by Mexican congressmen who interpreted the U.S. annexation of Texas as a hostile act (especially "Chapter One: Mexico and Texas").

[2] A New York lawyer named John O'Sullivan, known for his less-than-magnanimous character, coined the term to "justify North American ambitions" (Robinson, 202) as a means of motivating the American government to pursue its ideological moral duty. For additional information, see Robinson's *The View from Chapultepec,* Krauze's *History of Mexico,* and McAfee and Robinson's *Origins of the Mexican War.*

[3] For a detailed account of the Creole era presented from a Mexican perspective, see Robinson's "Introduction" and Krauze's "The Collapse of the Creoles" cited in this paper.

[4] Even the language of Mexican history books, which uses terms such as *Porfirismo* or *Zapatismo,* suggests the importance of an allegiance to a patron rather than to the nation of Mexico in and of itself (Krauze, xv). See Krauze's "Preface" and "Introduction" for a detailed discussion of the relationship between individual leaders and Mexican history from 1810. The subtitle of the book, "Biography of Power," underscores Krauze's premise that in Mexico the concept of 'nation' is historically linked directly to *patrones* rather than to political institutions. As I explain later in this paper, nations exist in infinite time, and, as a result, individuals are willing to die for the nation. This spirit of intense patriotism contrasts with the conception of nation in Mexico symbolized by the life(span) of a *patrón* (i.e., clearly delimited in time by birth and death dates).

[5] For additional information on discrimination against immigrant soldiers, see Dennis Wynn's "The San Patricio Soldiers" in *Southwestern Studies* as well as "The Race Question and Manifest Destiny" and "Not Only Irish, but Catholics Too" in Michael Hogan's *The Irish Soldiers of Mexico.*

[6] While it is unclear when the American military stopped inflicting the punishment of whipping and branding on deserters, it may have been meted out as late as the Civil War. See, for example, Simon Winchester's *The Professor and the Madman* (1998).

[7] See *Nations Unbound* by Linda Basch, Nina Schiller, and Christina Blue, "The Mexican-U.S. Border: The Making of an Anthropology of Borderlands" by Robert Alvarez and *Border Approaches* by Hastings Donnan and Thomas Wilson.

[8] To clarify, nations are not bounded chronologically; one regime inherits another so that there is no date of birth or death of a nation, as in the case of human beings (Anderson, 22-36, 204-6). As imagined communities, nations stretch infinitely backward and forward in time. As a result, citizens are more likely to sacrifice their lives for a nation than, say, other imagined communities (i.e., American Medical Association or Rotary Club).

[9] The root word of *unisonance* is *unison,* which is derived from the Latin terms *unus* (one) and *sonus* (sound). The term *unison* is often associated with "elements behaving the same way at the same time," such as a military platoon marching in unison.

[10] First-person narratives of U.S. soldiers, such as the one quoted here, compose the greater corpus of American writing on the Mexican American War. Among the 19th century writers canonized in this period, such as Emerson, Whitman, Thoreau, and Dickinson, few wrote about the war. Thoreau's most famous essay, "Civil Disobedience," expresses harsh disapproval of American aggression against Mexico. (He spent a night in a Concord jail to protest paying taxes that contributed to the war effort.)

[11]In my discussion concerning those inside and outside the imagined American community, I am referring to outsiders primarily as non-U.S. citizens. I acknowledge that U.S. citizens display a range of responses to the flag from reverence to loathing. My point, however, is to illustrate that those responding in unisonance to the flag perceive their reaction in contrast to outsiders, a perception American soldiers repeatedly describe in their accounts of the war. The exclusionary distinction of communities caused by unisonance creates a border that separates the people inside from those outside the imagined community.

[12]The hierarchical border that separates communities I propose may be linked to notions of identity. Exploring the relationship of borders and identity is a growing field in border studies; however, such a discussion exceeds the scope of this paper. For theoretical analyses of border identity, see Michael Kearney's "The Local and the Global," and Michael Rosler and Tobias Wendle's *Frontiers and Borderlands*.

[13]According to Dennis Wynn, the U.S. military, for relatively minor offenses such as drunkenness, meted out harsher punishments to immigrants (soldiers) than to non-immigrants. He writes, "an enlisted man found guilty of drunkenness and mutinous conduct might be shot, or he might be confined for thirty days. . . . the foreign-born soldier, especially if he happened to be Irish or German, automatically received a harsher sentence than a native American would for the same offense" (Wynn, 2). In fact, thirty-two of the San Patricios tried to defend themselves at the court-martial by explaining that they were drunk; they hoped for acquittal because (1) drunkenness was one of the most common infractions among the rank and file during the war and often resulted only in a mild reprimand, and (2) military law allowed for reduced sentencing based on mitigating factors such as drunkenness. Their defense was not successful. See Hogan's *The Irish Soldiers of Mexico* (162-67) and Miller's *Shamrock and the Sword* (94-96).

[14]According to Eisenhower, Mexico's northern provinces were sparsely populated wastelands that did not have a clearly demarcated border (196). Many American expansionists called the region the "Great American Desert" even though they still coveted the land (Eisenhower, 196). My conclusion is that the physical border separating the military from the civilian community was more heavily fortified than the border between the imagined national communities of Mexico and the United States in the mid-nineteenth century. Such a comparison of two different types of borders is less clear today. In other words, today, military installations are heavily protected due to the amount of high-tech weaponry, and, to some extent, the United States-Mexico border is equally militarized. To the contrary, however, large stretches of the United States-Canada border are not fortified today.

[15]Because I am analyzing the rhetoric of individuals in this study, it is important to contextualize each passage so that a reader may better understand the biases of the writer. I will thus provide a brief overview of each writer and text. Colonel Davis's autobiography is a first-person account of his experience as General Scott's aide-de-camp during the Mexican American War, written in retrospect at the age of approximately seventy-nine. He campaigned with Scott until the fall of Mexico City, at which time he was appointed secretary of state to General Quitman, the newly appointed Governor of the capital. Davis was born on 24 May 1810 in Malta, the son of Anna (Tucker) and George Davis, who, as a naval officer, served with the consul general of the United States to Tripoli. George Davis's family had a history of military service in which members occasionally placed political convictions above family loyalties; in the Revolutionary War, for example, two brothers fought for different armies. A lawyer by trade, Colonel Davis explains that he accepted his military commission for various reasons: he felt obligated to "rally at the call of our country, to aid in driving from our soil a foreign invader," and he feared the "stigma of insincerity as well as want of valor, that will be visited upon [his] children, and children's children during their whole lives" (97). At the end of the war, Davis served in the War Department as a chief clerk until he retired from the military and settled in New York, engaging in various commercial businesses, (such as railroads, newspapers, and manufacturing) (393). His autobiography was published posthumously by his legal representative, according to Davis's wishes.

[16]Two notes are applicable here. First, Americans were crossing into the territory of Vera Cruz (a seaport located on the Gulf of Mexico) that constitutes the land of contemporary Mexico on today's maps. Second, although Colonel Davis states General Shields was the first to set foot on Mexican soil at Vera Cruz, Eisenhower's text states General William Worth was the first to do so (259).

[17]For the purpose of this paper, "deterritorialized" refers to what Michael Rosler and Tobias Wendl have termed "figurative multisited borderlands," which are "neither spatially bounded" nor have "a particular location within national center-periphery frames." See Rosler and Wendl's *Frontiers and Borderlands*.

[18] In the *Iliad* and *Odyssey*, for example, Homer describes at length the enemies' military might, following the traditional catalogue format in epic poetry. In *Paradise Lost*, Milton similarly enumerates the military capabilities of the forces in heaven and hell at great length.

[19] Bustamante is well known for his widely published account of the Mexican American War titled *Historia de la invasión de los anglo-americanos en México*. He was born in Oaxaca in 1774 and served in the war of independence from Spain, after which he became a Mexican congressman for essentially the rest of his life (Robinson, 51). As a young man, he admired the United States for its economic progress and democratic political institutions. His position changed after witnessing numerous diplomatic attempts by the United States to acquire Mexican territory. At the time of this writing, he viewed the United States as a political enemy (Robinson, 51).

[20] By way of illustration, the current government in Mexico lays claims to the legitimacy of the country's Aztec ancestors, because a nation inherits to some extent its predecessors' concept of an imagined community. Modern nations continually reinforce such a chronological lineage, using tools such as maps, museums, and the census. See Anderson's *Imagined Communities* (155-62).

[21] Although several authors claim to have written this pamphlet, Mexican historians generally attribute the key ideas to Otero, who served as minister of external and internal affairs at the time of publication. Since the pamphlet was also serialized in the newspaper *El Monitor Republicano*, many historians note that it was probably read by a large number of Mexican citizens.

[22] For additional information, see chapter 6, "Life in the Camps," in Smith and Judah, *Chronicles of the Gringos*. This chapter contains firsthand accounts ranging from soldiers' daily schedules (i.e., drill, patrol, meals, etc.), to comments on the sheer boredom of camp life and descriptions of washing laundry. Also see the firsthand accounts of Zeh, George, Kirkham, and Sargent.

[23] With reference to Western literary traditions, crossing borders into the enemy camp is another theme prevalent in Homer's *Iliad* and *Odyssey* and in Shakespeare's *Henry V*. In these crossings, the protagonists learn much about their own humanity by witnessing "the other" engaged in basic human activities, such as eating, sleeping, and worrying about an upcoming battle. I point this out to illustrate some classic literary examples of border crossings; however, these allusions are distinct from the case study of the San Patricios, who do not conceal their identity once they have crossed into Mexican lines.

[24] For examples of such leaflets, see General Ampudia's and General Arista's writings in McAfee and Robinson, *The Origins of the Mexican War* (1:109, 122-23).

[25] As previously noted, many of the "facts" of the Mexican American War are disputed. Colonel Davis's journal states that Harvey hanged eleven San Patricios (228). Miller's text states that Harney hanged twenty-nine San Patricios (103). According to the front page of the *American Star*, sixteen deserters were hanged at San Angel and thirty-four were hanged at Miscoac [*sic*] ("Execution," 1). Similarly, facts vary concerning the number of actual troops that landed with General Scott's army in Vera Cruz. Eisenhower claims that approximately ten thousand U.S. troops landed (254); Smith and Judah and Miller state that nine thousand men landed (Smith and Judah, 172; Miller, 59).

[26] For another example of the hierarchy of American values in which familial claims supersede national ones, see letters by Lieutenant Meade, General Taylor, and General Ampudia in McAffee and Robinson's *Origins of the Mexican War* (121-34) that address the death of Colonel Trueman Cross, a deputy quartermaster-general in the army, who is killed when riding alone several miles from the American camp at Matamoros. Cross's son waits in vain for news of his father's return and "wins the sympathy and affection of the whole army by his manly deportment;" when his father's badly mutilated body is found, many soldiers want to avenge the Colonel's murder by attacking the Mexican soldiers at their camp opposite Matamoros because they feel badly for Colonel Cross's son.

[27] During Colonel Harney's twenty-nine year career in the U.S. Army, he was known, according to U.S. War Department records, for his "profanity, brutality, incompetence, peculation, recklessness, insubordination, tyranny and mendacity" (Miller, 105-7). His service record is punctuated by incidents such as occurred in St. Louis in 1843, where he was tried and acquitted for beating a female slave to death. By the time Harney was ordered to execute the San Patricios, he had a reputation of rapaciousness based on his service in the Seminole and Blackhawk Indian wars. Harney was Irish and a Roman Catholic (Hogan, 160). See the *Official Correspondence of Brigadier General W. S. Harney,* Hogan (180-96) and Miller (105-8).

[28]James Reilly wrote an essay called "An Artilleryman's Story" that was published in the 1903 edition of the *Journal of the Military Service Institution,* describing his experience with the San Patricios. Other than this article, little else is known about Reilly.

[29]Oddly, Reilly's word choice describing the San Patricios as being "launched into eternity" is identical with the words used on the front page of the *American Star* and in Colonel Davis's autobiography. It is not clear whether Reilly and Davis borrowed the phrase from the newspaper—a possible connection since thousands of servicemen subscribed to it—or whether it was a common euphemism for death in the nineteenth century. Nonetheless, the connection between time ("eternity") and sacrifice in the phrase cannot be ignored. The "traitors" (from the American perspective) are killed by the defenders of the nation, an imagined community that exists infinitely backward and forward in time. To extend the analogy, the San Patricios are "launched" forcibly into a temporal purgatory state—a sharp contrast to the common epigraph "Rest in peace."

[30]We may never know why the San Patricios cheered at the sight of the flag, as Reilly recounts, but Hogan speculates that they were simply glad the ordeal of Harney's execution would soon be over—they had waited for four and one half hours to be hanged. See the passage "A Long Morning at Mixoac" in Hogan's text (183-89).

[31]The *American Star* frequently reminded its readers, who were primarily U.S. military members, of the fate of the San Patricios by way of a deterrent. Thus in one column they published General Scott's warning: "Let all our soldiers, protestant and catholic, remember the fate of the deserters taken at Churubusco. These deluded wretches were also promised money and land; but the Mexican government, by every sort of ill usage, drove them to take up arms against the country and flag they had voluntarily sworn to support, and next placed them in front of the battle—in positions from which they could not possibly escape the conquering valor of our glorious ranks. After every effort of the General-in-Chief to save, by judicious discrimination, as many of those miserable convicts as possible, fifty of them have paid for their treachery by an ignominious death on the gallows!"

[32]Although my research does not refute Bustamante's claim, I found no American sources to corroborate his statement that Mexicans willingly flogged or hanged the San Patricios. According to the *American Star,* General Twiggs requested a Mexican muleteer to flog the men because he "deemed it too much honor . . . to be flogged by an American soldier." (The following line of the article describes Riley's reaction to the flogging somewhat caustically: "He did not stand the operation with that stoicism we expected" ["Execution, 1]).

[33]Bustamante places morality above citizenship in a rhetorical strategy akin to that of Thoreau in "Civil Disobedience."

[34]Alcaraz et al., *Apuntes para la historia de la guerra,* is a history of the Mexican American War written by fifteen Mexican scholars who had witnessed the war. The group talked frequently about the *desgracias del pais,* and decided to compile notes about the war to provide an accurate account of events from multiple perspectives for all to judge.

[35]Sargent was born in 1828 and enlisted in the army in Pennsylvania, his home state, on 24 December 1846. He was inducted into the Second Regiment on 7 January 1846 and mustered out on 14 July 1848. He carried his personal diary with him on the battlefield throughout the war, and did not intend for it to be published (hence the grammatical errors and shorthand). This fact lends a degree of authenticity to his writing, since he most likely considered the diary a private chronicle of his life during the war. After the war he started the Union News Company, an affiliate of the Pennsylvania Railroad, married, and had five children. He died in 1904. It is interesting to note that Sargent was proud of his plunder of a Mexican flag, a clear emblem of nationalism, which he brought home with him after the war.

Works Cited

Alcaraz, Ramón, et al. *Apuntes para la historia de la guerra entre México y los Estados Unidos.* Mexico, DF: Siglo Vientiuno Editores, 1977.

Anderson, Benedict. *Imagined Communities.* London: Verso Publishers, 1991.

Barcena, José María Roa. *Recuerdos de la invasión norteamericana (1846-48)*. 3 vols. México: Editorial Porrúa, 1947.

Bustamante, D. Carlos María. *El nuevo Bernal Díaz del Castillo o sea la historia de la invasión de los anglo-americanos en México*. Mexico, DF: Secretaría de Educación Pública, 1949.

Castronovo, Russ. "Compromised Narratives along the Border." In *Border Theory*, ed. Scott Michaelson and David E. Johnson, 195-220. Minneapolis: University of Minnesota Press, 1997.

Davis, George Turnbull Moore. *The Autobiography of the Late Colonel George Turnbull Moore Davis . . . from Posthumous Papers*. New York: Press of Jerkins and McCowan, 1891.

Eisenhower, John S. D. *So Far From God*. New York: Random House, 1989.

"Execution of Deserters." *American Star*, 20 September 1847, 1.

George, Isaac. *Heroes and Incidents of the Mexican War*. CA: Sun Dance Press, 1971.

Hogan, Michael. *The Irish Soldiers of Mexico*. Mexico, DF: Fondo Editorial Universitario, 1997.

Kearney, Michael. "The Local and the Global: The Anthropology of Globalization and Transnationalism." *American Review of Anthropology* 24 (1995): 547-65.

Kirkham, Ralph W. *The Mexican War Journal and Letters of Ralph W. Kirkham*. Ed. Robert Royal Miller. College Station: Texas A&M University Press, 1991.

Krauze, Enrique. *Mexico: Biography of Power*. Trans. Hank Heifetz. New York: Harper Perennial, 1997.

Martínez, Oscar J. *Border People*. Tucson: University of Arizona Press, 1994.

McAfee, Ward, and J. Cordell Robinson. *The Origins of the Mexican War: A Documentary Source Book*. 2 vols. NC: Documentary Publications, 1982.

Miller, Robert Royal. *Shamrock and Sword*. Norman: University of Oklahoma Press, 1989.

Otero, Mariano. "Consideraciones sobre la situación política y social de la República Mexicana en el año 1847." In *Obras*, ed. Jesús Reyes Heroles, 95-137. Mexico, DF: Editorial Porrúa, 1967.

Pratt, Mary Louise. "Scratches on the Face of the Country." *Critical Inquiry* 12, 1 (1985): 119-43.

Ramírez, José Fernando. *Mexico during the War with the United States*. Ed. Walter V. Scholes. Trans. Elliott B. Scherr. Columbia: University of Missouri Press, 1950.

Robinson, Cecil, ed. and trans. *The View from Chapultepec: Mexican Writers on the Mexican American War*. Tucson: University of Arizona Press, 1989.

Rosler, Michael, and Tobias Wendl. "Frontiers and Borderlands: The Rise and Relevance of an Anthropological Research Genre." *Frontiers and Borderlands: Anthropological Perspectives*. Unpublished manuscript. Institute of Ethnology and African Studies. Munich: University of Munich, n.d.

Sargent, Chauncey Forward. *Gathering Laurels in Mexico: The Diary of an American Soldier in the Mexican American War*. Ed. Ann Brown Janes. Lincoln, NE: Cottage Press, 1990.

Sassen, Saskia. *U.S. Immigration Policy toward Mexico in a Global Economy. Between Two Worlds*. Ed. David G. Gutiérrez, 213-28. DE: Scholarly Resources, 1996.

Selby, John. *The Eagle and the Serpent: The Spanish and American Invasions of Mexico in 1519 and 1846*. London: Hamish Hamilton, 1978.

Singletary, Otis. "San Patricios." In *The Mexican American War*, 90-91, 158. Chicago: University of Chicago Press.

Skidmore, Thomas E., and Peter H. Smith. *Modern Latin America*. Oxford: Oxford University Press, 1984.

Smith, George Winston, and Charles Judah. "Triumphs and Woes of the Victors." In *Chronicles of the Gringos*, 387-444. Albuquerque: University of New Mexico Press, 1968.

Wright, Marcus. "San Patricios." In *General Scott*, 237-39. New York: D. Appleton and Company, 1897.

Wynn, Dennis J. "The San Patricio Soldiers." In *Southwestern Studies*. El Paso: University of Texas Press, 1984.

Zeh, Frederick. *An Immigrant Soldier in the Mexican War*. Ed. William J. Orr and Robert Ryal Miller. Trans. William J. Orr. College Station: Texas A&M University Press, 1995.

Puerto Rico lírico

LA INFLUENCIA DEL "POETA DE AMÉRICA" EN EL NACIONALISMO PUERTORRIQUEÑO

Santiago Daydí-Tolson

UNIVERSITY OF TEXAS AT SAN ANTONIO

En 1913, cuando Puerto Rico llevaba ya quince años bajo control de los Estados Unidos, José Santos Chocano, el poeta peruano que reclamaba para sí las virtudes lírico-políticas de un Whitman hispanoamericano, visita la isla en una de sus tantas giras de poeta famoso y aclamado orador político. Desde principios del siglo, y en especial a partir de la publicación en 1906 de su libro *Alma América,* se le había identificado en Hispanoamérica y España como el poeta del continente. "Cantor de América" lo nombran la crítica y el público, admiradores de su obra poética de inspiración y propaganda mundonovistas y de su figura de hombre público, activo impulsor de los sentimientos americanistas de reafirmación de lo hispano que resultaron de la derrota española del 98.

Expulsado de México por Huerta en 1912 debido a la participación que había tenido en los primeros momentos de la revolución, se establece por un tiempo en Cuba, desde donde viaja a Puerto Rico a mediados de octubre del año siguiente, invitado por "varios redactores de la *Revista de las Antillas* y de otros periódicos puertorriqueños", según lo afirma Luis Llorens Torres, uno de los colaboradores de la revista y el principal promotor de la visita de quien él mismo identifica como "cantor de las glorias y grandezas de América y de toda la raza española" ("Vendimia" 89).

Si el motivo de la visita de Chocano a Puerto Rico fue principalmente económico — de servicio cumplido por contrato, ya que Chocano dependía en gran medida de los ingresos de sus presentaciones en público—, a juzgar por la invitación de sus anfitriones y por las actividades que desempeñó durante los casi tres meses de estadía en la isla, su presencia en ésta tuvo un decidido carácter político-literario. Sus varios recitales en diversas ciudades de la isla, sus declaraciones a la prensa y los infaltables discursos en tertulias, ceremonias, banquetes y convocatorias públicas fueron noticia y motivo de crítica en los periódicos y círculos intelectuales y políticos puertorriqueños.

Puerto Rico, territorio hispanoamericano absorbido por el expansionismo de los Estados Unidos, le ofrecía al poeta, en su dependencia política, el lugar más adecuado para cantar las grandezas de una América hispana histórica y futura diametralmente opuesta a la América del norte. En pocos sectores del continente una visita de Chocano podía alcanzar mayor significación. Como muy bien lo resume Luis Alberto Sánchez en *Aladino, o vida y obra de José Santos Chocano,*

> La isla se hallaba bajo el gobierno militar norteamericano, a consecuencia de la derrota de España por Los Estados Unidos y del Tratado de París de 1898. Vivía

en plena eclosión patriótica, embelesada en sus ensueños de independencia y sus afirmaciones hispanoamericanistas. La pugna entre ciertos intereses de los Estados Unidos y los fundamentos de la Revolución Mexicana, avivada bajo la presidencia de Taft y apenas atenuada con el advenimiento de Wilson, eran circunstancias favorables a la prédica y actitud del aventurero poeta. Este escogió y decidió bien su nuevo, aunque pasajero destino. (286)

Eligieron bien, así mismo, los intelectuales puertorriqueños nacionalistas, quienes viendo la oportunidad que la presencia de Chocano les ofrecería para fomentar en la isla sus objetivos políticos, lo invitaron a visitarla e hicieron de su estadía en ella motivo de especial celebración y demostración públicas de patriotismo nacional y panamericanismo hispánico. Si al poeta político le convenía una gira de recitales y conferencias que le produjera ganancias y acrecida fama, a los puertorriqueños, enfrentados a la necesidad de oponer su hispanismo a la creciente influencia norteamericana en la isla, la figura del poeta de América hispana les resultaba particularmente útil y valiosa.

Luis Alberto Sánchez, quién pesquisó detalladamente las diversas alternativas de la visita en las crónicas de los periódicos puertorriqueños del día, ha dejado en el capítulo "Puerto Rico frente al imperialismo y con España" de su libro *Aladino* (pp. 286-341) una bastante clara interpretación de lo que esas pocas semanas de fines de 1913 significaron para el poeta y para los puertorriqueños que lo tuvieron entre ellos y lo oyeron en varias ocasiones recitar sus entusiastas poemas enaltecedores del continente y dar fervorosos discursos políticos panamericanistas.

Otra fuente de información —bastante menos objetiva— sobre la presencia e influjo de Chocano en Puerto Rico la ofrece un volumen producido en 1914, poco después de cumplida la visita, y reeditado en parte y sin gran cuidado crítico en 1967. Se trata, en el primer caso, del volumen *Puerto Rico lírico y otros poemas*, que presenta, con prólogo de Luis Llorens Torres, una selección de quince poemas de Chocano sobre Puerto Rico, seguida de varios poemas de colecciones anteriores; y en el segundo, del volumen *Puerto Rico lírico*, producido por varios colaboradores bajo el sello editorial de la Academia de Artes y Ciencias de Puerto Rico. Incluye este último el prólogo original de Llorens Torres y las quince composiciones líricas de Chocano sobre Puerto Rico, así como varios textos de escritores y críticos puertorriqueños relacionados con la estadía y la obra de Chocano en la isla.

A diferencia de otros libros de Chocano, *Puerto Rico lírico y otros poemas* no parece ser resultado de su propia iniciativa, sino de la de quienes vieron en los poemas que escribiera durante su estadía en la isla una oportunidad de fomentar y propagar el nacionalismo independentista puertorriqueño al influjo de las fuertes tendencias hispanoamericanistas del momento en el resto de las naciones del continente. En su introducción al volumen Luis Llorens Torres alude a la decisión de Chocano de dejar que los poemas se publicaran como libro en Puerto Rico mismo y le atribuye a tal decisión una motivación quizás exagerada, pero del todo acorde con los objetivos políticos de quienes aceptaron el obsequio:

> Asombrado ante un palpable progreso que el poeta no había visto en España ni en ninguna república hispanoamericana, conmovido ante las bellezas naturales de esta isla tropical, y feliz en el amor de nuestro pueblo devoto del arte, Chocano dio a Puerto Rico lo que hasta ahora sólo le había dado a su gran patria América; nos dio un libro, este libro de bellísimas poesías. (14)

El mismo Llorens Torres hace explícito el valor político del libro al indicar en su nota de la *Revista de las Antillas* cómo los poemas que Chocano le dedicó a la isla le valdrían a ésta reconocimiento universal como patria hispanoamericana:

> Pero el poeta hizo todavía mucho más: algo que le vale hoy y le valdrá siempre la gratitud de todo buen puertorriqueño. Cantó las bellezas de esta tierra: de su cielo, de su mar, de sus campos, de sus ciudades y de sus recuerdos históricos. Las cantó como ningún otro poeta lo había hecho. Su libro titulado *Puerto Rico lírico y otros poemas*, que acaba de editarse en los talleres de la *Revista [de las Antillas]* es la más bella, la más alta y la más noble expresión de cuanto es bella y noble y poética esta isla de Puerto Rico. Este libro recorrerá todos los países de habla castellana y a todas partes llevará el nombre de nuestra isla y la fama de su belleza y su cultura. Más alto exponente no lo hemos tenido hasta hoy. ("Vendimia" 90)

Idéntica decisión hicieron los intelectuales puertorriqueños al publicar los poemas de Chocano en el volumen aptamente titulado *Puerto Rico lírico*. Les bastaba que la voz del poeta admirado dijera en sus versos, siempre efectivos en sus ritmos e imágenes, las bellezas naturales de la isla. En el canto personalísimo de quien había hecho de América su fuente de inspiración se enaltecía el lugar propio, ganando así, en comparación con el resto del continente, su identidad hispanoamericana. "En la lista de obras del inmortal poeta, debajo del sugestivo título *Alma América*, se leerá siempre este otro no menos sugestivo: *Puerto Rico lírico*" (Llorens 14) escribe Llorens Torres al final de su prólogo al libro, subrayando la inclusión de la isla en el mundo iberoamericano. Malamente podía haberse imaginado el entusiasta admirador del "poeta de América" que, por lo que a éste respecta, su predicción no había de cumplirse, ya que Chocano nunca incluyó el libro puertorriqueño en la lista de sus obras. En efecto, para él la colección no tuvo carácter de libro independiente; en obras posteriores incluye los poemas de la misma como parte de otros grupos de poemas y excluye el volumen puertorriqueño de la lista de sus obras publicadas (Sánchez 308).

Los textos líricos dedicados a Puerto Rico —no tan bellos para un oído menos subjetivo y retórico que el de Llorens Torres— debió componerlos (al menos trece de ellos, según Sánchez [308]) en la isla, a medida que los iba incluyendo en sus recitales públicos. Para el recital final del 7 de diciembre en el Teatro Municipal de San Juan se anuncia en los diarios, como un modo de atraer público a la función, la inclusión de siete de los textos que más tarde formarían parte de la colección de 1914:

> "Por los canales", descripción de los caños de Hato Rey; "Cielo estrellado", una noche en Ponce; "Tramontando", impresión de la niebla en Cayey; "Tarde antillana", sobre los campos de Mayagüez; "Bajo las palmas", evocación de las palmas de Santurce; "Campanas matinales", sobre la Iglesia de Santa Ana de San Juan; "Playa caribe", sobre la Boca de Cangrejos en Isla Verde, y "Ojos tropicales", dedicado a la mujer puertorriqueña . . . El programa —concluye irónicamente Sánchez— era un abre-boca nacional. Apetitoso sin duda. Poeta-empresario, Chocano se sabía de memoria los temas capaces de avivar el sentimiento y despertar la curiosidad y el entusiasmo de los públicos. (294)

Nada más de acuerdo con las características creativas de Chocano que escribir al correr de la pluma y al dictado inmediato de las circunstancias. Sus textos puertorriqueños son modelo de tal capacidad creativa, virtud o defecto de un poeta que conoció el éxito total y el total olvido, manifestaciones inequívocas de la reacción del público ante el carácter circunstancial y adocenado de tanto verso oportunista. Escritos con la certeza y desenfado de quien conoce demasiado bien su oficio, los poemas de Puerto Rico responden a los patrones comunes de la lírica de Chocano y, por lo mismo, consiguieron en su momento el efecto para el que los escribió: despertar en el público borinqueño un sentimiento de exaltación nacionalista.

Quienes oyeron a Chocano recitar por primera vez en los escenarios de la isla sus versos a la ciudad de San Juan y a los paisajes borinqueños pudieron reconocerlos inmediatamente como textos característicos del poeta de América y debieron sentir el flujo poderoso del orgullo patrio al saber que la misma voz que había cantado las grandezas de los parajes más soberbios del continente cantaba también las bellezas de ese paisaje nacional que un crítico supone habrá defraudado al poeta de los Andes majestuosos y las magníficas selvas tropicales: "En nuestra tierra sólo le esperaba el candor majestuoso de los cielos azules, unas montañas encintadas por la lejana humedad de la anochecida y las rubias arenas del litoral puertorriqueño" (Belaval 57).

No necesitó Chocano hacer poesía heroica en Puerto Rico. Dejó para los discursos la retórica del decir político y en el verso prodigó la función lírica —puro sentimentalismo—, que se prestaba mejor para sus efusiones expresivas del espíritu americanista que Puerto Rico reclamaba como necesario para su liberación.

La breve introducción que el poeta independentista Llorens incluye al comienzo de la colección, titulada muy significativamente "El poeta de América" (9-14), sirve de base perfecta para una lectura que valore a la colección como texto de mucho más alcance significativo que el de simple homenaje circunstancial a la isla. Leídas las composiciones en otro contexto que el de esta colección bien pueden entenderse como puramente descriptivas de una experiencia personal de viaje, carentes de todo contenido o impulso reivindicadores de una nacionalidad impedida. Leídas, en cambio, como textos escritos para la ocasión por quien representaba la unidad de raza y espíritu de Hispanoamérica, las palabras del poeta cobran importancia decisiva para la identificación de Puerto Rico como entidad cultural en una geografía política que se la arrebata: "En México, cantó a México —escribe Llorens—; en Colombia, cantó a Colombia; y en Puerto Rico, cantó a Puerto Rico. Porque en los tres países no vio más que su gran patria, América" (10).

Más explícito aún en su interpretación de la significación del verso de Chocano en Puerto Rico es Balaval, cuando escribe:

> Las campañas antillanas de nuestro José de Diego habían advertido a Hispanoamérica que el problema de conciencia que representaba Puerto Rico no se había solucionado dentro de la Pax Romana de nuestro continente. Cuando llega José Santos Chocano revive, en un largo estremecimiento poético, el problema de conciencia. (55)

Problema que el crítico parece advertir implícito en "La ciudad encantada" (17-18), poema a la ciudad de San Juan con que se abre el conjunto. Es éste el único de los quince del volumen en que se advierte cierta preocupación por la situación política de la isla: "Como todas las ciudades americanas descritas por Chocano —observa Belaval con respecto al poema—, la ciudad de Puerto Rico parece estar sujeta a un vago encantamiento, sacada de cordura, abandonada a un destino de perpetuo embrujamiento" (59). La referencia es, como el poema, oblicua; como es oblicua también la promesa de esa "tierna profesía de redención" que el crítico lee en la estrofa novena:

> Entre tu encantamiento silencioso
> Que el temblor de la luna envuelve en chales
> ¿No oyes gritos que enturbian tu reposo?
> ¿No ves sombras que inquietan tus cristales? (vv. 33-36)

y en la duodécima:

> Y yo sé que en tu mar tiembla un balido
> Que es angustioso afán de un derrotero:
>
> Cada copo de espuma retorcido
> Es tal vez un vellón de tu cordero . . . (vv. 45-48)

Coincide esta lectura optimista del puertorriqueño con la visión política que Chocano tiene de la condición presente y del desarrollo futuro de la isla, y que hace explícita en su discurso del banquete de despedida del 4 de diciembre (99-104) y en su conferencia del 25 del mismo mes organizada por la Biblioteca Insular de San Juan y leída en la Cámara de Delegados:

> Un millón doscientas mil almas que, hace quince años, fueron legadas a los dominios de Estados Unidos del Norte de América, han permanecido vigorosamente distintas de sus dominadores; aún reconocida la potencialidad de éstos, que, en las reservas de sus criterios, tendrán que conformarse con ser, pese a Washington y a Franklin y a Cleveland, dueños ocasionales del territorio de Puerto Rico, pero no de su espíritu nacional. (101)

Es ese espíritu nacional que perdura el que la lírica de Chocano promueve. Como lo afirma Cesáreo Rosa-Nieves, con la "presencia de Chocano en la isla, se reafirman poderosamente en la conciencia borincana [los] temas vernáculos"; y a partir de entonces los poetas puertorriqueños "empiezan a cantarle a la patria" (80). Por eso puede el crítico añadirle otra virtud al regalo que el poeta le dejó a la isla: "Nos regaló el poeta un libro de versos, una lírica influencia hacia lo aborigen que despertó a las arpas nativas hacia los temarios isleños: historia, naturaleza, política" (82). Ya el mismo Chocano les había dicho en su discurso a los poetas borincanos que la poesía americana "debe enseñarnos a amar la tierra" (102).

La colección que sustenta la admiración de los intelectuales de la isla es, sin embargo, pobre en originalidad, incluso para Chocano, a quien no le faltaban capacidades en el arte de las imágenes y la versificación. Salvo por lo que los poemas tienen de descriptivo de Puerto Rico, que fue causa suficiente para que se los admirara en años próximos al 98, nada hay en ellos que indiquen una sensibilidad del poeta a la circunstancia política de Puerto Rico, tan diferente a la de otras naciones hiapanoamericanas. Como el soneto escrito en Arecibo a causa de la muerte del poeta Vicente Palés y Anés, sucedida casi en el mismo escenario donde Chocano recitó sus poemas, los textos de *Puerto Rico lírico* carecen de convicción, son claramente composiciones de circunstancia, fórmulas sin mayor interés en una profundización poética.

No sorprende, sin embargo, que cincuenta años después de la visita de 1913, se reedite en Puerto Rico la serie de poemas que Chocano escribió sin mayor esfuerzo en sus días de exitosa estadía en la isla y se diga de ellos que no fueron "trabajo de ocasión, halago de viajero, breve sonar de la cítara dentro del tedio de las celebraciones" (61) porque para el lector puertorriqueño, necesitado de reafirmar continuamente su identidad cultural hispánica, los poemas de Chocano dedicados a la isla "encajan todos dentro de la poesía, que con gran solemnidad, y sujeta al plan de hacer un libro completo de una América largamente amada, escribía Santos Chocano" (61). Así, medio siglo después de esa visita "dinámica y fructífera en recitaciones, banquetes, veladas literarias y amores relámpagos de tipo platónico" (77), Puerto Rico recuerda todavía, con evidentes resabios de ese nacionalismo iberoamericanista de comienzos de siglo, la impronta que el poeta de América —olvidado ya casi del todo por el resto del continente que ensalzó— dejó entre los poetas puertorriqueños de un primer período de afirmación poética del espíritu nacional amenazado por la dominación geográfica de Norteamérica. "Puertorriqueños: amad a Puerto Rico" (100) fueron las palabras de despedida del cantor de la unidad hispanoamericana. Lo mismo dicen esos quince breves poemas que se perpetúan en la edición y reedición de *Puerto Rico lírico*.

Bibliografía consultada

Chocano, José Santos. *Puerto Rico lírico*. San Juan, P.R.: Academia de Artes y Ciencias de Puerto Rico. Cuaderno Núm. 2, 1967.

Escajadillo, Tomás G. "Las mil y una aventuras de Chocano". Prólogo a: *José Santos Chocano. Antología poética*. Lima: Editorial Universo, 1972; sin número de páginas.

Llorens Torres, Luis (Luis de Puerto Rico). "Vendimia Literaria". En *Puerto Rico lírico*, 89-90.

Rodríguez-Peralta, Phyllis W. *José Santos Chocano*. New York: Twayne, 1970.

_____. *Tres poetas cumbres en la poesía peruana: Chocano, Eguren y Vallejo*. Madrid, 1983.

Sánchez, Luis Alberto. *Aladino, o vida y obra de José Santos Chocano*. México: Libro Mex Editores, 1960.

Dialéctica histórica
EN EL TEATRO DEL PUERTORRIQUEÑO MANUEL MÉNDEZ BALLESTER

L. Teresa Valdivieso
ARIZONA STATE UNIVERSITY

> "Ayer pasé todo el día con los anteojos en las manos.... Desde Punta Borinquén hasta Punta Ponce, todo lo vi, lo miré, lo remiré, lo bendije y lo sentí.... Pensaba en lo noble que hubiera sido verla libre por su esfuerzo, y no lo triste y abrumador y vergonzoso que es verla salir de dueño en dueño sin jamás serlo de sí misma".
> —Eugenio de Hostos

Hasta ahora la crítica teatral no se ha ocupado mucho del dramaturgo puertorriqueño Manuel Méndez Ballester. Nacido en 1909 es uno de los dramaturgos más fecundos y firmes. Con su primer drama, *El clamor de los surcos* de 1930, galardonada con el premio Ateneo 1938, empieza Méndez Ballester a ahondar en la problemática insular. Más tarde en 1940 nos ofrece *Tiempo muerto* a la que la crítica ha valorado como una de las obras de más calidad hasta su momento, en el sentido que representa la tragedia puertorriqueña, se elimina el concepto heroico del hombre y se nos revela como producto de un sistema no sólo explotador sino deshumanizado. A este drama le siguen otros muchos, tales como *Nuestros Días*, *Encrucijada*, *Arriba las mujeres* y otros más. En 1970, en el Décimotercer Festival de Teatro Puertorriqueño, sube a las tablas el drama objeto de este estudio, *La invasión*, y en 1988 su tenacidad y vocación de dramaturgo hacen que vea la luz otro nuevo drama *Tambores en el Caribe* en donde se funden los temas políticos, sociales, lingüísticos y culturales (Babín 26).

Resulta interesante comprobar que en la obra de Méndez Ballester, a pesar de escribir hacia la segunda mitad del siglo XX y, por consiguiente, caminar por líneas dramáticas tan diferentes a las prototípicas del primer tercio de siglo, haya tantas coincidencias a la hora de expresar sus esperanzas e inquietudes con respecto a Puerto Rico.

En efecto, si la dramaturgia puertorriqueña de principios de siglo recogía la figura de un puertorriqueño plagado de interrogantes y nacido en medio del desgaje político de España, Méndez Ballester enfoca ese mismo desgaje para ofrecernos una obra como *La invasión* en donde se presenta la visión fría del desastre del 98. En ambas sagas de dramaturgos se revela el cambio de estructuras ideológicas, económicas y sociales, pero en Méndez Ballester se aprecia un buceo íntimo al tratar la Guerra Hispanoamericana de 1898.

Espléndido y terrible surge el drama *La invasión*. Drama de corte histórico en donde el dramaturgo nos lleva en viaje imaginario a los tiempos transcurridos de 1898 y una vez allí, colocados en el espacio escénico, Méndez Ballester despliega la visión que le brinda la historia, con objetividad, sin abandonar nunca el arte dramático para convertir su obra en panfleto político y, como tal, inverosímil. Y es ahí donde se revela el dominio que posee este dramaturgo a nivel de creación teatral porque si bien es verdad que la imaginación histórica se esfuerza por revivir lo que ya ha desaparecido, no lo es en el caso de Puerto Rico, ya que la huella de la historia está allí, totalmente viva.

Y llegados aquí nos preguntamos, ¿es este drama actualización histórica o documento? Ciertamente que los acontecimientos de la Guerra Hispanoamericana figuran en la diégesis de la obra, cierto también que algunos de los personajes y de los hechos han sido arrancados de páginas de la historia: el doctor Henna, Theodore Roosevelt, el general Miles, el presidente McKinley, la revolución de Lares, la plaza de Ponce; sin embargo, se carece del dato comprobable, del testigo, las cartas, las conversaciones, los periódicos. Mas, no obstante esa carencia, sostenemos como hipótesis que el drama *La invasión* de Manuel Méndez Ballester no es otra cosa que un reclamo simbólico contra la *desmemoria*, es decir, lo que se pretende es revivir la conciencia colectiva, rescatar los hechos del olvido. Por consiguiente, el dramaturgo se convierte en historiador que cuenta a los demás lo que todo el mundo necesita saber; en este caso, lo ocurrido aquel 21 de abril en el que dio comienzo la Guerra Hispanoamericana, el 12 de mayo cuando San Juan de Puerto Rico fue bombardeado por la escuadra norteamericana, el 25 de julio cuando se inicia la invasión por Guánica y el 18 de octubre cuando se hace entrega oficial de la isla, como botín de guerra, a los Estados Unidos.

Méndez Ballester concuerda con Benedetto Croce en que el historiador no es juez, ni le asisten razones morales para condenar a sus antepasados, los cuales pertenecen a la paz del pretérito; por lo tanto, no emite juicios, simplemente permite en su creación que unas criaturas, puertorriqueñas en su mayoría, se suban al tabladillo, se instalen en el presente del drama y restituyan la vida a unas efemérides que nadie debe olvidar.

La obra comienza a *medias res* en el sentido de que no se nos dice el porqué del descontento de los puertorriqueños frente a España, no se mencionan palabras como las de un Eugenio de Hostos cuando decía: "España no ha cumplido con América los fines que debió cumplir, y una tras otra las colonias del Continente se emanciparon de su yugo. La historia no culpará a las colonias" (cit. en Carreras 20). Y surge la pregunta inminente, ¿qué debía España a las Antillas? Dejemos que sea el mismo Hostos el que nos dé la respuesta: "Les debe los sacrificios pecuniarios para ayudar a la guerra de Africa; les debe el dinero con que se hizo la guerra de Santo Domingo, les debe, sobre todo, la mansedumbre de tres siglos de paciencia con que han esperado la libertad que necesitaban" (cit. en Carreras 21).

En unos breves apuntes, precisamente sobre Hostos, se refiere que estando éste en Nueva York un lunes, el 18 de julio de 1898, se entera por la última edición de *The New York Herald* que el general Miles salía de Cuba para Puerto Rico con tres mil hombres, y que el general Brook partiría el miércoles siguiente de Newport News con el resto de las tropas, para la invasión de la isla de Puerto Rico. Y el 25 de julio de ese fatídico 1898 desembarcaba el ejército norteamericano en Guánica. La invasión se había consumado. Aquí comienza el drama de Manuel Méndez Ballester y, como si el tiempo se hubiera detenido y la historia se repitiera circularmente, los personajes de la obra *La invasión*, como paralizados, contemplan el desembarco norteamericano como en el pasado contemplaron el hispánico (Montes 112).

La obra está dividida en dos actos y tiene como escenario la sala de una hacienda del siglo XIX, residencia de una antigua y rica familia de agricultores criollos. En ella viven Pijuán Bermúdez y su hermana Lupe con su hijo Diego. Pijuán y Lupe ya no son jóvenes, ya han recorrido la mitad de su vida. Y en la descripción de ese escenario radica el primer acierto del dramaturgo. En el reino de las imágenes es fácil sensibilizar cuán preciosa es para estos seres la casa, una casa que siempre les había albergado, una casa de la que se desprende una esencia íntima y concreta, esencia de memorias insondables. El telón se levanta en el atardecer del 12 de agosto, han pasado diecinueve días desde que se produjo la invasión y, a partir de aquel momento, para Pijuán la casa será no sólo su refugio sino todos los refugios. Sin esa casa, Pijuán sería un ser disperso, el espacio de la casa representa en el drama el papel del espacio interior que cierra y se encierra frente a poderes extraños y violentos. Pero en la base misma de este topoanálisis debemos introducir un matiz, la casa tiene una ventana y Pijuán, protegido ya del espacio exterior y seguro de sí mismo, trata de establecer la comunicación con el exterior a través de esa ventana, desde donde se divisan a lo lejos las trincheras españolas y la cuesta del Asomante.

Pero antes de continuar quisiera destacar el indiscutible acierto dramático de Méndez Ballester al recrear en Pijuán Bermúdez el mismo adolorido sentir de Hostos cuando éste contempla Puerto Rico desde la cubierta del "Philadelphia" y pronuncia las palabras que me sirvieron de epígrafe. Y digo esto porque Pijuán, al igual que Hostos, vive a plenitud la derrota de la historia.

Siguiendo el hilo conductor del drama, el dramaturgo erige la casa de Pijuán como un lugar privilegiado a donde concurrirán otras personas en busca de refugio y amistad, cuando no de amor; así vemos como llegan Sarmiento, coronel de las fuerzas españolas; Emilio, dueño de una hacienda colindante, ahora dedicado al periodismo; Gonzalo, el más americanizado, dicen que por saber inglés; y Pola, una joven de unos treinta años, de padre español y totalmente españolizada por vivir en España la mayor parte del tiempo. Pola no comulga políticamente con Pijuán por su ideología separatista. De hecho, la puerta de la casa adentra desde el exterior, pero la ventana revela desde el interior convirtiéndose así en objeto dinámico. El dramaturgo evoca todo ese dinamismo en una sola frase: "Pijuán, intrigado, toma los gemelos de campaña y observa por la ventana" (379).

A lo largo del drama, esa ventana aparece como algo más trascendente que una simple hendidura en la pared por donde se contempla lo que está pasando afuera —los movimientos de tropas, caballos que se acercan y que desaparecen y el incendio provocado de la hacienda de Pola. En realidad, esa ventana se presenta como un hueco humano, un hueco en el alma de Pijuán, queriendo verterse hacia afuera, sobre todo al contemplar la columna de los americanos dispuestos a repechar por la cuesta del Asomante: "Deseos no me faltan. . . . Lo que me falta son los arrestos de un guerrillero. Hace treinta años cuando la revolución de Lares yo era un muchacho . . . arriesgado y valiente. Hoy tengo cuarenta y cinco, un hombre a mitad de camino, sin entusiasmo y sin ilusiones" (383).

Según Montes Huidobro, la pregunta que nos hacemos todos, incluyendo al propio dramaturgo, es ¿por qué razón los americanos invadieron la isla? La respuesta, en términos escénicos nos la da Theodore Roosevelt a quien el espectador imagina avanzando hacia las candilejas para decirnos:

> We became colonial minded . . . Our ostensible reason for entering the war had been to gain for Cuba her independence. We found ourselves however, with a far more complex problem, for we had, in addition to Cuba, Puerto Rico and Philippines. The general attitude of mind . . . was that no nation with any pretense to importance should be without colonies. . . . We decided that we, too, would be an empire. (cit. Montes 114)

Dentro de este mismo pensamiento se podría incluir la concepción ideológica del *panamericanismo* de Monroe que ocultaba la idea de someter todo el continente americano a su tutela, una cuestión tan llena de dificultades.

Técnicamente y siguiendo a Brecht, Méndez Ballester conduce al espectador, a través de los juegos dramáticos, por sendas didácticas. Así el fuego de la hacienda de Pola nos lleva a otros fuegos más aterrantes: el fuego de la guerra: "Esta guerra es como una de esas pesadillas en que sorprendemos a dos ladrones en nuestra casa, queremos gritar, pero no nos sale la voz, sino un gruñido de impotencia" (382). Si se considera la obra desde esta perspectiva, su aspecto histórico cobra una dimensión muy diferente a una simple página de la vida de las naciones porque lo que Méndez Ballester está actualizando es un tema con reflejos directos de la realidad: el problema de las relaciones entre fuerzas antagónicas de la historia, problema que definiremos como "dialéctica histórica".

En aras de esta dialéctica y ocupando un puesto medio de equilibrio inestable, figura Pijuán, quien a pesar de representar lo mejor del "ser puertorriqueño", se encuentra ahora asediado por dos fuerzas antagónicas, o sea, en el vórtice de dos fuerzas coloniales —Estados Unidos y España— y ambas representan para él soluciones inadmisibles; de tal manera, que la única solución posible surge del ideario independentista, aunque como él mismo dice: "Los guerrilleros no cuentan conmigo para nada. Nadie cuenta conmigo" (439). Lo que en realidad le sucede a este hombre es que se encuentra atrapado en un juego de esfuerzos que será conducente a una parálisis que le impide actuar, de ahí que Pijuán se erija como ejemplo de la indecisión. Este fenómeno se recalca en el parlamento con su sobrino Diego durante el segundo acto. Diego es uno de los poquísimos revolucionarios y sueña con ir a la guerra. Aqu' sigue el parlamento que sostienen:

> Diego: Las revoluciones se hacen . . . con hombres valerosos y decididos que contagian con su entusiasmo a los demás. Como hiciste tú en la revolución de Lares. . . .
>
> Pijuán: Diego, aquélla era una situación muy distinta a ésta.
>
> Diego: La misma de ahora. Acabar con el coloniaje. Me has defraudado. Has renegado de la causa en que fundaste tu vida entera. (419)

Este parlamento queda ratificado en el cuadro siguiente por medio de Pola la cual se pregunta y nos pregunta:

> ¿Qué han hecho [los puertorriqueños]? ¿qué hacen en estos momentos en que un ejército extraño ha invadido su tierra? ¿Qué han hecho? Nada. Y yo no los culpo porque vosotros, los revolucionarios de profesión, tampoco habéis hecho nada, sino hablar, hablar y hacer notas en una libreta como si estuvieseis escribiendo una novela por entregas. ¿Qué es lo que tanto escribe Pijuán?

Y contesta Diego: "Las memorias de la Guerra Hispanoamericana en Puerto Rico", a lo que Pola replica: "Ahí le tenéis con la pluma en la mano cuando debiera tener el fusil en el hombro. ¡Ahí tenéis al guerrillero de papel!" (419).

Tales son los arriesgados principios sobre los que Méndez Ballester ha asentado su drama, arriesgados porque el dramaturgo ha transformado el concepto de lo dramático, concepto que ya no es un conflicto entre individualidades, el antagonismo no se da entre personas, sino que es centrípeto, del personaje hacia sí mismo y, a la vez, eminentemente trágico, es decir del personaje hacia aquello que le excede, hacia las fuerzas exteriores e interiores que lo presionan; es decir, para Pijuán Bermúdez, su suplicio de Tántalo es saber, entender, agonizar viendo la situación de su Puerto Rico y ser incapaz de resolver nada.

El cuadro cuarto del segundo acto recoge el final de la guerra con el bochornoso armisticio de París y el último cuadro cierra el círculo cuando vemos que Pijuán sigue mirando por la ventana y observando, no ya las trincheras españolas y la cuesta del Asomante, sino cómo los soldados americanos celebran su victoria con una gran borrachera, mientras que los españoles celebran su velorio. Pijuán ve que el pueblo entero está en la calle celebrándolo. Y no sólo Pijuán, Emilio, el periodista, también capta ese espacio exterior a través de la ventana y al ver cuán pronto los puertorriqueños se han pasado al bando norteamericano exclama: "¡Qué comedia! ¡Qué comedia divertida! A los puertorriqueños nos ha sucedido lo que a la prostituta de Coamo... que se acostó con un guardia civil y amaneció con un soldado americano" (446).

Esta construcción circular obliga a una precisa identificación de cuantos intervienen en la trama. Existe una especie de determinismo que inserta por necesidad y conscientemente a las criaturas escénicas en las condiciones sociales de ese momento histórico; y así, la indecisión que se trasluce en el protagonista Pijuán no es más que su condición de frustrado. El porqué de esa frustración viene determinado por las circunstancias históricas de Puerto Rico en donde a pesar de ciertos síntomas saludables, una especie de nihilismo hace que éstos se desvanezcan.

Ahora bien, la frustración creada por el dramaturgo no es tampoco una cortina de niebla que envuelva a todas sus criaturas, existe una esperanza, casi un horizonte ilusorio, una posibilidad abierta, un nuevo fervor caracterizado por Diego, cuando éste renuncia a volver a los Estados Unidos para seguir sus estudios porque como él mismo dice, "se [le] caería a pedazos la cara de vergüenza" (437); de ahí que opte por alistarse en la milicia de guerrilleros. Se adivina en el dramaturgo un ansia de buscar resortes ocultos que resuelvan la situación, o quizá, un ansia de patentizar el contraste entre la acción —Diego— y la parálisis —Pijuán. Sin embargo, el pesimismo radical que flota en el ambiente anula la existencia de esos resortes que se pretende descubrir y lo único que persiste es la unificación de los contrarios: lo que fue y lo que hubiera podido ser si todos los Pijuán hubiesen despertado a la acción.

La orografía de la superficie que hemos llamado histórica deja en la pieza suficientes marcas que reconocen la imagen de la derrota. La escena final es una durísima imagen que hace contrastar el entusiasmo de Diego y los contados revolucionarios que lo acompañan, y la frustración que se despliega en la materialidad del horizonte dramático. De tal manera, que las palabras de Lupe, la madre de Diego, reflexionando sobre la decisión de su hijo de lanzarse a la lucha, resuenan en el escenario.

Obras citadas

Babín, María Teresa. "Teatro de nuestro tiempo". En *Los cocorocos* y *Tambores en el Caribe*. Tomo 1 de *Teatro de Manuel Méndez Ballester. 1938-1966 Medio siglo de teatro puertorriqueño*, ed. Instituto de Cultura Puertorriqueña, 23-26. San Juan, PR: División de Publicaciones y Grabaciones, 1991.

Carreras, Carlos N. *Hostos, apóstol de la libertad*. San Juan, PR: Editorial Cordillera, 1971.

Maldonado-Denis, Manuel. *Puerto Rico. Una interpretación histórico-social*. México, DF: Siglo Veintiuno Editores, 1980.

Méndez Ballester, Manuel. *La invasión*. Tomo 1 de *Teatro de Manuel Méndez Ballester. 1938-1988 Medio siglo de teatro puertorriqueño*. Ed. Instituto de Cultura Puertorriqueña, 375-452. San Juan, PR: División de Publicaciones y Grabaciones, 1991.

Montes Huidobro, Matías. *Persona: vida y máscara en el teatro puertorriqueño*. San Juan, PR: Centro de Estudios Avanzados de Puerto Rico, 1984.

La hispanidad amenazada
RUBÉN DARÍO Y LA GUERRA DEL 98

Alberto Acereda

ARIZONA STATE UNIVERSITY

La guerra de 1898 entre España y los Estados Unidos de América del Norte representó políticamente el fin de las colonias peninsulares. Culturalmente supuso una amenaza para el concepto de hispanidad, con todas las connotaciones de comunidad lingüística y cultural pertenecientes a él. Así, al menos, lo vieron algunos de los poetas hispánicos del fin de siglo pasado y de forma muy especial, Rubén Darío (1867-1916), padre del fundamental movimiento estético-literario hispanoamericano denominado "Modernismo" y uno de los autores más importantes en el desarrollo de la literatura en lengua española.

Este trabajo abordará varias de las ideas sociales y políticas que en torno a la Guerra del 98 fue elaborando Darío como poeta y como periodista: como lírico, en algunos de sus libros más importantes publicados antes y después de 1898 y como prosista en sus crónicas literarias y textos enviados al diario *La Nación* de Buenos Aires. El análisis diacrónico y detenido de algunos de estos textos de Darío permitirá establecer algunas ideas sobre la visión que hace cien años se tuvo del llamado "desastre colonial". Desde tal perspectiva se extraerán ciertas reflexiones sobre el concepto aquí denominado "la hispanidad amenazada" y su recurrencia como tema y preocupación de los pueblos hispánicos frente al creciente imperio norteamericano. El tema de "la hispanidad amenazada" en relación con la Guerra del 98 a la luz del pensamiento y la poética de Darío está todavía por estudiar de forma completa, ya que la crítica se ha venido centrando con mayor exclusividad en otros autores más comprometidos de la época, como ocurre con la prosa ensayística del uruguayo José Enrique Rodó o las crónicas del cubano José Martí, por ejemplo, quienes fueron, además, amigos de Darío. En la singularidad del tema radica el posible interés de este trabajo y en la viabilidad de extraer también una dimensión artística dentro del marco de unos ideales étnicos noblemente comprometidos en favor del mestizaje de la raza hispánica.

Darío y la hispanidad

En las últimas décadas del siglo XIX los Estados Unidos de América experimentaron una pujanza política que llenó de temor al mundo hispánico y que concluyó con la derrota de España. Darío no estuvo ajeno a este problema, del que años después escribió Pedro Salinas:

> Problema agónico, también de vida o muerte, de desaparición o supervivencia, el mayor que les salía al paso a esos pueblos desde la Independencia, Darío, alma nunca estrecha, avara ni mezquina, vivió esta experiencia gigantesca de él y de los suyos, en algunas de sus más célebres poesías. Lo vivió en toda su dimensión, en sus alternativas, con dramáticos altibajos, exaltado ahora, desalentado después,

auscultando como oído que se pega a un cuerpo, todos los arrítmicos pálpitos de
la gran hermandad consciente hispana. (230-31)

La bibliografía dedicada al aspecto político de Darío es tan extensa como desigual. Destacan los trabajos de Salinas, de la Torre, Oliver Belmás, Torres-Rioseco, Anderson Imbert, Ancona Ponce, Edelberto Torres y Gómez Espinosa, por citar sólo algunos.[1] En muchos casos los críticos extraen conclusiones a partir del estudio de determinadas parcelas de la producción o de la biografía del nicaragüense. Interesa, sin embargo, estudiar la actitud política de Darío desde un sentido trágico porque muchas veces sus versos han sido vergonzantemente utilizados para fines parciales. Desde alguna antología de poesía marxista rubendariana hasta algún artículo presentando a un Darío favorable a la causa franquista, no han sido pocos quienes han utilizado la obra y el nombre del nicaragüense para ciertos propósitos politizantes. Es verdad que Darío nunca fue, estrictamente hablando, un pensador político y no tuvo un programa ideológico concreto. Gustó de sus cargos diplomáticos más como fuente económica, y no excesiva, que política. En este sentido, Vargas Vila afirmó de Darío que "tenía el horror de la política" (82). También es cierto que no fue precisamente su vida pública y privada un modelo de rigor y lo mismo cabría esperar de su ideología. Sin embargo, es inaceptable que sus textos poéticos de inspiración política e histórica sean, como afirma Octavio Paz, "textos para ser leídos en la tribuna, ante un auditorio de fiesta cívica" (55). Este mayor contenido declamatorio que riguroso sugerido por Paz para los poemas políticos del nicaragüense se explica, según el mismo crítico, porque en ellos Darío "tiene poco que decir y su pobreza se reviste de oropel... Los poemas de Darío carecen de sustancia: suelo, pueblo" (55). Una mirada atenta al sentido de los escritos rubendarianos revela, sin duda, al hombre que sintió profundamente la trágica angustia del ocaso hispánico, al individuo conmocionado y dolorido. Por su condición de incansable viajero y empedernido bohemio se ha dicho a menudo de Darío que no sintió realmente su mezcla de raíz hispana e indígena.[2] Hacia el final de su vida, el propio Darío confesó en *Historia de mis libros*: "En el fondo de mi espíritu, a pesar de mis visitas cosmopolitas, existe el inarrancable filón de la raza; mi pensar y mi sentir continúan un proceso histórico y tradicional" (210). Por ello, su pensamiento no es contradictorio, sino más bien, complejo. De lo que no hay duda, sin embargo, es de que Darío prefirió la poesía a la política; su literatura no se estrecha nunca por los márgenes del activismo político o el compromiso social. En palabras de Darío: "las plantas *trepadoras* conversan de política / las rosas y los lirios, del arte y del amor" (559, vv. 11-12),[3] dice en "Del campo". (El subrayado es mío; irónico equívoco el de Darío). Ese complejo carácter del pensamiento dariano político se comprueba mejor, en el ámbito de la producción poética dariana, desde una perspectiva diacrónica.

En sus primeros años, cabe buscar en el joven Darío la influencia del coronel Félix Ramírez, pues de él pudo llegarle la preocupación política, liberal, progresista y hasta revolucionaria. Ya en la primera parte de la década de 1880, con apenas quince años, Darío escribe varios poemas en favor de la unión centroamericana de las cinco repúblicas, ideas que luego llevará a las editoriales y artículos de opinión de algunos diarios como *El Correo de la Tarde* y en textos como los enmarcados en "El poeta civil", con varias composiciones apoyando la causa anexionista. Con tan sólo dieciocho años el joven Darío escribe el largo poema "El porvenir", en cuyo último verso expresa su esperanza en el futuro de la América hispánica: "¡América es el porvenir del mundo!" (387, parte IX, v. 17). En 1889 Darío fue director del periódico *La Unión* de Nicaragua, órgano de los unionistas centroamericanos y en cuya redacción se debieron tratar en varias ocasiones temas políticos. En octubre de ese mismo año Darío leyó el poema titulado, precisamente, "Unión Centro-americana". Tres años después, en 1892, Darío visitó España como enviado de *La Nación* de Buenos Aires para las fiestas del cuarto Centenario. Allí pudo respirar cierto ambiente de desencanto en el pueblo español y sus dirigentes.[4] En su *Autobiografía* Darío habla de la visita a España y recuerda su conversación con Emilio Castelar en estos términos: "Tengo presente que me habló de diferentes cosas referentes a América: de la futura influencia de los Estados Unidos sobre nuestras Repúblicas" (113). Seis años después de esa conversación, en 1898, España perdió, por la llamada Guerra de Cuba, sus últimas colonias. El fin del antiguo imperio español engendró en Darío un sentimiento que constituye el primer embrión de su tragedia política. Uno de los biógrafos de Darío, Oliver Belmás, afirma: "Es en 1898 cuando Darío cambia de actitud. La voladura del 'Maine', la intervención militar contra España y la derrota de los españoles le provocan reacciones antiyanquis" (570). Efectivamente, en su conciencia del mestizaje hispanoamericano Darío fue consciente de la nueva era que se iniciaba políticamente y que bajo el imperio norteamericano representaba una amenaza a la hispanidad. Sus poemarios son testimonio de ello, como se comprobará a continuación.

Hispanidad y literatura

Los libros poéticos que anteceden a la fecha clave de 1898, *Azul...* y *Prosas profanas y otros poemas* sobre todo, no dan, como era de esperar, demasiados indicios de un sentido de desengaño en el poeta. 1898 todavía no ha llegado, pero Darío deja entrever ya algunas ideas. Así, por ejemplo, uno de los sonetos de *Azul...*, el titulado "Caupolicán" en honor del héroe araucano, representa muy bien el tema del heroísmo y la exaltación de la raza autóctona del valle chileno, pero en él no hay lugar para la tragedia. Otro soneto del mismo volumen, el medallón "Walt Whitman", es un reconocimiento de admiración al poeta norteamericano; sin embargo, la influencia real de Whitman sobre Darío es mucho menor de lo que hasta ahora se ha venido sugiriendo, como ya demostró Derusha. Para éste la imagen de Whitman en Darío está arraigada más en un ideal juvenil de admiración heroica y modernista que en los escritos de Martí Sarrazín y Mayorga Rivas sobre el poeta norteamericano.[5]

Unos años después, ya en *Prosas profanas,* se anuncia algo de lo que vendrá después de forma más consolidada en *Cantos de vida y esperanza*. En las "Palabras liminares" de *Prosas profanas* Darío afirma: "Si hay poesía en nuestra América, ella está en las cosas viejas: en Palenke y Utatlán, en el indio legendario y el inca sensual y fino, y en el gran Moctezuma de la silla de oro. Lo demás es tuyo, demócrata Walt Whitman" (546). Darío opone la grandeza de la imperial sangre india a la vulgaridad del presidente y la cultura democrática. En *Historia de mis libros* repite una idea parecida: "Mas abominando la democracia funesta a los poetas, así sean sus adoradores como Walt Whitman, tendí hacia el pasado, a las antiguas mitologías y a las espléndidas historias" (209). Los términos de asco y espanto con que Darío califica también en esa misma exégesis la situación de su Nicaragua natal, y con ella de toda Hispanoamérica, nos dan ya una clave para vislumbrar su tragedia interior. Textualmente dice al comentar *Prosas profanas*: "Asqueado y espantado de la vida social y política en que mantuviera a mi país original un lamentable estado de civilización embrionario, no mejor en tierras vecinas, fue para mí un magnífico refugio la República Argentina" (209). Precisamente en Buenos Aires tendrá oportunidad de desarrollar sus facultades de artista y poeta, y así se explica en parte el gran amor de Darío por la

Argentina, amor expresado en el *Canto a la Argentina*. Ese lamentable estado de los pueblos hispanoamericanos está muy bien expresado por Darío en un poema de fines de 1892, "A Colón", incluido quince años después en el volumen *El canto errante*. "A Colón" revela ya el Darío escéptico ante el futuro de los pueblos hispanoamericanos. En sus versos se halla la queja dolorida:

> Un desastroso espíritu posee tu tierra:
> donde la tribu unida blandió sus mazas,
> hoy se enciende entre hermanos perpetua guerra,
> se hieren y destrozan las mismas razas. (703, vv. 5-8)

La desolada visión de los hispanoamericanos llega al final del poema: "Duelos, espantos, guerras, fiebre constante / en nuestra senda ha puesto la suerte triste" (704, vv. 53-54).

Volviendo a *Prosas profanas*, Darío elogia el pasado histórico y legendario de España en "Cosas del Cid", pero no se halla ninguna visión trágica ahí. Otro poema, "El país del Sol", está dedicado a una artista cubana y escrito al parecer durante la estancia del poeta en Nueva York en 1893. Todo él es un consejo de Darío a la artista para que regrese a su patria, el país del sol, la isla de Cuba, pues allí todo será más propicio a su espíritu que la dura "isla de Hierro", el Manhattan neoyorquino, horrible destierro de la muchacha. Sin embargo, estos poemas no son todavía una expresión trágica del dolor ante la hispanidad amenazada sino un adelanto de lo que vendrá después. Por eso, cuando José Enrique Rodó abrió su estudio sobre *Prosas profanas* diciendo que Darío no era el poeta de América acertó en parte. Darío está todavía gestando los poemas que constituirán su gran libro: *Cantos de vida y esperanza*. Es precisamente a partir de 1901 y hasta la publicación de ese libro en 1905 cuando Darío se acerca a una dimensión más definida, a la exaltación de la raza por vía de lo trágico, y con lo español como acervo de valores humanos, morales y culturales frente a la civilización anglosajona. Por ello precisamente, el prólogo del nuevo libro de poemas lo cierra Darío con estas palabras:

> Si en estos cantos hay política, es porque aparece universal. Y si encontráis versos a un presidente, es porque son un clamor continental. Mañana podremos ser yanquis (y es lo más probable); de todas maneras, mi protesta queda escrita sobre las alas de los inmaculados cisnes, tan ilustres como Júpiter. (626)

Con esta valiente y estética afirmación el vaticinio de Darío del inmediato dominio norteamericano se hace enérgica protesta porque Darío siente la paulatina pérdida de las señas de identidad de los pueblos hispánicos. Ese sentimiento lo confirma el mismo Darío en *Historia de mis libros*, al asegurar, refiriéndose a su libro de 1905: "Hay, como he dicho, mucho hispanismo en este libro mío" (219). Esos poemas se nutren de tragedia y dolor cuando Darío contempla justamente a esa hispanidad amenazada. En muchos de los poemas políticos de *Cantos de vida y esperanza* la obsesión por la aniquilación colectiva de lo hispánico produce en Darío una visión trágica. Darío se lanza al optimismo pero sus poemas son, en último término, más canto de dolor que de esperanza, más de muerte que de vida. Con motivo de la visita a España en marzo de 1899 del rey Óscar de Suecia, Darío publica el poema "Al rey Óscar" en *La Ilustración Española y Americana* de Madrid. El poema rebosa optimismo, pero es un optimismo causado por la inquietud del poeta ante el futuro de España y la América hispánica. Es la madre patria que acaba de perder sus colonias americanas, la España caída en el estiércol de su antigua gloria y humillada por los Estados Unidos. Por eso España es "morada que entristeció el destino" (634, v. 42). Sin embargo, emocionado por el grito de "Viva España" que el monarca lanzó al pisar territorio español, Darío busca todavía el consuelo y la alegría, y la abolición de la muerte desde "la morada que viste luto" (634, v. 43).

Cuatro años más tarde, Darío compone desde Málaga, en enero de 1904, la célebre oda "A Roosevelt". El poeta empieza por atribuirse a sí mismo la necesidad de usar un verso bíblico, o un verso de Walt Whitman. Roosevelt es cazador y así queda emparentado con Nemrod, cazador legendario y símbolo de la tiranía. Roosevelt encarna a los Estados Unidos, y dice Darío tajantemente:

> Eres los Estados Unidos,
> eres el futuro invasor
> de la América ingenua que tiene sangre indígena,
> que aún reza a Jesucristo y aún habla en español. (640, vv. 5-8)

Véase cómo, una vez más, los temas, aquí político y religioso, se complementan en la poesía de Darío.[6] Al decirle Darío a Roosevelt "te opones a Tolstoy" (640. v. 10), sentimos el contraste del humanitarismo del novelista ruso frente a la crueldad de Roosevelt. Tolstoy predicó la reforma social y en el modernismo representa el humanitarismo social ejemplificado en su propia vida al libertar a sus siervos y fundar una escuela donde él mismo enseñaba a los hijos de los antiguos siervos. Roosevelt representa, según Darío, una oposición a cualquier tipo de conciencia cívica. Funde también Darío la figura de Alejandro Magno con Nabucodonosor y después junta el don de la fuerza, Hércules, con el falso dios de la riqueza y de la avaricia, Mammón. Todo el poema, en definitiva, supone un canto contra el peligro del imperialismo norteamericano: "Los Estados Unidos son potentes y grandes. / Cuando ellos se estremecen hay un hondo temblor / que pasa por las vértebras enormes de los Andes" (640, vv. 19-21). Frente al imperio norteamericano, la otra América, la de Moctezuma, la de Colón, la católica española, la que sueña, vibra y ama. La América que no se rinde, y ante la que Darío advierte:

> Tened cuidado. ¡Vive la América española!
> Hay mil cachorros sueltos del León Español.
> Se necesitaría, Roosevelt, ser, por Dios mismo,
> el Riflero terrible y el fuerte Cazador,
> para poder tenernos en vuestras férreas garras. (641, vv. 45-49)

Y, al final, con despecho, Darío quiere creer que la condición católica hispana supone una amenaza más, si cabe, a la integridad anglosajona. A la vez, hay un orgullo de religiosidad trascendente de los pueblos hispánicos frente al pragmatismo norteamericano: "Y, pues contáis con todo, falta una cosa: ¡Dios!" (641, v. 50). En este final la fe católica adquiere categoría de arma política.

Todo el poema evidencia una actitud política frente a la amenaza anglosajona, como lo reconoce Darío en *Historia de mis libros*: "En 'A Roosevelt' se preconizaba la solidaridad del alma hispanoamericana ante las posibles tentativas imperialistas de los hombres del Norte" (220). No me parece que haya en este poema retórica, a pesar de la metáfora del león español y los cachorros hispanoamericanos. Sin embargo, eso no importa para reconocer que Darío siente hondamente estos versos. También en la oda "A Roosevelt" vuelve a aparecer la obsesión por la muerte cuando Darío relaciona la muerte con los Estados Unidos. Ellos son generadores de destrucción: "Y domando caballos o asesinando tigres" (640, v. 11). Y poco después se enfrenta a la concepción norteamericana de la vida, que representa Roosevelt: "Crees que la vida es incendio / que el progreso es erupción, / que en donde pones la bala / el porvenir pones. No" (640, vv. 15-19). La idea de cataclismo que traen los

Estados Unidos sobre Hispanoamérica se repite en la "Salutación del optimista".[7] Pedro Salinas ya vio este poema en términos de tragedia, al enfrentar Darío a hispánicos y anglosajones "en su fatal situación antagónica ... y en eso consiste lo trágico del problema" (235). Los ataques al presidente Roosevelt se repiten también en el ámbito de la prosa de esas mismas fechas. Una de las crónicas para *La Nación*, compuesta sólo unos meses después de la oda "A Roosevelt", lleva el título, insinuantemente burlesco, de "El arte de ser presidente de la República". Todo él rezuma un fino cinismo que va desde la pintura de la familia presidencial a la ridiculización de las ocupaciones de Roosevelt.[8] La inquina de Darío hacia este hombre continuó cuando ya no ocupaba el puesto de presidente. Por eso ocho años después, en la crónica "Roosevelt en París", escrita en la capital francesa e incluida en *Todo al vuelo*, Darío echa mano otra vez de un fino cinismo y se ríe de Roosevelt y aun de Francia entera por la grata acogida que le han dispensado.[9]

En la madrugada del 28 de marzo de 1905, Darío, hinchado de alcohol, parece que terminaba de escribir la hermosa "Salutación del optimista" que tenía que leer horas después en el Ateneo de Madrid. Aparte del magnífico acierto métrico de sus versos, todo el poema está concebido bajo una doble disposición ideológica. Por un lado, el elogio de lo hispánico y, por otro, la idea del poeta como vate o profeta del porvenir. Junto a ello, se percibe una crítica a los Estados Unidos. La alabanza a lo hispánico, a lo español en concreto, salpica todo el poema: "Ínclitas razas ubérrimas" (631, v. 1), "Hispania fecunda" (v. 2), "lenguas de gloria" (v.4), "vigor español" (v. 30), "la nación generosa, coronada de orgullo inmarchito" (632, v. 34), "el antiguo entusiasmo" (v. 42), "el espíritu ardiente" (v. 42), etc. El vate está presente cuando Darío propone la unión de los pueblos hispánicos:

> Únanse, brillen, secúndense, tantos vigores dispersos;
> formen todos un solo haz de energía ecuménica.
> Sangre de Hispania fecunda, sólidas ínclitas razas,
> muestren los dones pretéritos que fueron antaño su triunfo. (632, vv. 38-41)

La mirada a la muerte se une al tema de la raza y constituye otro grito ante la hispanidad amenazada. A pesar de todo, al hacer revivir las antiguas glorias pasadas, Darío contempla la muerte como algo en parte vencible, controlable: "mágicas ondas de vida van renaciendo de pronto; / retrocede el olvido, retrocede engañada la muerte" (631, vv. 5-6). Es la muerte anunciada de la hispanidad amenazada a la que se engaña porque Darío quiere y desea la revalorización de la raza, la llegada de un "reino nuevo" (631, v. 7) y la aparición de "la divina reina de luz, la celeste Esperanza" (631, v. 11). Darío identifica la vida con la unión hispánica y la muerte con la pervivencia de un mundo que desprecia lo hispánico: el anglosajón, y, especialmente, los Estados Unidos, país al que atacó casi siempre Darío. En este poema, Darío es "español de América y americano de España" (218), como él mismo reconoce en la exégesis de sus libros. La "Salutación del optimista" expresa, dice el poeta, "mi confianza y mi fe en el renacimiento de la vieja Hispania en el propio solar y del otro lado del Océano, en el coro de naciones que hacen contrapeso en la balanza sentimental a la fuerte y osada raza del Norte" (218).[10]

El primero de los poemas de la sección "Los cisnes", incluida en *Cantos de vida y esperanza*, recoge también la angustia ante la destrucción de lo hispánico por manos anglosajonas. En el poema Darío se dirige en nombre de todos los poetas al cisne, símbolo aquí portador de la esperanza y del porvenir. En el comentario de sus propios libros, Darío dijo de este poema que "por el símbolo císnico torno a ver lucir la esperanza para la raza solar nuestra" (221). Darío, desde el principio, deja clara su condición y raíz hispanoamericana: "Soy un hijo de América, soy un nieto de España..." (648, v. 11). Desde esa filiación, vuelve a expresar su desencanto en versos enormemente musicales: "Brumas septentrionales nos llenan de tristezas, / se mueren nuestras rosas, se agotan nuestras palmas, / casi no hay ilusiones para nuestras cabezas, / y somos los mendigos de nuestras pobres almas" (648, vv. 17-20). La desilusión turba a Darío y en la conciencia del ocaso de lo hispánico surge la tragedia política: "La América española como la España entera / fija está en el Oriente de su fatal destino" (649, vv. 29-30). Y en la siguiente estrofa ataca la lengua de los invasores y enfrenta la nobleza y el honor de caballeros e hidalgos a la barbarie que representan los Estados Unidos: "¿Seremos entregados a los bárbaros fieros? / ¿Tantos millones de hombres hablaremos inglés? / ¿Ya no hay nobles hidalgos ni bravos caballeros? / ¿Callaremos ahora para llorar después?" (649, vv. 33-36). Darío es, pues, consciente de la realidad de su raza, de su pueblo, el hispánico. El desengaño es patente hacia el final del poema, donde se recoge nuevamente la imagen del león, ya utilizada en la oda a Roosevelt, ahora con la connotación de fuerza, de poderío en declive; junto al león viejo español la cobardía de los países hispanoamericanos: "He lanzado mi grito, Cisnes, entre vosotros, / que habéis sido los fieles en la desilusión, / mientras siento una fuga de americanos potros / y el estertor postrero de un caduco león" (649, v. 40). Pero junto al desengaño, se halla el canto de vida, de esperanza en la última estrofa, como en la "Salutación del optimista", que surge de la caja de Pandora y que aquí pregonan dos cisnes: "...Y un Cisne negro dijo: 'La noche anuncia el día.' / Y uno blanco: '¡La aurora es inmortal, la aurora / es inmortal!' ¡Oh tierras de sol y de armonía, / aún guarda la Esperanza la caja de Pandora!" (649, vv. 41-44). La hispanofilia de Darío también se corrobora en otros poemas de *Cantos de vida y esperanza*, aunque sin alcanzar en ellos una visión hondamente trágica. En "Retratos", por ejemplo, el poeta evoca figuras del antiguo apogeo. "Trébol" es un homenaje a las glorias españolas, específicamente Góngora y Velázquez. En otro poema elogia a Francisco de Goya, y a Cervantes le dedicará una composición en la que lo presenta como fuente de alegría. "Allá lejos" es un recuerdo de paisajes tropicales y una evocación de su tierra natal nicaragüense. Por su parte, el poema "Letanía de Nuestro Señor Don Quijote", elaborado con un fino humorismo y con una meditada técnica poética, es una agria crítica a la sociedad y a la cultura de los primeros años del siglo XX, sin descartar lo español.

Con *El canto errante* (1907), el pensamiento político de Darío parece hacerse incoherente y contradictorio respecto a las ideas expuestas en los poemarios anteriores. Ya en el prefacio, "Dilucidaciones", elogia a Roosevelt por sus alabanzas a la poesía. Dice Darío: "El mayor elogio hecho recientemente a la Poesía y a los poetas ha sido expresado en lengua 'anglosajona' por un hombre insospechable de extraordinarias complacencias con las nueve Musas. Un yanqui. Se trata de Teodoro Roosevelt.... Por esto comprenderéis que el terrible cazador es un varón sensato" (691). Estas palabras de encomio se amplían a todo lo que representan los Estados Unidos en el manido poema "Salutación al Águila" del mismo volumen. El poema fue escrito en Río de Janeiro, donde Darío asistió en calidad de Secretario de la Delegación de Nicaragua a la Conferencia Panamericana celebrada en 1906.[11] El poema lleva ya el significativo subtítulo en inglés, del poeta brasileño Fontoura Xavier, "...May this grand Union have no end!" (707). Darío se dirige al águila, símbolo de los Estados Unidos, a la que da la bienvenida de parte de la América hispana:

> Bien vengas, mágica Águila de alas enormes y fuertes,
> a extender sobre el Sur tu gran sombra continental,
> a traer en tus garras, anilladas de rojos brillantes,

> una palma de gloria, del color de la inmensa esperanza,
> y en tu pico la oliva de una vasta y fecunda paz. (707, vv. 1-5)

Darío poetiza la unión de las dos Américas, la hispánica y la anglosajona, a partir del símbolo del Águila y del Cóndor: "Águila, existe el Cóndor. Es tu hermano en las grandes alturas" (709, v. 39).

Las reacciones al poema no se hicieron esperar, y no fueron pocos los escritos de desencanto e indignación por parte de los poetas amigos de Darío. El primero de ellos fue Rufino Blanco Fombona, que en una carta desde Holanda el 3 de agosto de 1907 calificó el poema de infame, y poco después (según dice la carta recogida por Alberto Ghiraldo): "¡Cómo no lo han lapidado a usted, querido Rubén! Le juro que lo merece, ¿Cómo? ¿Usted, nuestra gloria, la más alta voz de la raza hispana de América, clamando por la conquista . . . ?" (141). La "Salutación al Águila", efectivamente, choca frontalmente con todo lo que antes había dicho Darío en *Cantos de vida y esperanza*. De ahí que los comentaristas de Darío se dividen y hasta se confunden al interpretar su pensamiento político. La respuesta de Darío dos semanas después de la carta de Blanco Fombona es harto significativa: "¿Saludar nosotros al Águila, sobre todo cuando hacemos cosas diplomáticas . . . ? No tiene nada de particular. Lo cortés no quita lo Cóndor . . ." (Ghiraldo, 337). Unos meses después, en la "Epístola a la Sra. de Lugones", Darío confesaba desde Mallorca: "*Et pour cause*. Yo pan-americanicé / con un vago temor y con muy poca fe" (747, parte I, vv. 11-12). Según Francisco Contreras, biógrafo y amigo de Darío, la explicación del cambio tan brusco radicaba en el carácter débil de Darío, tímido y doblegable:

> tuvo miedo, sin duda, de haber ido demasiado lejos en su apóstrofe "A Roosevelt", y su "Salutación del optimista" . . . Darío aprovechó, pues, la ocasión de aquella Conferencia para desagraviar a la poderosa nación adversaria . . . Y cuando yo solía hablarle de esta "Salutación" manifestándole mi sorpresa y mi descontento, me replicaba invariablemente: "¡Qué quiere, amigo! Ellos son los más fuertes". (258)

Si tenemos en cuenta los dos citados comentarios del propio Darío, el dirigido en verso a la esposa de Lugones y la respuesta a la carta de Blanco Fombona, podemos concluir que la "Salutación al Águila" surgió simplemente como consecuencia del clima diplomático de la conferencia en cuestión. Son versos más de circunstancias que verdaderamente sentidos porque Darío siempre fue defensor del derecho de los pueblos pequeños frente al imperialismo de las grandes potencias. Darío perdió definitivamente su fe en la política norteamericana en 1910 cuando el presidente Taft intervino en Nicaragua y ayudó a la caída del gobierno, por lo que Darío no fue reconocido como representante de su país natal en las fiestas de la Independencia de México. De ahí surgirá el folleto político rubendariano de 1911, "Refutación al Presidente Taft".

Testimonio de la conciencia dariana ante la hispanidad amenazada es la disconformidad que mostró el nicaragüense frente a la política de los Estados Unidos, según es comprobable en otros varios artículos y crónicas. Ya en 1898, antes de que Rodó utilizase parecidas ideas en *Ariel*, Darío había escrito para *El Tiempo* de Buenos Aires el artículo "El triunfo de Calibán", que denunciaba la agresión bélica de los Estados Unidos contra España. Darío no había olvidado los abusos cometidos en Texas, Panamá, las Antillas y en Centroamérica en general y escribió: "No, no puedo, no quiero estar de parte de esos búfalos de dientes de plata. Son enemigos míos, son los aborrecedores de la sangre latina, son los Bárbaros . . . No, no puedo estar de parte de ellos, no puedo estar por el triunfo de Calibán . . ." (Anderson Imbert, 152).

Entre los escritos dispersos recogidos de periódicos porteños y editados por Pedro Luis Barcia destacan dos, compuestos desde París para *La Nación*. El primero de ellos, de fines de diciembre de 1901, lleva el título de "La invasión de los bárbaros del Norte" y cons-tituye una llamada de atención a las varias modas norteamericanas que paulatinamente se iban imponiendo en Francia. El otro artículo, "La invasión anglosajona. Centro América Yanqui", aparecido en abril de 1902, surge a raíz del convenio para la construcción del canal de Panamá. Darío afirma: "Lo que es un hecho, es que dentro de no lejano tiempo, la tierra en que he nacido . . . pasará a ser dependencia de la gran república del norte; el resto de Centro América lo será después; ya se sabe cuál es la manera pacífica de conquistar que tienen los hombres de los ferrocarriles y de los dollars" (131). Casi todo el artículo reproduce las opiniones del por entonces ex presidente de Honduras, Marco A. Soto, quien le aseguraba a Darío, entre otras cosas: "El poder económico de los Estados Unidos se hará sentir por todas partes. La América española no podrá librarse de su dominación, y menos los países centroamericanos, que están tan próximos al coloso de Norte América" (134). Las ideas de Soto debieron turbar a Darío, quien cierra su crónica lamentándose: "desaparecerá también la raza, la savia latina; la ola invasora lo destruirá todo" (135). Este y no otro es el concepto y la conciencia dariana de la hispanidad amenazada.

Final

Rubén Darío, en definitiva, despreció por completo la política imperialista norteamericana y sin embargo nunca la llegó a odiar desde el activismo político, sino que más bien la temió. En su interior, pese a todo, Darío admiró el pragmatismo y la constancia de los Estados Unidos. Elogió a sus grandes poetas, a sus hombres de ciencia, y, en general, a los hombres de buena fe, y a su libertad, su autodeterminación, su independencia. Darío no era ajeno al exceso de palabrería política en Hispanoamérica. Era además consciente de las necesidades de esos pueblos. Por eso, detrás de la lisonja de la "Salutación al Águila" se hallan algunos versos sinceros, versos de hermandad cultural: "Tráenos los secretos de las labores del Norte, / y que los hijos nuestros dejen de ser los rétores latinos, / y aprendan de los yanquis la constancia, el vigor, el carácter" (708, vv. 31-33). Darío admiró en parte a los Estados Unidos, y en *Peregrinaciones*, volumen publicado en París en 1901, incluyó un artículo, escrito en agosto de 1900, titulado "Los anglosajones", donde afirmaba:

> No; no están desposeídos esos hombres fuertes del Norte del don artístico. Tienen también el pensamiento y el ensueño. Los hispanoamericanos todavía no podemos enseñar al mundo en nuestro cielo mental constelaciones en que brillen los Poe, Whitman y Emerson. Allá donde la mayoría se dedica al culto del dólar, se desarrolla, ante el imperio plutocrático, una minoría intelectual de innegable excelencia . . . Entre esos millones de Calibanes nacen los más maravillosos Arieles. (57-58)

Pese a todo, al poner Darío su mirada en los pueblos hispánicos se angustió. Su ilusión de una hermandad panamericana exenta de exclusivos intereses económicos nunca se llegó a realizar. Darío sufrió ante el panorama de Hispanoamérica, vaticinó el trágico futuro de los pueblos hispánicos y su visión de la hispanidad amenazada pervive todavía hoy como lección y testimonio.

Notas

[1] Una visión panorámica de las aproximaciones críticas a estos aspectos políticos puede verse en el segundo capítulo del libro de Keith Ellis. Para la crítica coetánea a Rubén Darío—Eduardo de la Barra, Paul Groussac, Manuel Gondra y José Enrique Rodó—vale la pena consultar el artículo de Juan Loveluck.

[2] Una aportación destacada sobre el concepto de lo político y de la hispanidad en Darío es el libro de Mario Ancona Ponce, dividido en tres partes: una primera visión del poeta y el hombre en su medio y su época; una exposición de sus ideas políticas; y unas conclusiones. Para Ancona Ponce, Darío pasó paulatinamente de una visión de la hispanidad como unión centroamericana a una visión como ideal hispanoamericano y de ahí a una concepción de unión panamericana. Martín Alberto Noel dedicó en 1972 un trabajo a estudiar las raíces hispánicas en Darío desde lo vital, lo literario, lo pictórico y lo histórico. Entre las conclusiones a las que llegó Noel destaca la de que "el hispanismo de Darío es principalmente vital y accesoriamente literario. En Darío lo hispánico se presenta como parte integrante e inseparable de una americanidad primordial" (81).

[3] Todas las citas de los libros poéticos de Darío siguen siempre la edición de *Poesías completas*.

[4] La última década del XIX, como casi todos los fines de siglo, fue para España época de profunda crisis. Un estudio de la prensa nacional de la época, que debió conocer Darío, podría confirmarlo. En el ensayismo político también se comprueba este talante de desengaño nacional. Ya desde la promoción o grupo de los del 68 hasta los regeneracionistas, Ángel Ganivet, Lucas Mallada, Macías Picavea y Joaquín Costa, los ejemplos se multiplican. José Luis Abellán ha estudiado con acierto algunos de estos aspectos.

[5] Cuando Darío alaba a Whitman en *Azul*, su elogio se dirige más bien al gran poeta, al mítico patriarca, al demócrata neoyorquino. Whitman es casi una idea concebida por Darío más que realmente conocida. Piénsese que por esos años, antes de 1890, Darío apenas comprendía el inglés. Por otro lado, una lectura de *Leaves of Grass* (1855) de Whitman demuestra lo lejos que estaba el pensamiento político de uno y otro autor. En Whitman hay una creencia de que los norteamericanos están llamados a cumplir una misión civilizadora sobre todos los pueblos a los que juzga inferiores y, entre ellos, Hispanoamérica. En el poema "Starting from Paumanok", del citado libro, hay una clara actitud de superioridad por parte de los Estados Unidos. Por eso, en la parte cuarta escribe Whitman: "Take my leaves America, take them South and take them North, / . . . / Surround them East and West, for they would surround you . . ." (18, vol. 1, parte 4, vv. 1 y 3). Esto no es otra cosa que el llamado "Manifest Destiny" por el que los Estados Unidos cumplirán su destino de expandirse en todas las direcciones. Y más adelante en el mismo poema, "Yet sailing to other shores to annex the same . . ." (29, vol. 1, parte 14, v. 58). En otro poema del mismo libro, el terrible "Salut au monde!", considera a América, que para él son los Estados Unidos, como luz y guía del resto de las naciones. Por eso concluye: "Toward you all, in America's name, / I raise high the perpendicular hand, I make the signal, / to remain after me in sight forever, / for all the haunts and homes of men" (176, parte 13, vv. 18-21). En otro poema, "Pioneers! O Pioneers!", Whitman considera la expansión americana como propósito divino. La prosa de Walt Whitman es aún más explícita al abogar por la necesidad de que los Estados Unidos dominen el mundo. En las últimas páginas del ensayo "Democratic vistas", muy anterior a la guerra contra España, Whitman confía en que antes del año 1976 Canadá y Cuba sean partes integrantes de los Estados Unidos. Para Whitman es inevitable la expansión de los Estados Unidos hacia la América hispánica y, aún más, no duda de la aceptación de los países hispánicos. Textualmente dice: "Long ere the second centennial arrives, there will be some forty to fifty great states, among them Canada and Cuba . . . The Pacific will be ours, and the Atlantic mainly ours . . . The individuality of one nation must then, as always, lead the world. Can there be any doubt who the leader ought to be?" (130, vol. 5). En definitiva, la influencia de Whitman sobre Darío es casi nula e incluso, más de adorno que de sentimiento, porque Darío nunca aceptó la superioridad yanqui. En palabras de Will Derusha: "Lo que interesa a Darío no es Whitman, sino lo que Whitman simboliza, su función de icono; la razón por la cual el gran viejo no cambia nunca, desde los primeros escritos hasta los últimos. La fama, la figura pública, la nobleza poética corresponden al perfil heroico del modernista" (145).

[6] No puede dejar de insistirse en que esta mezcla de temas en Darío es constante. También lo político se une, por ejemplo, con lo sexual. Así, en "Carne, celeste carne" el poeta supedita cualquier fuerza política a lo femenino. Por eso, al dirigirse a la mujer, sublime carne, dice el poeta: "Inútil es el grito de la legión cobarde / del interés, inútil el progreso / yankee, si te desdeña. / Si el progreso es de fuego, por ti arde. / ¡Toda lucha del hombre va a tu beso, / por ti se combate o se sueña!" (669, vv. 34-39).

⁷En torno a la oda "A Roosevelt" se ha escrito mucho. Me limito a señalar los artículos de Aurora de Albornoz, Publio González-Rodas, Luis Monguió y Keith Ellis. Juan Ramón Jiménez en *Mi Rubén Darío* ofrece interesantes detalles sobre la composición de este poema.

⁸Textualmente dice Rubén, según recoge Pedro Luis Barcia, "Y así quieren los yanquis a su presidente, que lo mismo se pone la toga oscura y el cuadrado gorro de la universidad de Yale, como coge la carabina y se va al monte, gran cazador delante del Eterno; . . . Y en tal señalado día se deja triturar la diestra presidencial por los innumerables ciudadanos de los Estados Unidos, que van a estrecharle la mano; . . . da gracias a Dios oficialmente un día al año, en la libertad de todos los cultos y en comunión con todas las razas de la tierra que se funden en el crisol anglosajón; . . . pero, y esto es lo grave para nosotros los hispanoamericanos, constituyendo un peligro para la América conquistable, el peligro de un director de apetitos imperialistas que se han manifestado desde Filipinas y Puerto Rico, hasta la reciente broma de Panamá" (*Escritos dispersos* 216).

⁹Escribe Darío irónicamente: "Los franceses han apreciado en su verdadero valor, algunos de los principios rooseveltianos, y sobre todo éste: El hombre, el ciudadano, como la nación, lo primero a que debe dedicarse es a hacer dinero. Una vez hecho el dinero puede hacer lo que le venga en deseo" (158). Y al final concluye: "Y apenas ha habido aquí en los periódicos espacio para hablar de otra gloria yanqui, que acaba de desaparecer: Mark Twain" (159).

¹⁰La "Salutación del optimista" da muestra, según Juan Larrea (61), de las posibilidades proféticas de Darío porque su anuncio cataclísmico precedió a la Guerra Mundial de 1914.

¹¹Rubén Darío llegó a Río de Janeiro en julio de 1906. Fue gratamente recibido por la intelectualidad brasileña y elogiado por el escritor Elizio de Carvalho; también de esta época data la leyenda de sus amores con "la Condesa de Río de Janeiro".

Obras citadas

Abellán, José Luis. *Historia crítica del pensamiento español*. Tomo V. Madrid: Espasa-Calpe, 1989.

Albornoz, Aurora de. " 'A Roosevelt': un poema muy actual de Rubén Darío". *Cuadernos Americanos* 117 (1961): 255-58.

Ancona Ponce, Mario. *Rubén Darío y América (El nuevo mundo como realidad política en la poesía rubeniana)*. México: Parresia, 1968.

Anderson Imbert, Enrique. *La originalidad de Rubén Darío*. Buenos Aires: Centro Editor de América Latina, 1967.

Contreras, Francisco. *Rubén Darío. Su vida y su obra*. Santiago de Chile: Ediciones Ercilla, 1937.

Darío, Rubén. *Autobiografía*. Madrid: Shade, 1945.

_____. *Escritos dispersos de Rubén Darío (Recogidos de periódicos de Buenos Aires)*. Ed. Pedro Luis Barcia. Tomo 2. La Plata: U Nacional de La Plata, 1967.

_____. *Historia de mis libros. Páginas escogidas*. Ed. Ricardo Gullón. Madrid: Cátedra, 1986. 197-225.

_____. *Peregrinaciones*. Madrid: Imprenta G. Hernández y Galo Sáez, 1922.

_____. *Poesías completas*. Ed. Alfonso Méndez Plancarte y Antonio Oliver Belmás. Madrid: Aguilar, 1975.

_____. *Todo al vuelo*. Madrid: Renacimiento, 1912.

Derusha, Will. " 'El gran viejo' de Rubén Darío". *Rubén Darío. La creación, argumento poético y expresivo*. Ed. Alberto Acereda. Barcelona: Anthropos, 1997. 141-45.

Ellis, Keith. "Un análisis estructural del poema 'A Roosevelt' ". *Cuadernos Hispanoamericanos* 212-13 (1967): 523-28.

_____. *Critical Approaches to Rubén Darío*. Toronto: U of Toronto P, 1974.

Ghiraldo, Alberto. *El archivo de Rubén Darío*. Buenos Aires: Losada, 1943.

Gómez Espinosa, Margarita. *Rubén Darío, patriota*. Madrid: Turner, 1966.

González-Rodas, Publio. "Rubén Darío y Theodore Roosevelt". *Cuadernos Americanos* 168 (1970). 185-92.

Jiménez, Juan Ramón. *Mi Rubén Darío (1900-1956)*. Ed. Antonio Sánchez Romeralo. Moguer: Ediciones de la Fundación, 1991.

Larrea, Juan. *Intensidad del canto errante*. Córdoba: U Nacional de Córdoba, 1972.
Loveluck, Juan. "Rubén Darío y sus primeros críticos (1888-1900)". *Revista Iberoamericana* 64 (1967): 209-35.
Monguió, Luis. "El origen de unos versos de 'A Roosevelt' ". *Hispania* 38 (1955): 424-26.
Noel, Martín Alberto. *Las raíces hispánicas en Rubén Darío*. Buenos Aires: U de Buenos Aires, 1972.
Oliver Belmás, Antonio. *Este otro Rubén Darío*. Barcelona: Aedos, 1960.
———. "Lo social en Rubén Darío". *Asomante* 23 (1967): 58-63.
Paz, Octavio. *Cuadrivio: Darío, López Velarde, Pessoa, Cernuda*. México: J. Mortiz, 1965.
Rodó, José Enrique. *Obras completas*. Buenos Aires: Zamora, 1956.
Salinas, Pedro. *La poesía de Rubén Darío: ensayo sobre el tema y los temas del poeta*. Buenos Aires: Losada, 1957.
Torre, Antonio M. de la. "Consideraciones sobre la actitud político-social de Rubén Darío". *Revista Iberoamericana* 19 (1954): 261-72.
Torres, Edelberto. *La dramática vida de Rubén Darío*. Barcelona: Grijalbo, 1966.
Torres-Rioseco, Arturo. *Vida y poesía de Rubén Darío*. Buenos Aires: Emecé Editores, 1944.
Vargas Vila, José María. *Rubén Darío*. Barcelona: Ahr, 1972.
Whitman, Walt. *The Complete Writings of Walt Whitman*. 10 vols. 1902. New York, London: Grosse Pointe, Mich., Scholarly Press, 1968.

Mapping Empire in Omaha and Buffalo

WORLD'S FAIRS AND THE SPANISH-AMERICAN WAR

Sarah J. Moore
UNIVERSITY OF ARIZONA

When the United States' battleship *Maine* exploded under mysterious circumstances while anchored in Havana Harbor on the night of 15 February 1898, plans were already well underway for two world's fairs: the Trans-Mississippi and International Exposition, Omaha, and the Pan-American Exposition, Buffalo. With the declaration of war with Spain in the spring of that year, organizers of the Omaha exposition feared it would be delayed or canceled. That the exposition opened, as scheduled, on 1 June 1898 prompted at least one observer to consider Omaha's achievement as nothing less than Admiral George Dewey's decisive victory over the Spanish fleet in Manila Bay.[1] Indeed, the presence of the Spanish-American War and its implications of colonialism were unmistakable at the Omaha exposition with respect to the fair's ideological assumptions, exhibitions, and official, as well as critical, discourse. In contrast to the Omaha exposition's aspiration to the status of an international world's fair based on the triumphant model of the World's Columbian Exposition of 1893 in Chicago, the Pan-American Exposition was conceived as a Western Hemispheric world's fair whose concern was exclusively "the Americas." Originally scheduled to open in 1899 to "crown a century of progress that had witnessed the emergence of the Western Hemisphere as a leading and independent force in the world,"[2] the Spanish-American War of 1898 caused plans for the opening of the fair to be postponed until 1901.[3] In addition to being historically contiguous, these two events, the Spanish-American War and the 1901 Pan-American Exposition, had profound ideological resonances, each redefining American national identity within a colonial context. In fact, the physical and conceptual presence of empire that informed the Pan-American Exposition was directly proportional to the political and territorial conquests of the 1898 war. Carefully crafted as an elaborate allegory of the so-called New World's coming of age, the Pan-American Exposition revealed the heady confidence of the United States at the beginning of the new century with respect to advances in technology, industry, and science, and as a new imperial world power and a culture in the full flush of civilization. This paper addresses the Omaha and Buffalo expositions of 1898 and 1901, respectively, as cultural performances, suggesting the degree to which they collided with the realities and implications of the Spanish-American War while corroborating contemporary assumptions about national identity, progress, race, the frontier, and empire.

Perhaps nowhere is the cultural production of meaning and identity clearer than at the international expositions of the late nineteenth and early twentieth centuries. Performing the role of great summarizers of culture, world's fairs molded the world into an "ideologically coherent symbolic universe, confirming and extending the authority of the [host] country's . . . leadership."[4] As a structure of legitimization and producer of meaning, the world's fairs had a didactic mission while evoking an "imagined community" in which national and cultural profiles and boundaries were fixed.[5] As many contemporary scholars have noted, "almost without exception the major international exhibitions were sponsored by nations with colonial dependencies. Each displayed its colonies, or its internally colonized peoples, to its home population, to its rivals, and to the world at large."[6] The displays of colonial possessions in particular and of the expositions in general were informed by a kind of ideological mapping in which boundaries and identities became essentialized and authoritative so as to require no definition other than self-assertion.[7] The expositions in Omaha and Buffalo proved no exception to this rule, although their respective construction of empire differed decisively; the former articulated an internal colonial model in its emphasis on westward territorial expansion, whereas the latter defined empire within an international context. Indeed, the two expositions can be read as parallel trajectories of the United States' excursion into empire building that in 1898 made a decisive shift beyond its geopolitical boundaries.

The heady confidence in the progress of American civilization that informed the Trans-Mississippi and International Exposition was expressed perhaps nowhere more clearly than in the remarks of the official spokesman of the Omaha fair, James Baldwin, on 1 June, opening day, who observed, "The Exposition has become the instrument of civilization. Being a concomitant to empire, westward it takes its way."[8] Casting the historical context of the Omaha fair within the westward trajectory of previous international exhibitions—London (1851), Philadelphia (1876), and Chicago (1893)—Baldwin situates the Trans-Mississippi and International Exposition within an imperial context and offers the Little White City, as the fair was often referred to, as inexorable proof of America's conquest of its internal colony, that is, the Trans-Mississippi West. Baldwin's statement concisely summarizes many of the organizing principles that fueled United States' westward expansion and belief in manifest destiny throughout the nineteenth century and resonates with many visual images from the period, perhaps none more so than the bombastic mural study for the United States Capitol, *Westward the Course of Empire Takes Its Way*, by Emanuel Leutze in 1861. Critical discourse about the Omaha fair regularly repeated Baldwin's official appraisal and referred to the astonishing speed with which the Trans-Mississippi region was transformed from a "wilderness into twenty-four states and territories . . . [with] nearly one-half of the wealth and one-third of the population of our country."[9] Another contemporary observer described the Omaha exposition as nothing less than a "miracle . . . rising in what but yesterday seemed one of the earth's waste places" and concluded confidently that the fair "should strengthen the faith of Anglo-Saxons in the potency of their race and its institutions."[10]

Physically and ideologically modeled on the World's Columbian Exposition of 1893 in Chicago, which traced America's progress of civilization to Columbus's so-called discovery of the New World four hundred years earlier, the exposition's fairgrounds were dominated by the Grand Canal, or Grand Court, as it was often called, an artificial lagoon, replenished every day by an estimated one million gallons of water pumped from the nearby Missouri River,[11] stretching nearly half a mile and surrounded by the prominent buildings of the fair: Mines and Mining, Machinery and Electricity, Manufacturers, Liberal Arts, Agriculture, and Fine Arts. Paralleling the east-west axis of Chicago's Court of Honor, which corroborated contemporary assumptions about the frontier and the directional flow of civilization, the Grand Canal's main entrance was at the eastern end of

the fairgrounds and was punctuated by the Arch of the States, which included a display of the coats of arms of each of the twenty-four Trans-Mississippi states and territories and was crowned by the great shield and golden eagle of the United States.[12] The United States Government Building terminated the western edge of the Grand Canal and was crowned by a colossal gilded dome bearing a reproduction of Bartholdi's Statue of Liberty; her gigantic electric torch was held some 178 feet above the ground and dazzled viewers each night as its spotlight illuminated the entire lagoon.[13]

The prominent position of the United States Government Building at the western edge of the Grand Canal was suggestive of contemporary assumptions about the frontier and demonstrated the degree to which the Omaha fair was engaged in a dual construction of empire as contained within and extending beyond the geopolitical boundaries of the United States. Coming only five years after the bold declaration of the historian Frederick Jackson Turner that the empire was officially closed—not coincidentally at the World's Columbian Exposition—the Omaha fair institutionalized westward expansion and the colonization of the American continent and its indigenous populations as an accomplished fact rather than a national imperative. At the same time, the United States Government Building contained numerous artifacts and exhibitions that related directly to the Spanish-American War, including a model of the battleship *Maine* near the main entrance of the building with the banner above it reading "Remember the *Maine*," and displays designed to educate the viewer about recent colonial acquisitions as a direct result of the war. As such, the distinction between the continental and imperial frontier was collapsed, the latter being construed as a logical and inevitable extension of the former.[14]

Allusions to imperialism at the Omaha fair were not limited to the broadly interpreted neoclassical style of the buildings along the Grand Canal, including the United States Government Building, whose air of permanence and authority was directly linked to its predecessor in Chicago in 1893, nor to the ideological topography of the fairgrounds that located progress on an east to west trajectory. Indeed, the construction of the United States as an imperial power, with both internal and external colonies, was perhaps nowhere clearer than in the displays on the Midway, sometimes referred to as the Passing Show. As with previous world's fairs, the Midway featured numerous amusements, sideshows, and idle curiosities for the pleasure and diversion of the fairgoer. One contemporary observer noted, "There is a kaleidoscopic jumble of grotesque shapes and flaring colors along the Midway streets. There is a fanfare of trumpets and drums penetrating the ear from noon to night."[15] At the same time, there was a host of so-called educational and scientifically sanctioned ethnological displays that demonstrated the efficacy of the United States' imposition of control over its internal colony, that is, the Trans-Mississippi West and its native populations, and the expediency of its new excursion into empire building as a result of the Spanish-American War.

The Midway displays were located at the northern boundaries of the fairgrounds and featured, among others, the so-called Scenic Railway that transported riders underground and included a representation of the Battle of Manila and the triumphs of Admiral Dewey on the walls of the tunnel, a scaled miniature model of the bombardment of Cuban forces, and, as the historian Robert Rydell has noted, "a spectacular performance, complete with stereopticon slides, music, and fireworks, depicting the passage of the battleship *Maine* from New York to Havana, the destruction of the ship, and the funeral of the soldiers. . . . A flotilla of naval vessels and portraits of generals followed, and the show concluded with President McKinley's portrait."[16] Contemporary ideas about racial hierarchy were corroborated by the many living ethnological displays, as they were called, on the Midway; the Philippine Village in particular confirmed the widely held racist image of Filipinos as uncivilized savages whose only hope for redemption was through assimilation with their benevolent new colonial ruler. A contemporary advertisement for Pears' Soap, which features Admiral Dewey aboard ship washing his hands, suggests the prevalence of these ideas and their popular appeal to a broad audience. The text of the advertisement reads, "The first step towards lightening The White Man's Burden is through teaching the virtues of cleanliness. Pear's Soap is a potent factor in brightening the dark corners of the earth as civilization advances, while amongst the cultured of all nations it holds the highest place." The central image of Dewey is surrounded by vignettes of ships in Manila Bay, a missionary offering a bar of soap to a crouching Philippine native, and a cargo ship unloading cases of Pears' Soap. The latter image refers directly to Dewey's requisition of six thousand pounds of soap for the Philippines in the summer of 1898 and ideologically to the United States' recent excursion into imperialism that Rudyard Kipling welcomed with the poem "The White Man's Burden: The United States and the Philippines" in February 1899.[17]

The Midway display that attracted the largest audience and inspired numerous written commentaries was the so-called Indian Congress, held on a multiacre tract to the north of the Midway. Given the post-Turnerian assumption about the end of the frontier, it is no wonder that the Indian Congress offered a retrospective view of what one con-

temporary observer called "a great meeting of a vanishing race."[18] Indeed, as Robert Rydell noted, the Indian Congress was self-consciously modeled after colonial exhibits at recent European world's fairs and was designed to present the colonization of Native Americans as a fait accompli.[19] Moreover, the Indian Congress was a scientifically sanctioned ethnological display whose legitimacy was underscored by the participation of the Smithsonian Institution's Bureau of American Ethnology. In addition, the display benefited from the financial support of the United States Congress, although the forty-thousand-dollar appropriation was delayed due to the outbreak of the Spanish-American War, causing the Indian Congress to open on 4 August, more than two months after the official opening of the fair. Some thirty-five different tribes of Native Americans, largely from the Trans-Mississippi region, were represented at the Indian Congress; the display featured living encampments and a large arena for regular performances of mock battles and war dances, the latter were designed to underscore the Native Americans' savagery and included "various kinds of tortures, including burning at the stake, [and] scalping."[20] The current assumption that savagery, by definition, destined the Native American populations to extinction underscored many contemporary discussions of the Indian Congress: Octave Thanet found the spectacle of the "doomed" race "full of interest, full of sadness"; William Allen White observed that "the exhibit of the savage makes the show of the civilized man more significant. The representatives from each of the existing tribes exemplify its manner of aboriginal life, its savage customs, its barbaric industries. . . . But Democracy cannot civilize the Indian. In barren soil, the mustard seed dies."+ Such a construction of the Native Americans served not only to legitimate their subjugation but as a litmus test for the efficacy and expediency of American colonial rule. As the historian Walter Williams has observed, "[the] clear pattern of colonialism toward Native Americans [during the nineteenth century] . . . served as a precedent for imperialist domination over the Philippines and other islands occupied during the Spanish-American War."[22]

The unanticipated success of the Omaha fair, with respect to the number of visitors—more than 2.7 million—and its financial return to its stockholders, led local businessmen to reopen it the following summer. Under the new banner of Greater America Exposition, the definition of American national identity within an imperial context that had underscored the Trans-Mississippi and International Exposition became the 1899 fair's overtly stated organizing principle.[23] An official poster advertising the Greater America Exposition featured Uncle Sam embracing a globe encircled by a garland that read "The White Man's Burden" and pointing to territorial acquisitions in the wake of the Spanish-American War; the text of the poster read "The First Colonial Exhibit." Outside of the potential reference to McKinley's reported first response to the news of Admiral Dewey's victory over the Spanish fleet in Manila—he rushed to the globe to discover just where the Philippines were located—the 1899 fair proclaimed, as Rydell notes, "the centrality of colonialism to continued American progress"[24] and laid the path for future expositions to engage in demonstrations of the United States' imperial prowess and new position of leadership in the international arena. Moreover, the Greater America Exposition can be considered within the broader context of the nationwide celebrations of Admiral Dewey's triumphant return from the Philippines in 1899 in the wake of the Spanish-American War. That same year, the Dewey Arch was commissioned in New York City and, as the art historian Michele Bogart has noted, "not only did it [the triumphal arch] honor Dewey's wartime feats; like the admiral's own actions, the arch was an expression of America's expansionist policies."[25]

As the first world's fair hosted by the United States in the twentieth century, the Pan-American Exposition, held in Buffalo in 1901, ushered in the new century with aplomb and heady confidence in the preeminence of the United States. Unlike its distinguished predecessors, which were international in orientation, the Buffalo exposition was restricted to the Western Hemisphere and ostensibly embraced, indeed celebrated, Pan-Americanism. However, in its design to stimulate trade between the United States and other nations in the Americas and to secure foreign markets for United States corpo-

rations, the Pan-American Exposition's supposed demonstration of hemispheric unity was present only in official discourse, as national chauvinism and American cultural imperialism informed the general structure and displays of the fair.

Following the enormous success of the World's Columbian Exposition, the Pan-American Exposition presented a carefully constructed view of the United States, organizing the principal buildings of the fair around a central court from which radiated a triumphant message of the United States as the true heir of Western civilization and the locus of progress. As with the Court of Honor of the World's Columbian Exposition, whose east-west axis symbolized the flow of culture and civilization from east to west and alluded to the United States as poised on the western frontier, the hemispheric orientation

of the Pan-American Exposition informed the so-called Court of Fountains as well; its north-south axis resonated with the hemispheric scope of the fair. Moreover, the location of the principal buildings was carefully crafted so as to confer authority. At the south end stood the Triumphal Bridge, the sole entrance to the fair; the north end was punctuated with the Electric Tower, the fair's ultimate symbol of American progress and ascendancy. Just north of the triumphal bridge, whose four massive pillars were topped with equestrian sculptural groups suggestive of Roman imperial chariots, a traverse court running east and west broadened the approach to the Court of Fountains and was bracketed by, among others, the United States' Government Building, giving it a position of authority and prominence that was not shared by other government buildings, whose location at the southern fringe of the fairgrounds put them well off the beaten track. The Court of Fountains was surrounded by the six other principal buildings: the Temple of Music, Ethnology, Machinery, Manufacturer and Liberal Arts, Electricity, and Agriculture.[26]

Of perhaps even greater interest was the allegorical sculpture that filled the Court of Fountains and its aesthetic obedience to the ideological assumptions that formed the armature of the fair in general. Designed to "tell a story in sculpture", according to Paul W. Bartlett,[27] the director of sculptural decorations at the fair, and to be read as a visual affirmation of the United States' preeminence on the world stage, the south end of the court featured "The Genius of Man"; the north end of the court was bracketed by the "Fountain of Abundance," whose baroque flourish and promise of great richness had striking parallels with the "Triumph of Columbia Fountain," which occupied essentially the same position in the Court of Honor at the 1893 exposition. Unlike the World's Columbian Exposition, however, where the Court of Honor was punctuated by the pastiche, neo-classicial Administration Building, the Court of Fountains in Buffalo was terminated by the Electric Tower, which confirmed progress—and its rightful heir, civilization—as the United States' own.

Given the prominence of electricity as the most defining invention of modern times, it is not surprising that the Pan-American Exposition, located just fifteen miles southeast of Niagara Falls, would select electricity as its central theme. Capitalizing on the electricity generated by the first hydroelectric power station at Niagara Falls, the Pan-American Exposition was the first world's fair to be primarily an evening spectacle thanks to the hundreds of thousands of incandescent lights that outlined the perimeter of most of the buildings, fountains, as well as much of the sculpture.[28] Indeed, the presence of Niagara Falls at the Pan-American Exposition was not gratuitous nor seen as a geographical coincidence but rather functioned as the centerpiece in the fair's elaborate allegory of the United States' rise to power and prominence in the international arena.

Beginning with images as early as 1800, Niagara Falls played a prominent role in the construction of American national identity, such as the design after *An Emblem of America* (1800), or *Science Unveiling the Bounties of Nature to the Genius of America* (1814), in which the great cataract appears in the background. As the embrace of manifest destiny grew ever more feverish throughout the middle years of the nineteenth century, such prominent artists as Frederic Church looked to Niagara Falls as a source of national identity, pride, and unlimited power. His panoramic, pre–Civil War painting *Niagara* of 1857 depicts North America's unrivaled natural wonder as a veritable national icon suggestive of the United States' somewhat paradoxical identity as both a new Eden and a heroic technological powerhouse able to subdue even the most sublime and omnipotent natural forces. *Niagara As Seen From Different Eyes,* an 1873 illustration in *Harper's Weekly*, suggests the degree to which Niagara Falls had become a defining feature of American culture; the foreground is filled with a range of American types: tourists, mill owners, lovers, poets, patriots, artists, geologists, and Native Americans, among others.

The Electric Tower, literally and figuratively, embraced the power of Niagara Falls and offered the final authoritative word on progress as a willed national agenda. The tower itself stood four hundred feet high, three times taller than all other exposition buildings, and in its embrace of architectural modernity—the tower looked more like an American skyscraper than the variously interpreted Spanish-Renaissance style of the rest of the architecture at the fair—proclaimed itself as a symbol of American progress.[29] The center of the tower featured a seventy-four-foot model of Niagara Falls, which released thirty-

five thousand cubic feet of water per minute[30]—the spectacle was enhanced by the ninety-four searchlights that shone on the artificial cataract—while twin sculptural groups by George Gray Barnhard on either side of the carved falls depicted the triumph of humankind over nature as well as of Euro-American culture over that of Native Americans: on one side stood *The Great Waters in the Days of the Indians,* in which primeval nature is prominent; on the other side stood *The Great Waters in the Days of the White Man,* in which the natural wonder has been harnessed and subdued. The whole ensemble was crowned by Herbert Adams's *The Goddess of Light,* a blithe young victory figure symbolizing electricity, and a grouping of searchlights that beamed toward the falls, the real falls, that is. Employing electric elevators to carry exuberant visitors to new heights and a commanding view of the entire fairgrounds, the Electric Tower was the most stunning and defining architectural ensemble of the exposition and unquestionably situated the United States in a position of supreme authority within the international arena of 1901.

The Electric Tower was not the only ideologically situated site at the Pan-American Exposition. Indeed, suggestions of and assumptions about empire abounded throughout the fairgrounds, although perhaps nowhere more blatantly than on the Midway. Following the great popularity of the Midway Plaisance at the World's Columbian Exposition, the organizers of the Buffalo fair decided to further integrate the ethnological displays and varied amusements of the Midway into the overall ensemble of the exposition—the Midway could be accessed from various sites at the fairgrounds as it formed a U-shaped arc around its western section—thus blurring the boundaries between the more authoritative displays around the Court of Fountains.[31] In addition to its portion of curiosities and amusements, including the aeriocycle, which transported its riders to an elevation of 235 feet, or the so-called Trip to the Moon,[32] which featured a number of reportedly convincing illusions and offered an extraterrestrial, if quite unintentional, parallel to the theme of imperial expansion that dominated the fair as a whole, the Midway included a number of so-called living ethnological displays that celebrated the United States' imperial gains, including a Cuban, Hawaiian, and Philippine display, the latter was the largest display with more than one hundred people on an eleven-acre site.[33] Even in the displays that were not defined by the United States' new colonial possessions, such as the Streets of Mexico or Cairo Street, assumptions about racial hierarchies were prominent and offered, as the architectural historian Zeynap Celik has observed, multiple meanings, "making a claim to scientific authority and accuracy while nourishing fantasy and illusion" about the "exotic" other.[34]

The imperial logic that informed the fair in general can be seen at work in the fine arts display as well. The display was held in a temporary structure on the southeast end of the fairgrounds. The Albright Art Gallery, with its derivative, neo-classical style, was intended to house the fine arts display and afterward to be a permanent gallery for the collection of the Buffalo Fine Arts Academy; however, the building was not completed on time. As it was, the display in the fine arts building did not officially open until 15 June, nearly one month after the official dedication day. The building contained sixteen galleries and had three principal exhibitions: one for the United States, one for Canada, and a so-called international section for works by artists of South American birth. In contrast to the more than eleven hundred feet of line devoted to the nearly seventeen hundred works by 620-odd artists from the United States, the international—read Pan-American—section had only three hundred feet of line. The nearly crushing presence of the United States affected the outcome of the medals awarded as well, with over 150 awards going to United States' artists in contrast to the 10 awarded to South American artists.[35] Indeed, as the contemporary art critic Charles Caffin noted, there was very little "Pan" represented in the fine arts display.[36]

Facing the entrance to the fine arts gallery was a cast of the *Sherman Monument* by Augustus Saint-Gaudens; this equestrian statue of the Union general William Sherman, led by an angel of victory with a palm frond in her hands, had been displayed at the 1900 Universal Exposition in Paris to great acclaim. Upon entering the fine arts gallery, visitors were greeted by Saint-Gaudens' *Shaw Memorial,* which formed a dialogue with the equestrian statue in the entryway. Recording the heroism of the Union officer Robert Shaw, who led black soldiers during the Civil War and lost his life in the battle at Fort Wagner, as did many of his men,[37] the two pieces suggested reunification of North and South and resonated not only with the recent history of the United States but with the official discourse of the fair, which, if only on paper, linked North America—read United States—and South America in one great union. Moreover, the works were resonant, even if indirectly, with current assumptions that the war with Spain would "reunify the nation by bringing together the North and South against a common external enemy."[38]

Although critical discussion of the Pan-American Exposition tended to concentrate on its technological marvels, the issue of Pan-Americanism, the specter of the Spanish-American War, and the United States' recently acquired status as an imperial power were not lost on all contemporary commentators. In a 1901 article on the Buffalo fair, which included a section on Latin America, for example, Walter Page lamented the United States' gross ignorance of its neighbors to the south and suggested that for political and commercial reasons, a "community of interest" must be constructed. He argued, "Our war with Spain may for a time have caused in Central and South America a misunderstanding of our purpose. It was perhaps not unnatural that for a brief period the fear may have got abroad that we might take a mood of foreign conquests—an idea that was repeated in certain European quarters and even at home by unbalanced and irresponsible men and journals. There was never a more absurd idea." Alluding to the Pan-American Conferences, an international forum organized in 1889 to stimulate trade and commerce between North and South America, the author suggested that the exposition in Buffalo was uniquely positioned to extol the potential of a "peaceful community of interests . . . that is not merely commercial in a narrow sense, but in that large sense in which commerce becomes an agency of civilization."[39]

Attempting to diminish the contemporary notion of the United States as a potential tyrant and oppressor, Page boldly and uncritically proclaimed the United States' colonial displays as educational and "striking proof of our expansion of sympathy and interest." He continued, "The people would not . . . have gained in many years as definite a knowledge of life in Porto [sic] Rico, the Hawaiian Islands, and the Philippines as they will learn from the Government's exhibit of the products of these outlying wards of ours as well as the customs and character of the people. One of the wings of the Government's group of buildings is given to these exhibits; and the crowds of visitors show the greatest interest in them."[40] That the author concluded his article by noting, without further comment, that there were Hawaiian and Philippine villages on the Midway demonstrates the degree to which the presence of American colonies at the fair was part of a broader effort to reconfigure American national identity as well as the continuation of American progress within a colonial context. Expressing parallel concerns in an article entitled "Educational Influence of the Exposition," Nicholas Butler called for closer intellectual, ethical, and cultural relations between nations on American soil. He argued: "The South and Central American must be taught that their gigantic northern neighbor is a comrade and friend . . . and the inhabitant of the United States must learn that his nation's size and strength and wealth do not make unnecessary or unworthy the serious efforts of Latin . . . neighbors to the south of us to build American institutions of their own. If the Pan-American [Exposition] can put these thoughts, and those that flow from them, into some thousands of heads, it will have greatly promoted the peace, prosperity and good will of the New World. This is surely education."[41] The author concluded that the director general of the fair, William I. Buchanan, had the perfect credentials to carry out such a task, as Buchanan had considerable knowledge about Latin America, given his role as United States foreign minister to Argentina under President Cleveland.

Of all the events that took place during the six months of the fair, none was characterized by such high expectations, elaborate pageantry, and self-congratulatory discourse as President's Day in early September. President McKinley was greeted by throngs of admirers and visitors as he made his triumphal entry into the fairgrounds. McKinley believed, as did the organizers of the fair, that "progress was synonymous with America's material growth and economic expansion," which was, in turn, predicated on and demonstrated by its new role as a colonial power.[42] Emphasizing the fair's didactic mission to encourage peace and economic cooperation between the American nations and "charting the course to future utopia through the establishment of reciprocal relations with Pan-American nations,"[43] McKinley delivered what would become his most memorable speech, in which he declared, "Expositions are the timekeepers of progress. They record the world's advancement."[44] The following day, while shaking hands with the crowd in the Temple of Music, President McKinley was shot by Leon Czolgosz, a reported anarchist. The shooting triggered the arrests of anarchists and socialists across the country and, since

Czolgosz was the son of recent Polish immigrants, escalated nationwide demands for immigration restrictions. In a contemporaneous issue of *Harper's Weekly*, the cover featured an angry Uncle Sam tossing a would-be immigrant/assassin brandishing a pistol and a bomb off a ship named *United States;* the caption reads "No Room on This Ship."[45] Indeed, President McKinley's death, which took place eight days after the attempted assassination, exposed the deeply embedded ethnic and class rifts that defined American

society and, as such, highlighted the degree to which the Pan-American Exposition was an elaborate performance of national cohesion and a shared cultural tradition that had very little to do with the lived reality of many inhabitants of the United States.

The Trans-Mississippi and Pan-American Expositions were not to have the last word on national identity or on visions of empire. Indeed, before the gates closed in Buffalo in November of 1901, plans were underway for the 1904 Louisiana Purchase Exposition to be held in Saint Louis. Following the ideological model of the 1898 Omaha exposition and its construction of an internal colony, the Saint Louis fair was designed to commemorate the centennial of the beginning of the United States' westward expansion and featured a living ethnological exhibit of Native Americans, borrowing the scientific authority while diminishing the sideshow tawdriness of the Omaha fair's Indian Congress.[46] That the American Indian Reservation was immediately adjacent to the Philippine Reservation, a "living exhibit" of more than one thousand Filipinos at the center of the fairgrounds—both organized by the United States' government—underlined the contemporary assumption that the United States' past experience with continental expansion and the suppression of Native Americans and its recent colonial exploits were but two markers on the same trajectory of progress. At the same time, the Louisiana Purchase Exposition's eyes remained fixed on the Western Hemisphere in hopes of an early completion of an isthmian canal, paralleling the Pan-Americanism orientation of the Buffalo fair of 1901. It would not be until 1915, however, at the Panama-Pacific Exposition in San Francisco, that the completion of the Panama Canal would be celebrated as yet another example of progress and empire building as a willed activity of the United States.

The Trans-Mississippi and International Expositions and the Pan-American Exposition of 1898 and 1901, respectively, bracket the beginning of an era of self-conscious imperialist expansion of the United States beyond its geopolitical boundaries and demonstrate the degree to which the politics of colonialism are well served by such public constructions of culture and national identity. Given the current critical debates about the politics of culture, the construction of knowledge in the public sphere, and the often politically charged and ideologically saturated relationship between power, discourse, aesthetics, history, and display, the expositions of the late nineteenth and early twentieth centuries provide compelling case studies in which to examine the cultural production of meaning and identity. Hovering at the edge of the twentieth century, the Trans-Mississippi and the Pan-American Expositions were informed by contemporary assumptions about empire, race, gender, national identity, class, and progress, among others, that continue to resonate to this day.

Notes

[1] Henry Wysham Lanier, "The Great Fair at Omaha: The Trans-Mississippi and International Exposition, June 1 to November 1, 1898," *American Monthly* 18, no. 1 (July 1898): 53.

[2] William Irwin, *The New Niagara: Tourism, Technology, and Landscape of Niagara Falls, 1776-1917* (University Park: Pennsylvania State University Press, 1996), 156.

[3] *Leslie's Weekly* 92, 11 May 1901, 449.

[4] Robert W. Rydell, *All the World's a Fair: Visions of Empire at American International Expositions, 1876-1916* (Chicago: Chicago University Press, 1984), 3.